The ICJ and Multi-*forum* Litigation Strategy

Queen Mary Studies in International Law

Edited by

Malgosia Fitzmaurice

VOLUME 59

The titles published in this series are listed at *brill.com/qmil*

The ICJ and Multi-*forum* Litigation Strategy

By

Nikolaos Voulgaris

BRILL | NIJHOFF

LEIDEN | BOSTON

Library of Congress Cataloging-in-Publication Data

Names: Voulgaris, Nikolaos, *author.*
Title: The ICJ and multi-forum litigation strategy / by Nikolaos Voulgaris.
Other titles: International Court of Justice and multi-state litigation strategy
Description: Leiden ; Boston : Brill Academic Publishers, Inc., 2025. | Series: Queen Mary studies in international law, 1877-4822 ; volume 59 | Includes bibliographical references and index.
Identifiers: LCCN 2025024548 (print) | LCCN 2025024549 (ebook) | ISBN 9789004704558 (hardback) | ISBN 9789004704565 (pdf)
Subjects: LCSH: International Court of Justice. | Jurisdiction (International law) | International courts. | Actions and defenses.
Classification: LCC KZ6275 .V68 2025 (print) | LCC KZ6275 (ebook) | DDC 341.5/52--dc23/eng/20250523
LC record available at https://lccn.loc.gov/2025024548
LC ebook record available at https://lccn.loc.gov/2025024549

Typeface for the Latin, Greek, and Cyrillic scripts: "Brill". See and download: brill.com/brill-typeface.

ISSN 1877-4822
ISBN 978-90-04-70455-8 (hardback)
ISBN 978-90-04-70456-5 (e-book)
DOI 10.1163/9789004704565

This book is printed on acid-free paper and produced in a sustainable manner.

To Alkis, may he always follow the light and to Dimitra who is always there to show him the light

Contents

Foreword

In a time when global institutions are deadlocked, denounced or defunded, the International Court of Justice (ICJ) has been busier than ever. It is being asked by a record number of States to resolve contentious bilateral disputes in accordance with international law and requested by UN bodies to provide advisory opinions on questions essential to the fulfilment of their mandates (even if certain of these requests may mask inter-State disputes). At the time of writing, two-thirds of UN Member States are involved in cases before the ICJ as parties, interveners or participants in advisory proceedings.

In this comprehensive account of the ICJ's authority as a judicial institution, Professor Voulgaris explores the role of the Court as part of a multi-*forum* litigation strategy. Because while States are turning to the ICJ in unprecedented numbers, they are also pursuing litigation in other *fora*. He reveals and dissects the strategic choices of States and reflects on the implications for the ICJ when it is instrumentalised as part of this strategy. Is the ICJ merely another diplomatic platform for States to air grievances or is it one of remaining bastions of multilateralism in a fragmenting world? Or, in the analytical framework adopted by Professor Voulgaris, is the Court a 'pivotal judicial institution', a 'political dispute-settler', 'crisis-manager' or 'rule-maker'?

With incisiveness and clarity, Professor Voulgaris takes the reader through ten disputes where the ICJ formed part of a multi-*forum* litigation strategy. He makes the wise decision not to limit himself to pure legal analysis but also to draw upon literature on the decision to litigate and the roles played by national interests and the relative gains expected from litigation. His analysis is not limited to one viewpoint; he reflects thoughtfully on the varying perspectives of the Court's multiple constituencies. International lawyers may relish the Court's engagement in ongoing crises in Ukraine and Palestine because it encourages us 'to cast ourselves grandly in an heroic mould'.[1] However, ICJ Judges and Registry officials may feel more overworked and under resourced than ever. And the positions of various stakeholders – from government officials to survivors of war crimes – will vary depending on the outcome of each urgent request for provisional measures.

1 Hilary Charlesworth, 'International Law: A Discipline of Crisis' 65(3) (2002) Modern Law Review 377, 387.

In certain national systems, courts are under attack. United States officials have decried 'radical rogue judges' and denied judicial authority to review executive orders.[2] Indian officials have criticised the Indian Supreme Court as acting as a 'super Parliament'.[3] Responding to statements by British politicians, the United Kingdom Attorney-General has warned, 'We are entering a dangerous moment in which not simply on social media but indeed on the floor of the House of Commons, people are attacking judges on a personal basis.'[4] These are recent examples but attacks on judicial independence and competence are a constant theme in domestic politics.

The ICJ is not immune from criticism, and Professor Voulgaris rightly warns that roles implanted on the Court may create tension with its legal nature and thereby affect its sociological legitimacy and the normative value of its decisions. The responsibility for maintaining legitimate authority lies not only with the Court but also with States who are using it as a piece in their litigation strategies. It is understandable that Ukraine has pursued a 'web of accountability'[5] for violations of international law committed by Russia, but such a web also risks entangling and weakening the Court by raising legitimacy concerns and eroding its authority.

After navigating the reader through the potential pitfalls of multi-*forum* litigation, Professor Voulgaris leaves us on a hopeful note. International law being centre-stage (with the ICJ in the spotlight on that stage) means that peaceful dispute settlement is also at the forefront of many States' thinking about their rights, duties and disputes. This book is an essential guide to thinking by States and scholars not just about the evolving roles of the International Court of Justice, but about the international legal system as a whole.

Philippa Webb
Professor of Public International Law
University of Oxford, April 2025

2 https://www.rollingstone.com/politics/politics-news/donald-trump-judges-criticize-illegal-musk-vance-bondi-1235296835/

3 https://www.indiatoday.in/india/story/parliament-is-supreme-jagdeep-dhankhar-again-condemns-judiciary-supreme-court-encroachment-2712698-2025-04-22

4 https://www.theguardian.com/politics/2025/apr/02/british-attorney-general-says-mps-attacks-on-judges-a-huge-threat-to-the-rule-of-law

5 A term used at the International High-Level Conference on 3–5 March 2023 in Lviv, Ukraine organised by the Office of the Prosecutor General of Ukraine: https://rm.coe.int/programme-u4j-lviv-conference-3-5-march-2023/1680aa72e0

Preface

This book is the result of research I carried out between early 2022 and late 2024 in several academic institutions and with different capacities. The idea to make multi-*forum* litigation the central concept of the monograph was conceived when reading the Ejil:talk! post: *Multi*-Forum *Strategies to Tackle Climate Change and Other Complex Problems: A Note from Practitioners* (1 November 2022). The foundations of this monograph had been laid earlier though. During the 2022 spring term I organized and taught a seminar for the University of Athens Law School LLM entitled: 'Parallel proceedings in international law: adjudication of the same dispute in different judicial proceedings'. On account of the Ukraine-Russia judicial saga that commenced *in tandem* with the seminar, under my guidance, students had to identify and analyze inter-State disputes that were brought for adjudication before more than one international judicial *fora*. By the end of the academic term, I realized two things: a. such disputes have been proliferating in the last twenty years, to the extent that a trend is in a state of formation, and b. no academic treatise has explored this in a holistic fashion. Having in mind to close this gap in academic literature, I have been working on the writing of a relevant monograph in a triple capacity: from October 2022 as a post-doctoral fellow at the National and Kapodistrian University of Athens, since June 2023 as a fellow at the Centre for International Governance and Dispute Resolution at King's College London (KCL) and throughout this period as a Professor of International Law at the European Law and Governance School. Some preliminary findings were presented in September 2023 at KCL where Prof. Yuval Shany and Dr. Yusra Suedi provided valuable insights.

With this publication, my objective is twofold. First, to close a gap in literature. No books on inter-State multi-*forum* litigation exist. A wealth of literature tackles parallel or consecutive proceedings in international investment or commercial arbitration. Alas, such proceedings differ greatly from the ones examined in the proposed book because the courts involved therein operate on the basis of a distinct rationale (arbitration rather than litigation) and the disputing parties include private entities alongside States. This limits the room for a *mutatis mutandis* examination of relevant considerations (*lis pendens*/ *forum non conveniens*/ *res judicata*/ abuse of rights) and attests to the fact that the research agenda is set up differently with respect to inter-State disputes at the ICJ. Second, to produce a body of work that converses with legal and political science scholars. I have a legal background but lately, I have taken a great interest in the intersection between law and politics. The interdisciplinary focus of the monograph should be placed in this context. It forms part of a long-standing attempt to understand how these two disciplines intersect.

In order to offer an integrated account of multi-*forum* litigation I engage with both the legal and political science scholarship on the international judicial function. From a legal standpoint, I analyse the main characteristics of every aspect of ICJ jurisdiction. But yet, the legal analysis can paint only part of the picture. Relevant strategic considerations such as why States resort to multi-*forum* litigation in the first place, and what gains do they expect to reap from using the ICJ in this context, may be better understood by drawing insights from the literature on the behaviour of litigants. Due to the limited availability of information around State motives and expectations in this respect, the book engages with the rationalist perspective of international law and relations. And at the same time, it endorses the realist assumption whereby a decision to litigate may be informed by the national interests at stake and the relative gains that may be achieved from litigation. I strongly believe that a meaningful engagement with both disciplines is necessary to put the analysis in perspective.

Like every work that focuses on dispute settlement, the proposed book risks being outdated by running events. I believe that I have minimized this risk. First, the argument presented here relies upon recent ICJ caselaw. If legal certainty is safeguarded, it will not become outdated any time soon. Second, I selected disputes that are recent but now closed to illustrate the argument in Chapters 3 and 4. Third, the ongoing *Ukraine v. Russia* dispute is utilized in Chapter 2 because it is an exemplary case of a multi-*forum* litigation strategy. Developments are expected in this case, and they will likely run in the headlines for the next two years at least (unless settlement in all pending proceedings occurs before that time, which is highly unlikely at this point in time). However, the twofold purpose of its inclusion is independent of any judicial outcome: first, to demonstrate the turn inter-State dispute resolution has taken towards multi-*forum* litigation and further, to expose the characteristics of this strategy and its effects on international dispute settlement (how it is – not – analogous to a concomitant strategy in a private v. State dispute, what objectives Ukraine expects to achieve by pursuing such a strategy and how it will affect the legitimacy of the ICJ). So, the final outcome in this dispute, which – as far as the ICJ proceedings is concerned – is expected after the book's completion, will not affect the soundness of the argument. The 15th of December 2024 marks the final day of research. Any developments after this date are not incorporated in the analysis.

The subtitles in Chapters 2, 3 and 4 are inspired from the NBC sitcom 'Friends'.

Acknowledgments

I want to thank Mr. Tommaso Lusuardi, Mr. Botond Kunkli, Ms. Wanqing He and Ms. Zhang Huan Yi for their assistance with indexing.

The cover illustration *'Τοίχος'* ['Wall'] belongs to Mr. Theotokis Zervos. I am grateful for the generous gesture of allowing me to use it.

Several people have been there for me throughout this journey and they deserve a special mention. I feel indebted to Philippa Webb for her long-standing support. Her resolve to fight for what is good and just, is for me a source of inspiration. The Athens international law family game me courage and strength to go on. Among them, Anastasios Gourgourinis, Sotiris Lekkas, Panos Merkouris, Taygeti Michalakea and Akis Papastavridis were around whenever I wanted to pester them with queries about international law, music and travels. Special credit is due to Orfeas Hassapis-Tassinis – who always listens with an attentive ear – for the book's Conclusion. I know that his passion for ideas will not wane any time soon and it is comforting to know that our conversations will continue. Photini Pazartzis has been a mentor throughout my post-doc career. I cannot repay her help and wise advice.

My family is a beacon of love and without them this book would not have been possible.

CHAPTER 1

Multi-*forum* Litigation Strategy in an Inter-state Setting: What Is, Thrust of, Systematization

1 The Changing Landscape of Inter-state Litigation: Litigation as Diplomacy

Justice is an elusive concept. As understood in the international arena it provides a framework for thinking about the rights and duties of States.[1] The latter pursue such justice by different means and in different settings; in buzzing diplomatic corridors, in sterile courtrooms and in mud-filled battlefields. These settings are engaged in a parallel fashion, rendering thus litigation 'a phase in the unfolding of a political drama'.[2] Situated amidst informal exchanges and crude violence, judicial proceedings constitute a performative ritual, a structured spectacle that aims to generate normative commands to its addressees. The theatrical aspect of delivering justice through judicial proceedings not only justifies enforcement with judicial outcomes,[3] at the same time it transforms the courtroom to an agent of political communication, a stage for political debate.[4]

Nevertheless, courts are resisting their transformation into political battlefields or – even further – into political agents, as this is in tension with their judicial function.[5] The attempt to get rid of the political from the judicial process rests upon a 'pure' conceptual construction of justice untainted from policy underpinnings. Compared to the understanding of justice in a domestic context, in the international realm such eradication of politics from the delivery of justice is all the more impossible. For, in the absence of a global consti-

1 FD Hjorthen, 'International justice' in W Thompson (ed.), *Oxford Research Encyclopedia of Politics* (OUP, 2022), 1.

2 M Shaw, *Rosenne's Law and Practice of the International Court 1920–2015 vol. I* (Brill, 2016), 3.

3 J Allen, 'Theater of International Justice' 3 (2012) *Creighton International and Comparative Law Journal* 121.

4 C Stahn, *Justice as Message*: Expressivist Foundations of International Criminal Justice (OUP, 2020), 250ff.

5 J Odermatt, 'Patterns of avoidance: political questions before international courts' 14 (2018) *International Journal of Law in Context* 221; C Bradley and E Posner, 'The Real Political Question Doctrine' 75 (2023) *Stanford Law Review* 1031.

 | DOI:10.1163/9789004704565_002

tution defining the contours of international justice, international courts have traditionally been used for the furtherance of policy objectives as part of a diplomatic campaign. To complicate things even more, the ability of international judicial institutions to navigate the *amour impossible* between legal proceedings and politics will determine how kindly history will judge them.[6] The present book embraces this entangled perception of international justice, while understanding that the instrumentalization of this idea has been possible in an international setting via legal processes. That is, via processes administered by organs that exercise their functions on the basis of legal rules and make their findings by applying legal rules.

To avert the catastrophic ramifications of military engagement, the International Court of Justice (ICJ or the Court) has been created by United Nations members to administer international justice via adjudication, a structured rule-based process. And it was given the necessary powers to perform its function. And it was armed with the necessary arsenal (human and material resources) to fulfil its task. Lately, the Court has become highly relevant in adjudicating global affairs. As relevant as it has ever been. As these lines are written, facets of the three deadliest conflicts of 2024 – Ukraine, Palestine and Myanmar – are examined by the Court. One can add to this list the Syrian civil war and the war over Nagorno-Karabakh, which may not reach the previous ones in fatalities, however their geopolitical importance is beyond dispute. Beyond conflicts, proceedings on matters of interest transcending the interests of litigating States are either already pending before the ICJ (e.g. the request for an advisory opinion on climate change) or States have declared their intention to bring them before the Court (e.g. the situation of women in Afghanistan). Then, a cursory look at the ICJ's docket indicates that the international community has placed upon the Court most of its hopes for the resolution of high-profile inter-State disputes and more generally, the delivery of international justice. Otherwise said by the Court's President in his 2024 UN General Assembly address: 'the international community's reliance on the Court has never been greater'.[7]

---

6 The Permanent Court of International Justice has been 'but a footnote [in the political history of the League of Nations], partly because it did not deal with the main political issues of the day', O Spiermann, *International Legal Argument in the Permanent Court of International Justice: The Rise of the International Judiciary* (CUP, 2005), 132.

7 *Speech of HE Judge Nawaf Salam, President of the International Court of Justice, On the Occasion of the Seventy-Eighth Session of the United Nations General Assembly*, 24 October 2024, available at: https://www.icj-cij.org/sites/default/files/press-releases/0/000-20241024-sta-01-00-en.pdf, 13.

Being the principal judicial organ of a political organization, the Court performs its functions within the general framework of the political organization of the international society. Under this prism, the ICJ is a *medium* of diplomacy. And the decision to resort to the Court ('decision to sue') is a political one.[8] Since the 1990s the engagement of the Court for the political added value it generates has become more overt.[9] States rely all the more on litigation as part of a broader advocacy campaign. This engagement of the Court as a means to achieve policy objectives will be called 'instrumentalization' or 'utilization' throughout this book. This book examines the phenomenon of ICJ instrumentalization in the context of a – lately very trendy – litigation strategy: multi-*forum* litigation.

In order to do so, the analysis will move around two axes. Each one develops around a fundamental question. First axis of analysis: what are *the limits* of ICJ instrumentalization in the context of a multi-*forum* litigation strategy? To understand these limits two interconnected issues must be examined: the policy objectives States pursue when utilizing the ICJ in the course of such a strategy. And then, the extent to which resort to the ICJ can accommodate these objectives. Otherwise put, to what extent is multi-*forum* litigation an effective strategy for the promotion of policy objectives? Second axis of analysis: what *ramifications* ensue from such instrumentalization? These pertain to the Court's institutional authority. How does this instrumentalization affect State perception on the Court's role? And further, what impact does this new perception have on the Court's authority?

To come to grips with this, starting point of the analysis will be the rationale behind the decision to sue. Deciphering this is no easy feat. Some speculation in constructing motives is inevitable in the first place, and the related commentary targeting State motivation in engaging the ICJ does not provide much clarification.[10] States resort to judicial dispute settlement with the purpose to score points in a political controversy, so this decision is often multi-factored and animated by complex policy objectives. For example, domestic considerations may be decisive. Engaging the Court to settle a long-standing dispute via a judgment is an easy way of evading the responsibilities ensuing from decision-making: politicians will emerge victorious in case of a positive outcome and will pass the buck to the Court for any concessions that must be

8 T Gill, *Litigation Strategy at the International Court: A Case Study of the Nicaragua vs. United States Dispute* (Brill, 1989) 74.

9 Shaw, *supra* note 2.

10 See *infra* this Chapter Section 3.

made in the opposite scenario.[11] Then, because such instrumentalization of a judicial organ must be done against the backdrop of its functions, it is equally important to examine the framework within which the Court exercises such functions. The decision to request provisional measures is consonant with the objective of swiftly settling a dispute and submitting it to the attention of international public opinion.[12] On the other hand, lobbying for an ICJ advisory opinion accommodates better the desire to have the Court clarify or develop the law, and thus contributes to the 'setting of the conditions to negotiate solutions at the political level'.[13] If, instead, the sole animating factor is the public articulation of a political grievance, the introduction in 2004 of live video coverage of Court sessions, renders all oral ICJ proceedings a great public platform of communication.[14]

Lately, the Court is increasingly utilized as an agent of political pressure, not necessarily as a legal dispute settler. States capitalize on the Court's capacity to have an impact on the dispute not because it can generate legal normative commands to litigants, but rather because it can be politically influential via other means; as a *medium* of communication and as a promoter of a historic narrative. In disputes where the respondent is not expected to comply with Court outputs, judicial proceedings may promote policy objectives in different ways. And arguably, lately States do not focus exclusively on the ICJ's role as a determinative way of settling a dispute, because they do not always expect the Court to fulfil this role. Of course, this is directly relevant to the nature of cases that make their way to the Court. So, by modifying their expectations, States implant new roles in the Court. Roles that are connected to the Court's instrumentalization. The book does not argue that States instrumentalize the Court exclusively in this way, rather that this aspect is becoming all the more prevalent nowadays.

Certain indicia testify to the heightened State interest in utilizing international courts for their potential to exercise political pressure. First, it has

11 H Lauterpacht, *The Development of International Law by the International Court* (CUP, 2011), 4.

12 T Treves, 'The Political Use of Unilateral Applications and Provisional Measures Proceedings' in JA Frowein *et al* (eds) *Negotiating for Peace, Liber Amicorum Tono Eitel* (Springer, 2003) 463.

13 V Lowe, 'The Function of Litigation in International Society' (2012) 61 *International and Comparative Law Quarterly* 209, 213.

14 Introduced 'in response to the exceptional interest shown by the general public, civil society organizations and the media worldwide' (UN Doc. A/59/4, 51[266]) video coverage is a sign that the Court is more and more concerned by the need to establish better public relations, R Kolb, *The International Court of Justice* (Hart, 2013), 1197.

become an ever more common practice for international legal actors to recharacterize, compartmentalize, disaggregate, or reframe their dispute so as to fall within the Court's jurisdiction.[15] The respondent's opposition to the engagement of a judicial body to rule upon a dispute (termed here as 'defective consent'[16]) forces the applicant to engage in this practice. In such cases, the only option the applicant State is left with, is to invoke the compromissory clauses of multilateral treaties as the basis of ICJ jurisdiction. And when these treaties are of a humanitarian character, such as the Convention for the Elimination of Racial Discrimination (CERD) or the Genocide Convention, the Court and public opinion are exposed to claims regarding egregious human rights violations.[17] So, the jurisdictional clause becomes a convenient tag for disputes that essentially have little connection with the substance of the conventions invoked and where the parties are arguably more interested in drawing international attention to their plight than the settlement of the dispute.[18] For example, the engagement of the ICJ by Ukraine (examined in Chapter 2) and by Qatar (examined in Chapter 3) was based on such conventions. However, in both cases the claims presented to the Court derive from broader disputes with substantial political implications that cannot be submitted as such to the Court because of jurisdictional limitations. The opposition of attitudes in Middle East conflicts and the determination of spheres of influence, including links to Iran or the United States, are the background of the Qatari legal campaign. Sovereign claims over Ukrainian territory by the Russian Federation is the controversy underlying Ukraine's campaign. Such shoehorning pivots the discussion to "what is the dispute really about?",[19] and brings to the forefront issues of ICJ instrumentalization.

The same question and concomitant inquiries regarding judicial instrumentalization have lately surfaced with respect to other international judicial bodies too. Two examples are pertinent in this respect. In an unprecedented move, Azerbaijan made use in 2023 of the Bern Convention Arbitration whereby it sought an order that Armenia cease all ongoing violations of

15 L Hill-Cawthorne, 'International Litigation and the Disaggregation of Disputes: Ukraine/Russia as a Case Study', 68 (2019) *International and Comparative Law Quarterly*, 779.

16 Gill has called this lack of 'real consent', *supra* note 8, 64.

17 T Treves, 'Litigating global crises. Setting the scene: Legal and political hurdles for State-to-State disputes' 85 (2001) *Questions of International Law, Zoom-out* 5, 9.

18 Ph. Okowa, 'The International Court of Justice and the Georgia/Russia Dispute' 11 (2011) *Human Rights Law Review* 739, 740.

19 See ICJ, *Allegations of Genocide* (*Ukraine v. Russia*), Order, Provisional Measures, 16 March 2022, Separate Opinion of Judge Robinson, 242, 246[13]

the Convention on the Conservation of European Wildlife and Natural Habitats, and pay full reparation for environmental destruction in Nagorno Karabakh.[20] And in 2018, Qatar initiated arbitration under Article 32 of the Constitution of the Universal Postal Union against Bahrain, Egypt, Saudi Arabia and the United Arab Emirates.[21] Qatar challenged the closure of borders to postage as an effect of the 2017 Gulf diplomatic crisis. The employment of dispute settlement bodies that have never been used before and at the same time they have little to do with the underlying subject-matter of the overall dispute suggests that States are determined to utilize international judicial mechanisms as necessary components of a diplomatic campaign.

Both aforementioned extraordinary proceedings formed part of a litigation campaign spanning across several jurisdictions. This points to the second indication that international courts, and the ICJ in particular, are being increasingly sought for their potential to generate political pressure. Lately, States employ a litigation strategy whereby they use as many judicial *fora* as possible to have a saying on a broader dispute. With the ICJ usually playing a coordinating, key role in it. Such strategy has featured prominently in several high-profile inter-State conflicts; Ukraine has employed it in its decade long confrontation with Russia over Crimea and Eastern Ukraine, Georgia utilized it against Russia on the war over Abkhazia and South Ossetia, Armenia against Azerbaijan (and vice versa) over Nagorno-Karabakh and Palestine in its confrontation with Israel. However, it has proven pertinent in factual circumstances beyond those related to armed conflicts as a means of influencing underlying negotiations. Qatar made use of it in its attempt to lift the blockade it suffered from a Quartet of neighboring States, Timor-Leste when trying to vindicate from Australia its rights over the oil and gas reserves of the Timor Sea, and also Mauritius in order to reclaim from the UK its sovereign rights over the Chagos archipelago.

It is tempting to understand this increasing judicialization of inter-State disputes as a side-effect of shoe-horning. Since jurisdictional barriers prevent comprehensive settlement of a dispute, resort to more than one *fora* is inevitable. In this book however, it is viewed under a different lens. Not as the side-effect, but rather as the root-cause of shoehorning. This is so, because the

---

20 PCA, *Bern Convention Arbitration* (*Azerbaijan v. Armenia*), case no. 2023–60, available at: https://pca-cpa.org/en/cases/314/.

21 PCA, *Arbitration pursuant to Article 32 of the Constitution of the Universal Postal Union* (*The State of Qatar v. The United Arab Emirates*), case no. 2020–28, available at: https://pca-cpa.org/cn/cases/253/; *Qatar v. Bahrain*, case no. 2020–25; *Qatar v. Egypt*, case no. 2020–26; *Qatar v. Saudi Arabia*, case no. 2020–27.

factors animating such recourse to many judicial proceedings are sometimes unrelated to legal dispute settlement. In disputes of asymmetrical conflict for example, i.e. when the military capabilities of belligerent powers are not simply unequal but so significantly different that they cannot launch attacks of a similar scale and forcefulness against each other,[22] the weaker party to the conflict wages war on many fronts. The legal one being a key area of confrontation. Nevertheless, expectations of compliance with judicial commands in such cases are meager, if non-existent. Instead, this practice of transferring the conflict from the ground to the courts, has put in the spotlight the role of international tribunals in advancing strategic or military gains. If States utilize international judicial institutions for purposes other than dispute settlement, strategic resort to a litigation campaign can be seen as the mainspring – not the effect – of shoe-horning. In other words, States engage this strategy not *because* they have to salami-slice their disputes, rather, they are fixated on engaging more than one judicial *fora* and to do so they have to disaggregate their disputes.

The urge to resort to as many judicial institutions as possible may spiral in an antagonism of claims by both sides. This is exemplified in the legal confrontation between Armenia and Azerbaijan over Nagorno Karabakh.[23] It started off in September 2020 as an application by Armenia for provisional measures before the ECtHR for the reignition of the conflict in and around the region of Nagorno-Karabakh. And until the filing of the sixth inter-State application before this mechanism in August 2022 – the second one was brought by Azerbaijan – the ICJ had been employed to have a saying on the conflict's development. Armenia filed first an application against Azerbaijan before the ICJ in 16 September 2021, again coupled with requests for provisional measures. The application was countered – a week later (*sic*) – by Azerbaijan, which brought its own case against Armenia, much as it did before the ECtHR. Further, Azerbaijan upped the ante by resorting in 2023 to the Bern Convention arbitration, and to the (first inter-State) Energy Charter Treaty arbitration both administered by the Permanent Court of Arbitration. By overusing international judicial proceedings Azerbaijan is likely protesting too much in an attempt to 'give the impression that [it] is the true victim',[24]

22 A Paulus and M Vashakmadge, 'Asymmetrical war and the notion of armed conflict – A tentative conceptualization' 91 (2009) *International Review of the Red Cross* 95.

23 I Plakokefalos, 'The conflict in Nagorno-Karabakh before international dispute settlement bodies' *ELIAMEP Policy Paper #148/2023*.

24 ICJ, *Application of the International Convention on the Elimination of All Forms of Racial Discrimination (Azerbaijan v. Armenia)*, CR 2021/25, 12[2] (Kirakosyan).

while Armenia is possibly trying to micromanage a conflict via consecutive decisions of international courts. Be that as it may, the motivations underlying judicial instrumentalization are indicative of State perceptions regarding the role of such institutions, but also of international law as 'a system of claims'.[25]

The present book examines the engagement of the ICJ in the context of such a litigation strategy. It is the latest turn international dispute settlement has taken, yet, it is under-studied. Because a trend is in a state of formation, it is no longer appropriate to ignore it. The next Section will label such strategy as 'multi-*forum* litigation strategy' and after defining its essential characteristics it will distinguish it from the concepts of lawfare and strategic litigation. Further, this introductory chapter outlines the book's objectives. It sets the questions underlying the research agenda that has opened up by virtue of the utilization of this strategy. Then, the last Section explains how the book goes about in answering these questions.

2 Defining 'Multi-*forum* Litigation Strategy'

'Multi-*forum* litigation strategy' is not a term of art in international law, but it has been floating around in legal scholarship for quite some time. In science, like in art, parthenogenesis is rare. In dispute settlement scholarship – a scholarship reactive to the phenomenon of judicial practice – 'multi-*forum* litigation' has been used, often interchangeably with 'multi-jurisdictional litigation', in order to describe the judicial practice of pursuing a similar claim in multiple judicial *fora*.[26] In a domestic context, the term has been used to describe the filing of identical civil claims in more than one US state courts (hence the related term 'multi-district litigation').[27] In international adjudica-

25 P d'Argent, 'International Law as a System of Claims. What Can International Law Do to Stop the War?' 107 (2024) *Questions of International Law* 9.

26 M Myers, 'Fixing Multi-*Forum* Shareholder Litigation' (2014) *University of Illinois Law Review* 467; E Micheletti and J Parker, 'Multi-Jurisdictional Litigation: Who Caused this Problem, and Can it Be Fixed?' 37 (2012) *Delaware Journal of Corporate Law* 1.

27 J Stengel and A Calamari, 'Complex Multi-*Forum* Litigation' 36 (1996) *International Commercial Litigation* 21. Congress established in 1968 the Judicial Panel on Multidistrict Litigation a special body with the authority to determine whether civil actions pending in two or more federal judicial districts should be transferred to a single such court for pretrial proceedings. The problem is pervasive across the US and according to the statistics report published by this body, as of 1 November 2024, there are 325, 303 cases pending in 173 multidistrict litigations in 48 transferee districts before 145 district judges, available at: https://www.jpml.uscourts.gov/pending-mdls-0.

tion, Schneider utilized the term in 1990 to describe "all those disputes where the same or related facts or issues are tried before several different *fora*".[28] While he attempted to comprehensively categorize all such "disputes with which internationally practising lawyers are concerned", the latter related only to private vs. State cases.[29] Until today, a prolific scholarship targets the practice of investors to initiate simultaneous arbitrations under different investment treaties and contracts for the same dispute.[30] However, no detailed examination of such practice in the resolution of inter-State disputes can be found in international scholarship.

'Multi-*forum* litigation strategy', is understood here as the parallel or consecutive engagement of more than one international judicial *fora* to rule upon the same factual matrix as a strategic choice of a State. The idiosyncrasies of inter-State dispute settlement render multi-*forum* litigation at the inter-State level inherently different and more intricate than multi-*forum* litigation involving other actors. States are peculiar political actors, therefore peculiar litigants, with a hoist of factors shaping and affecting their litigation objectives and strategies. Inter-State disputes are usually multi-faceted, therefore more easily disaggregated into an array of factually connected but legally unrelated claims. Also, the *fora* engaged in the context of such a strategy are diverse as to their nature and their jurisdiction. All the above testify to the need to examine closely inter-State multi-*forum* litigation strategy. The essential characteristics of this strategy are analyzed right away. One caveat is necessary from the outset: while the subjective attitude of States is not a defining characteristic of the strategy examined here, it is presumed that States pursue multi-*forum* litigation in order to achieve some goals. Otherwise, such resort to judicial institutions cannot be understood as a strategic action. A strategy presupposes the pursuance of aims.

2.1 *Essential Characteristics*

2.1.1 A *Litigation* Strategy

Litigation, or the process of carrying on a lawsuit,[31] involves the use of judicial mechanisms to raise an issue and, usually, secure an outcome. This however, does not premeditate the nature of the *fora* involved in the context of this

---

28 M Schneider, 'Multi-Fora Disputes' 6 (1990) *Arbitration International* 101.

29 Ibid. 101–7.

30 For a recent account *see* M Reisman and M Arsanjani, 'The Multiplicity of Parallel Procedures in International Law' in Ch. Brower et al. (eds) *By Peaceful Means* (OUP, 2024) 323.

31 *Black's Law Dictionary* (10th ed. 2014).

strategy. The organs that may form part of such strategy include all those institutions that meet the following criteria: they have been established by an international legal instrument, they render decisions on the basis of international law, they follow certain procedural rules in rendering their decisions and these decisions are legally binding.[32] Such organs shall be termed here, interchangeably, as: 'international judicial organs', 'judicial institutions', 'international courts', 'international judicial mechanisms' or 'international judicial *fora*'.

2.1.2 A *One Actor* Strategy

This book is about a particular litigation strategy utilised by a State. It does not examine the use of international courts when this does not constitute the premeditated choice of one State as a user of international courts. That is, where this actor has been actively involved in planning and devising the respective lawsuits. Sometimes, applications instituting proceedings are brought in multiple international *fora*, even concurrently, concerning the same facts, nevertheless they are brought independently by different interested parties. Hence, they do not form part of a comprehensive strategy. For example, applications pertaining to Senegal's refusal to prosecute or extradite Hissene Habré, the former Chadian President, were filed before the African Court on Human and Peoples' Rights, the Court of Justice of the Economic Community of West African States ('ECOWAS Court'), and the ICJ.[33] Before the ICJ, Belgium initiated proceedings regarding Senegal's failure to prosecute Habré or extradite him. Belgium sought a ruling from the ICJ that Senegal submit 'without delay the Hissene Habré case to its competent authorities for prosecution; or ... failing that, ... [extradite] Mr. Habré to Belgium'.[34] National prosecution in Senegal was stalled by a judgment from the ECOWAS Court after Mr. Habré himself had petitioned the Court claiming that his prosecution would run counter to his human rights.[35] Finally, it was a Chadian

32 I borrow here four of the five criteria used by C Romano, 'The Proliferation of International Judicial Bodies: The Pieces of the Puzzle' 31 (1999) *NYU Journal of International Law and Politics*, 709, 713–4. This definition comes close to the understanding of 'international judicial institutions' by A von Bogdandy and I Venzke, 'Beyond Dispute: International Judicial Institutions as Lawmakers' 12 (2011) *German Law Journal* 979.

33 S Shah, 'Questions Relating to the Obligation to Prosecute or Extradite (Belgium v. Senegal)' 13 (2013) *Human Rights Law Review* 351, 352–5.

34 ICJ, *Questions Relating to the Obligation to Prosecute or Extradite* (*Belgium v Senegal*) Merits, 20 July 2012 [13].

35 ECOWAS Court, *Habré v Republic of Senegal*, 18 November 2010, ECW/CCJ/JUD/06/10.

national residing in Switzerland who filed an application to the African Court on Human and Peoples' Rights claiming that the legislative amendments and the initiation of proceedings against Habré was in violation of the African Charter on Human and Peoples' Rights.[36]

Relatedly, the possibility open to both individuals and States to vindicate violations of international law arising from the same factual circumstances against the same respondent State is a phenomenon that lies, almost entirely, outside the scope of this book.[37] Almost entirely, because strangely enough, not only inter-State judicial institutions may form part of a State's litigation strategy. International courts may be used by private parties as proxies of the State or under State influence in order to accommodate State interests. For jurisdictional or other reasons, a State may, as a strategic choice, force other litigants to step forward and request the triggering of responsibility of the opposing State. For example, it has been convincingly argued that prompting investors to resort to international investment arbitral tribunals may effectively promote State interests in the course of a litigation strategy.[38]

2.1.3 A *Multi*-forum Strategy

Further, more than one international judicial institutions are engaged in the context of this strategy. Temporally, this may be done either in a parallel or in a consecutive fashion. While it is not necessary that the claims before different *fora* overlap in substance,[39] it is important that all judicial proceedings are based on the same factual matrix.[40] This connection between proceedings ensures that the latter target the same overarching dispute, hence they form part of a comprehensive strategy. A dispute is understood in the broadest possible terms per Articles 2(3), 33 and 36 of the UN Charter, as a set of facts that generate "a higher degree of tension between two States than a mere

36 African Court of Human and People's Rights, *Michelot Yogogombaye v. Senegal*, 15 December 2009, Application No 001/2008

37 J Howley, *Overlapping Individual and Interstate Claims in International Law* (OUP, 2024).

38 This has arguably been the case with respect to Ukrainian investors and the annexation of Crimea, E Chang, *Lawfare in Ukraine: Weaponizing International Investment Law and the Law of Armed Conflict Against Russia's Invasion* (National Defense University Press, 2022); C Miles, 'Lawfare in Crimea: treaty, territory, and investor–state dispute settlement', 38 (2022) *Arbitration International* 135. Anecdotal evidence suggests that Ukraine continues this strategy with respect to the war in Eastern Ukraine, *see* Chapter 2.

39 A Nollkaemper, 'Conversations among Courts: Domestic and International Adjudicators' in C Romano, K Alter, and Y Shany (eds), *The Oxford Handbook of International Adjudication* (OUP, 2014) 523, 529.

40 Howley, *supra* note 37, 3.

'situation'" that does not threaten international peace and security.[41] The connecting factor rendering different judicial proceedings part of the same strategy is stronger than proceedings "that are linked in some ways, or which have some similarities",[42] but weaker than proceedings "arising from the same conduct."[43] The latter is too restrictive because inter-State disputes are multifaceted and they can be easily compartmentalized into various smaller disputes. Thus, judicial claims targeting different State conduct may still be part of an integrated litigation strategy regarding a single overarching dispute. On the other hand, the former is too generic as legally related but factually unconnected legal proceedings must not be understood as forming part of an integrated litigation strategy.

2.2 *Multi-*forum *Litigation Strategy as a Concept Distinct from 'Lawfare' and 'Strategic Litigation'*

Subjective elements are not defining features of a multi-*forum* litigation strategy. The motivation underlying resort to such a strategy or the objectives pursued are not relevant in order to classify certain strategic State actions as multi-*forum* litigation strategy. So, the concept is merely descriptive of a recurring State practice without any normative understanding as to its key objectives or the outcomes it produces. As noted above, litigation has always been a political phenomenon and concomitantly the use of legal argument to create the 'political leverage' to advance policy objectives has always formed part of a State's political arsenal.[44]

The possibility of using international legal norms in the courtroom or outside of it to try to achieve or to consolidate political gains has been the target of two strands of scholarship; one on 'lawfare' and another one on 'strategic

41 D Caron and Chr. Tomuschat, 'Article 2(3) UN Charter' in A Zimmermann et al. (eds) *The Statute of the ICJ: A Commentary* (OUP, 2012), 130 [22]; T Giegerich, 'Article 36 UN Charter' in *Ibid.* 189–191[24]–[29].

42 T Gazzini and A Pietrobon, 'Parallel Proceedings Concerning Investment and Human Rights Claims' in *The Changing Character of International Dispute Settlement* (CUP, 2023), 45, 46; G Cuniberti, 'Parallel litigation and foreign investment disputes settlement' (2006) ICSID *Review* 381, 382; H Wehland, *The Coordination of Multiple Proceedings in Investment Treaty Arbitration* (OUP, 2013), [1.20].

43 J Crawford, 'Overview of Part Three of the Articles on State Responsibility' in J Crawford et al. (eds), *The Law of International Responsibility* (OUP, 2010) 931, 932; A Roberts, 'Triangular Treaties: The Extent and Limits of Investment Treaty Rights' (2015) 56 Harvard International Law Journal 353, 383.

44 M Becker, 'Lawfare: Law as a Weapon of War. By Orde F Kittrie' (2017) *British Yearbook of International Law* 199, 201.

litigation'.[45] Dunlap introduced lawfare in 2001 to denote 'law as a weapon of war',[46] but since then its use has been unsystematic and conceptually the term has lost any solidity.[47] In fact, lawfare suffers from two inherent defects that render it not only useless as a concept for present purposes, but also dangerous as to its after-effect if over-used. First, it seems to be little 'more than a rhetorical gambit to attack challenges to the legality' of State behavior, because it carries with it a particular stigma of illegitimate recourse to legal remedies.[48] Second, due to its indeterminacy it is unclear where lawfare ends and 'the rest of the practice of international law begins'.[49] If every use of international law can be labeled as 'lawfare', the term is prone to abuse and to the creation of confusion. In other words, the labelling of some State behavior as 'lawfare' does not leave us wiser as to the evaluation of such conduct, it only puts into question the motivation behind such labelling.

Equally unhelpful in analyzing inter-State disputes is the scholarship on 'strategic litigation' as it is practically impossible to distinguish it from litigation that is non-strategic. Commonly associated with human rights litigation,[50] 'strategic litigation' has been defined in multiple ways.[51] Common attribute of these definitions and what makes 'strategic litigation' stand out is its objective to be politically influential and thus foster institutional, legal and political change.[52] But, in the context of inter-State litigation examined here, isn't this the case with all judicial initiatives undertaken by States? In

45 O Kittrie, Lawfare: law as a weapon of war (OUP, 2016), 5; M Ramsden and Kr. Gledhill, 'Defining Strategic Litigation' 38 (2019) *Civil Justice Quarterly* 407.

46 Ch. Dunlap, 'Law and Military Interventions: Preserving Humanitarian Values in 21st Conflicts', 29 November 2001, available at: www.people.duke.edu/~pfeaver/dunlap.pdf.

47 Goldenziel identified five sub-types of lawfare, J Goldenziel, Law as a Battlefield: The U.S., China, and the Global Escalation of Lawfare' 106 (2021) *Cornell Law Review* 1085, 1099–1100.

48 WA Schabas, 'Gaza, Goldstone and Lawfare' 43 (2010) *Case Western Reserve Journal of International Law* 307, 309.

49 D Guilfoyle, 'Litigation as Statecraft: Small States and the Law of the Sea' (2023) *British Yearbook of International Law* 1, 6.

50 But *see*, Fl. Jeßberger and L Steinl, 'Strategic Litigation in International Criminal Justice: Facilitating a View from Within' 20 (2022) *Journal of International Criminal Justice* 379.

51 *Compare* Ramsden and Gledhill, *supra* note 45, 407–416 and H Duffy, *Strategic Human Rights Litigation: Understanding and Maximising Impact* (Hart, 2018), 4–5.

52 In a subtle admission of the relaxed conceptual *contours* of the term, Hondora suggests that it is interchangeable with 'public interest litigation', 'test-case litigation', 'impact litigation' and 'cause-lawyering', T Hondora, 'Civil Society Organisations' Role in the Development of International Law through Strategic Litigation in Challenging Times' 25 (2018) *Australian International Law Journal* 115.

other words, all State litigation has a strategic component and making this the defining characteristic of resort to judicial proceedings has limited analytical value for present purposes.

While neither term provides an adequate conceptual framework to analyze State litigation practice, the book will delve into the potential of multi-*forum* litigation strategy to promote change in inter-State relations. It is not the objective of this book to de-politicize the discourse regarding State resort to international judicial institutions. Nor to attempt a relevant discussion without putting forward an understanding of State motivations, State objectives and the potential outcomes from such use of international judicial institutions. To the contrary, it strives to do so without at the same time characterizing such practice as either 'lawfare' or 'strategic litigation'.[53]

3 Book Objectives

The engagement of many judicial institutions to rule upon an inter-State dispute opens a research agenda that remains largely unexplored and the book aims to unearth. In particular, the intention is to assess two things. First, how the ICJ, the most authoritative inter-State juridical forum and the only one of general jurisdiction, is instrumentalized in the context of this strategy (the *limits*). And further, how this utilization and incorporation in a multi-*forum* litigation strategy impacts the Court's perceived role, its legitimacy and authority (the *ramifications*). To do so, the book investigates all inter-State disputes where the ICJ formed part of this strategy. Ten such disputes constitute the empirical backbone of the book, nine of them appearing in the Court's docket in the last 20 years (see Table 1.1). Using the ICJ to have a saying on a dispute can be visualized as a tug-of-war between the resorting State (be it an applicant State in the course of contentious proceedings or a State that lies behind the initiative to pose a question to the Court for the rendering of an advisory opinion) and the Court. The latter is increasingly sought for the advance of political gains and not for the overall resolution of the dispute in a determinative way, as would happen in e.g. a delimitation dispute. For example, such objective underlay Yugoslavia's requests in the *Use of Force* cases where the Court clearly lacked jurisdiction for a pronouncement on the NATO intervention in Kosovo. From the Court's perspective, in such dis-

53 Guilfoyle suggests the use of the term 'legal statecraft' instead, for 'it involves a shift in emphasis', *supra* note 49, 6.

putes it is increasingly difficult to keep both sides happy when reacting to such instrumentalization, i.e. to render Solomonic decisions that have a greater compliance potential.[54] So, the ICJ is caught amidst heavily politicized, polarized and high-stakes disputes.

This does not negate the importance of inter-State disputes where multi-*forum* litigation has been pursued, that have not made their way to the ICJ. For example, the fishing rights dispute between the Faroe Islands and the European Union underscores how different areas of international law may be brought to bear on a complex international problem. In 2013, the small island territory of Denmark asserted a right to a larger share of the annual herring catch due to changes in the stock's migration pattern. The EU answered by unilaterally imposing economic sanctions against the Faroes. Denmark brought simultaneously a WTO dispute challenging these measures as a violation of the trade rules,[55] and initiated arbitration under the UN Convention on the Law of the Sea alleging violations of this instrument.[56] In an *exemplaire* that recourse to international judicial processes is a weapon of the weak,[57] the Faroe Islands created favorable negotiating conditions and achieved swiftly their stated objectives. In the decentralized international legal order State consent to judicial mechanisms is provided sparingly. Thus, due to lack of jurisdiction the ICJ is not always an available *forum*. Nevertheless, pursuing such a strategy is a one-way street for States that wish to capitalize on the political pressure generated by multiple judicial proceedings.

What is more, the practical significance of this strategic use of international judicial *fora* has been emphasized lately in addressing issues of global concern.[58] The employment of mechanisms scattered across different international legal instruments to deal with an issue of common concern

54 N Grossman, 'Solomonic Judgments and the Legitimacy of the International Court of Justice' in Cohen et al. (eds) *Legitimacy and International Courts* (CUP, 2018), 43.

55 WTO, *EU-Herring,* case no. DS469 (mutually agreed solution on 21 August 2014).

56 PCA, *The Atlanto-Scandian Herring Arbitration* (*The Kingdom of Denmark in respect of the Faroe Islands v. The European Union*), case no. 2013–30, Termination Order, 23 September 2014.

57 D Guilfoyle, 'The South China Sea Award: How Should We Read the UN Convention on the Law of the Sea?' 8 (2018) *Asian Journal of International Law* 51, 56; B Kingsbury, 'International Courts: Uneven Judicialisation in Global Order' in J Crawford and M Koskenniemi (eds), *The Cambridge Companion to International Law* (CUP, 2012) 217–8.

58 D Raju et al., 'Multi-*Forum* Strategies to Tackle Climate Change and Other Complex Problems: A Note from Practitioners', *Ejil:talk!* 1 November 2022, available at: https://www.ejiltalk.org/multi-forum-strategies-to-tackle-climate-change-and-other-complex

TABLE 1.1 Inter-state disputes where a multi-*forum* litigation strategy was pursued (order by date of presentation of claims to the ICJ)

State initiating strategy	Opponent(s)	Factual matrix	ICJ Engagement (case name and date of presentation of claims)	Other judicial *fora* engaged
Democratic Republic of the Congo	Rwanda, Uganda and Burundi	Second Congo War	Armed Activities on the Territory of the Congo, 23 June 1999	African Commission on Human and Peoples' Rights
Georgia	Russia	August 2008 Russo-Georgian War	Application of the International Convention on the Elimination of All Forms of Racial Discrimination, 12 August 2008	European Court of Human Rights
Timor Leste	Australia	Exploitation of natural resources in Timor Sea	Questions relating to the Seizure and Detention of Certain Documents and Data, 17 December 2013	Article 298 and Annex V of the United Nations Convention on the Law of the Sea (PCA)
Colombia	Nicaragua	Maritime delimitation and related rights	Alleged Violations of Sovereign Rights and Maritime Spaces in the Caribbean Sea, 17 November 2016 (counter-claims)	Inter-American Court of Human Rights
Ukraine	Russia	Annexation of Crimea	Application of the International Convention for the Suppression of the Financing of Terrorism and of	European Court of Human Rights, International Investment Tribunals, International Criminal Court

TABLE 1.1 Inter-state disputes where a multi-*forum* litigation strategy was pursued (order by date of presentation of claims to the ICJ) (*cont.*)

State initiating strategy	Opponent(s)	Factual matrix	ICJ Engagement (case name and date of presentation of claims)	Other judicial *fora* engaged
			the International Convention on the Elimination of All Forms of Racial Discrimination, 16 January 2017	
Mauritius	UK and Maldives	Status of Chagos Archipelago	Legal Consequences of the Separation of the Chagos Archipelago from Mauritius in 1965, 23 June 2017 (advisory opinion)	Article 287 and Annex VII, Article 1 of the United Nations Convention on the Law of the Sea (PCA), International Tribunal on the Law of the Sea
Qatar	UAE/ Bahrain/ Saudi Arabia/Egypt	2017 Qatar diplomatic crisis	Application of the International Convention on the Elimination of All Forms of Racial Discrimination (only vs. UAE), 11 June 2018	Article 32 of the Constitution of the Universal Postal Union (PCA), Committee of the International Convention on the Elimination of All Forms of Racial Discrimination, WTO Panels
Palestine	Israel	Israeli-Palestinian conflict/ Status of Palestine	Relocation of the United States Embassy to Jerusalem (vs United States of America), 28 September 2018 +	International Criminal Court, Committee of the International Convention on the Elimination of All Forms of Racial Discrimination

TABLE 1.1 Inter-state disputes where a multi-*forum* litigation strategy was pursued (order by date of presentation of claims to the ICJ) (*cont.*)

State initiating strategy	Opponent(s)	Factual matrix	ICJ Engagement (case name and date of presentation of claims)	Other judicial *fora* engaged
			Legal Consequences arising from the Policies and Practices of Israel in the Occupied Palestinian Territory, including East Jerusalem, 19 January 2023 (advisory opinion)	
Armenia	Azerbaijan	Second Nagorno Karabakh War/ Status of Nagorno Karabakh	Application of the International Convention on the Elimination of All Forms of Racial Discrimination, 16 September 2021	European Court of Human Rights
Azerbaijan	Armenia	Second Nagorno Karabakh War/ Status of Nagorno Karabakh	Application of the International Convention on the Elimination of All Forms of Racial Discrimination, 23 September 2021	European Court of Human Rights, Energy Charter Treaty Arbitration, Bern Convention Arbitration
Ukraine	Russia	War in Eastern Ukraine	Allegations of Genocide under the Convention on the Prevention and Punishment of the Crime of Genocide, 27 February 2022	European Court of Human Rights, International Criminal Court, International Investment Tribunals

(the compartmentalisation of disputes) may be a means to integrate international law, rather than compartmentalise it. The fight against climate change is a case in point. Sometimes, bringing such matters to justice will necessitate the leveraging of areas of law that were not specifically designed to address these matters.[59] Whether this will eventually bear fruit largely depends on the attitude of courts. As things stand, it is probably the only way for international justice to adapt to rapidly changing circumstances. Such litigation efforts however, do not constitute the strategic choice of one actor as they often require coordinated action by many States and mayhaps other constituencies too.[60] The complexity in analysing the engagement of many judicial *fora* to litigate global matters is multiplied and so, such multi-actor strategies fall outside the scope of this book.

In order to offer an integrated account of multi-*forum* litigation, the book engages with both the legal and political science scholarship on the international judicial function. From a legal standpoint, it analyses the main characteristics of every aspect of ICJ jurisdiction (to follow the order they will be examined in the book: main proceedings, provisional measures and advisory opinions). Answers to questions such as: 'what is the normative effect of advisory opinions?', 'what connection must exist between the provisional measures requested and the rights subject to litigation?' and 'under what conditions may a State intervene in ongoing contentious proceedings?', set a working framework as to what the Court is legally empowered to do when it is seized of a dispute. Only once the limits of the ICJ's powers are clearly defined, can one understand what its users may request from it, what they may expect to get in return from using the Court and how the Court may react to its utilization. But yet, the legal analysis can paint only part of the picture. Relevant strategic considerations such as why States resort to multi-

-problems-a-note-from-practitioners/; J Bendel and Y Suedi, *Public Interest Litigation in International Law* (Routledge, 2023).

59 C Heri, 'Climate Change before the European Court of Human Rights: Capturing Risk, Ill-Treatment and Vulnerability' 33 (2022) *European Journal of International Law* 925.

60 The initiative for an ICJ advisory opinion was led by Vanuatu, see: https://www.vanuatuicj.com/. Eventually, 18 States jointly drafted the question put to the Court and in total 105 States co-sponsored the UNGA resolution making the request, UNGA, 'Request for an advisory opinion of the International Court of Justice on the obligations of States in respect of climate change', *UN Doc. A/RES77/276*, 4 April 2023. The respective request to the International Tribunal on the Law of the Sea came from the Commission of Small Island States on Climate Change and International Law (COSIS), composed of six States from the Caribbean and Pacific regions, ITLOS, 'Request for an Advisory Opinion of 12 December 2022', available at: https://shorturl.at/twRkw.

forum litigation in the first place, and what gains do they expect to reap from using the ICJ in this context, may be better understood by drawing insights from the literature on behaviour of litigants. Due to the limited availability of information around State motives and expectations in this respect, the book accepts the liberal premise that the so-called 'decision to sue' may be driven by both domestic and international considerations. And at the same time, it endorses the realist assumption whereby a decision to litigate may be informed by the national interests at stake and the relative gains that may be achieved from litigation.

As noted above, the analysis will move around two axes. First, around the legal and policy issues that arise from the utilization of the ICJ as part of a multi-*forum* litigation strategy. In other words, to bring to the forefront all these issues that relate to the limits of the Court's instrumentalization in such occasions. To do this, the book will not attempt to address in a comprehensive manner all the complexities of developing a litigation strategy in the first place. Or, to analyze all the tactical decisions to be made in order to effectively construct such a strategy. This requires an appreciation of a multitude of factors (choice of a litigation team and of an *ad hoc* judge, determination of the strengths and weaknesses of a case and of argumentative tactics etc) and exceeds the scope of the argument presented here.[61] Instead, the book strives to understand the phenomenon of multi-*forum* litigation as a strategic choice of States. This will be done while having in mind that political and legal considerations are interconnected in inter-State judicial settlement and both inform a State's litigation strategy.[62] As mentioned above, using the ICJ can be visualized as a tug-of-war between the resorting State and the Court itself, so the analysis will be informed by both vantage points.

From the applicant's point of view, the analysis begins from a fundamental question: why States resort to this strategy? In particular, what are their objectives and why do they employ the ICJ as part of this strategy? Or, what type of gains are they expected to reap when utilizing the ICJ (to issue Advisory Opin-

---

61 For litigation tactics before the ICJ *see* A Pellet and T Barsac, 'Litigation Strategy' (2019) *Max Planck Encyclopedia of International Procedural Law;* A Watts, 'Preparation for International Litigation' *in* TM Ndiaye and R Wolfrum (eds), *Law of the Sea, Environmental Law and Settlement of Disputes: Liber Amicorum Judge Thomas Mensah* (Martinus Nijhoff, 2007), 327; 106 (2012) *Proceedings of the American Society of International Law* (contributions by Wood, Reichler, Pratt, Kinnear, Berman); S Ugalde and JJ Quintana, 'Managing Litigation before the International Court of Justice' 9 (2018) *Journal of International Dispute Settlement*, 1.

62 T Gill, *supra* note 8, 56.

ions, provisional measures Orders or Judgments) as part of this strategy? And, finally, how effective is this strategy for the attainment of policy objectives? The 'decision to sue' has been touched upon by both lawyers and political scientists for quite some time now.[63] Nevertheless, the Court's powers have changed significantly over the past twenty years; the Court has underscored the binding nature of its provisional measures and advisory opinions are perceived to possess 'legal effect'. Such changes influence State expectations when using the Court and respectively inform the decision to resort to the ICJ. Recent studies that take into consideration these changes have not examined the decision to sue in a comprehensive manner, and they seldom make reference to multi-*forum* litigation.[64] The proposed book draws insights from this scholarship and offers a comprehensive review of State objectives and how they may be accommodated when utilizing all three aspects of ICJ jurisdiction. To understand the limits of Court instrumentalization, the book outlines first the contours within which the Court exercises each aspect of its jurisdiction (main proceedings, provisional measures and advisory opinions). Then, against this background, it suggests how utilization of the Court in this strategy may effectively accommodate State objectives

Under this prism, it aims to assess the limits of multi-*forum* litigation in promoting State policy objectives. The latter can be grouped in three

63 The only dedicated book-length treatise is quite outdated, see Gill, *supra* note 8. Most important articles include: W Coplin, 'The World Court in the international bargaining process', in R Gregg and M Barkim (eds) *The United Nations and its Functions* (Princeton, 1968) 313; A Rovine, 'The National Interest and the World Court', in L Gross (ed.), *The Future of the International Court of Justice* (Oceana, 1976) 313; D Fischer, 'Decisions to Use the International Court of Justice' 26 (1982) *International Studies Quarterly* 251; I Brownlie, 'Why Do States Take Disputes to the International Court?' in Nisuke Ando et al (eds) *Liber Amicorum Judge Shigeru Oda* (Brill, 2002), 829; Chr. Gray, 'Why states resort to litigation in cases concerning the use of force', in N Klein (ed.), *Litigating International Law Disputes: Weighing the Options* (CUP, 2014), 305; Sh. Scott, 'Litigation versus dispute resolution through political processes' in N Klein (ed.) *Litigating International Law Disputes:Weighing the Balance* (CUP, 2014) 24; E Leonhardsen, 'Trials of Ordeal in the International Court of Justice: Why States Seek Provisional Measures when non-Compliance Is to Be Expected' 5 (2015) *Journal of International Dispute Settlement* 306; D Guilfoyle, 'The Chagos Archipelago before International Tribunals: Strategic Litigation and the Production of Historical Knowledge' 21 (2021) *Melbourne Journal of International Law* 749.

64 Exceptions to this are Guilfoyle, *supra* note 49; B Batros and T Khan, 'Thinking Strategically about Climate Change' in C Rodrıguez Garavito (ed), *Litigating the Climate Emergency: How Human Rights, Courts, and Legal Mobilization Can Bolster Climate Action* (CUP, 2021), 104.

categories: to resolve the dispute in one's favor, to garner international support/multilateralize the dispute and to delegitimize the opponent's position/legitimize its own position. To this end, the following questions are particularly apposite. Under what terms, can ICJ advisory opinions be incorporated in such a litigation strategy in order to promote the resolution of a bilateral dispute? This has been a major issue in the *Chagos* opinion and in the latest advisory proceedings on Palestine. Further, are ICJ provisional measures Orders an efficient tool to influence other dispute resolution proceedings running in parallel? In *Qatar vs UAE* for example, the ICJ provisional measures orders likely influenced the CERD Committee decisions on jurisdiction and admissibility against the UAE and Saudi Arabia. Or finally, to what extent are ICJ judgments clothed with a *de facto res judicata* effect? With respect to the situation in Eastern Ukraine for example, how likely is it for the ICC or the ECtHR to rely on relevant ICJ *dicta* regarding factual circumstances?

Albeit, achieving such objectives via judicial organs may come at a cost for these institutions. From the Court's viewpoint, its employment as part of this strategy may have institutional ramifications as to its authority. And the book aims to shed light to them. To do so, the book first examines how the ICJ may react to this instrumentalization. Otherwise said, how much wiggle-room does the Court have to accommodate or resist State interests when dealing with such disputes? Is the incorporation of the request for an advisory opinion in a multi-*forum* litigation strategy for the resolution of a bilateral dispute a good enough reason for the Court to deny to answer such a request? This argument has been the UK's first line of defense in *Chagos*. Further, when may the request for an ICJ pronouncement be considered abusive on account of its underlying motive? The Court has never found this to be the case, but the consecutive requests by South Africa for the indication of provisional measures in the context of the same dispute and in a short time-span has tempted the Court to revisit its position. In addition, how relevant is the theory of *lis pendens* – applied by international courts to regulate multi-*forum* proceedings in private vs. State disputes – in inter-State litigation? And further, the fact that an ICJ judgment, order or advisory opinion forms part of a series of related decisions by international courts may somehow affect its substance? In what way did the ICJ take into account in *Qatar vs. UAE* the interpretation of Article 1(1) CERD effectuated by the CERD Committee against the same factual background 18 months earlier?

Having outlined that *est modus in rebus*, the argument proceeds to the second axis of the analysis. That is, the impact such strategy may have on the Court's authority. Irrespective of the aspect of ICJ jurisdiction instrumentalized, multi-*forum* litigation impacts the Court's authority in a twofold way. Negatively, when the instrumentalization targets the Court as a *forum* for political advocacy. That is, when the ICJ is instrumentalized for the by-products of its authority; for power that does not ensue directly from the exercise of its judicial function (e.g. the ability to act as a platform of communication or its potential to create a historic narrative). Such utilization implants in the Court a role that is in tension with its judicial function. And positively, when the instrumentalization targets the Court's legitimate authority, or its capacity to produce normative commands (e.g. the capacity to create a domino of like-minded rulings and the potential to create the 'shadow of the law'). This utilization accords with the Court's judicial function and reaffirms its pivotal role as an authoritative institution in the international dispute settlement system. As noted above though, the decision to sue is a complex one. Most times the intention is to utilize the ICJ in both ways described above, so that measuring the impact on authority is increasingly more complex.

4 Book Structure

The argument develops in the following steps. In this introductory Chapter the theoretical concept is constructed ('inter-State multi-*forum* litigation') and the claim is made that multi-*forum* litigation strategy has developed into a fashionable litigation strategy. The empirical part follows in Chapters 2, 3 and 4. Each Chapter targets a different aspect of ICJ jurisdiction used in the course of such a litigation strategy, respectively main proceedings, provisional measures and advisory opinions. Therein, the monograph analyzes the limits of ICJ instrumentalization in each of them and also the ensuing concerns over the Court's authority. Finally, in the concluding fifth Chapter the book summarizes previous findings and, in this synthesis makes a claim on the Court's future days as an authoritative judicial body.

Further, each of the Chapters 2, 3 and 4 that constitute the book's backbone, develops around a running example. Chapter 2 around the ongoing Ukraine v. Russia military dispute. Chapter 3 around the Mauritius v. UK dispute over Chagos. And Chapter 4 around the Qatar v. UAE/Bahrain/Saudi Arabia/Egypt dispute regarding the 2017 sanctions. These disputes guide the argumentation as they are recalled time and again during each Chapter and any new knowledge is applied to them. Finally, these examples showcase how the ICJ may be incorporated in a multi-*forum* litigation strategy and whether this strategy constitutes an effective method of pursuing public diplomacy objectives.

Chapter 2 fleshes out the complications, at the legal and the policy level, that derive from the use of the ICJ to deliver a judgment on the merits as part of a multi-*forum* litigation strategy. In order to do so, Chapter 2 uses Ukraine v. Russia (re: Eastern Ukraine) as a running example because arguably this is the main motivation underpinning Ukraine's request. The legal issues arising from multi-*forum* proceedings have been dealt with extensively in literature with respect to disputes between private entities and States (i.e. international investment disputes). And they can be grouped in three categories: *lis pendens*, *res judicata* and abuse of rights. The first two pertain to inter-institutional relationships, while the third to the ability of the parties to engage a particular judicial forum in a dispute. By juxtaposing the two categories of disputes (State v. State and private v. State) the Chapter claims that they are not comparable and examination of the aforementioned legal issues cannot occur on a *mutatis mutandis* basis. The Chapter then considers the legal reasons why *lis pendens* and abuse of rights are unknown to ICJ jurisprudence, while the principle of *res judicata* operates with a much more limited scope.

The Chapter also showcases that main proceedings before the Court accommodate two main policy objectives. They provide a publicized way of garnering international support via interventions, and also they further the construction of a historic narrative by forcing litigants to engage in storytelling. This is possible since the Court can effectively be used as a means of communication with different audiences; domestic constituencies, third States and the general public. When such instrumentalization is coupled with a respective stance before other judicial institutions, as Ukraine did with the staging of ECtHR interventions, the strong cooperation with the ICC prosecutor and the encouragement of Ukrainian investors to seek multimillion investment awards, such a judicial campaign constitutes an effective means for the promotion of policy objectives. Especially for States that are engaged in disputes with intransigent opponents and do not count on the capacity of judicial institutions to foster compliance, the pursuance of a multi-*forum* litigation strategy may be proven impactful. To pursue such objectives, Ukraine's judicial campaign required some skillful lawyering and also a handful of proceedings. The Court's coordinating role in it cannot be stressed enough, and neither the hopes the international community has placed in the ICJ for a 'spark that will inspire other competent international organs and agencies to take the further steps'.[65] Seen together with the recent turn

65 ICJ, *Allegations of Genocide under the Convention on the Prevention and Punishment of the Crime of Genocide* (*Ukraine v. Russia: 32 States Intervening*) CR 2022/5, 61[16] (Koh).

towards public interest litigation, it looks as if the international legal community entrusts the Court with a central role in advancing international justice.[66]

For the ICJ though, its instrumentalization as part of a multi-*forum* litigation strategy can prove to be a double-edged sword. The *de facto* pivotal part the Court plays in the international dispute settlement system suggests that its decisions may provoke a domino effect of like-minded rulings. So, it is an affirmation that the ICJ is an authoritative – hence an influencing – institution. On the other, its instrumentalization as a *forum* for political advocacy could impact its legitimate authority. In fact, the utilization of the ICJ in the context of such a litigation strategy is a strong sign that another role (apart from that of a dispute-settler) is implanted in the Court by litigants: that of a political agent of dispute resolution. And because the ICJ is a place for legal dispute settlement, not for other kinds of dispute resolution, such a perception around the Court's role is potentially harmful as to its sociological legitimacy, i.e. the way it is viewed by its clientele. Since there is no legal framework in place that regulates the political use of the ICJ, it is impossible to put this use in check. So, how the Court reacts to this is critical for its future. The ICJ may cherish the opportunity to influence global affairs, but it does not do so at the expense of its judicial function. Then, the Court may be careful not to push the envelope and engage in policy-making or law-making (in other words to go beyond its statutory functions). Nevertheless, if it is perceived by engaged audiences as a political battlefield it will end up facing issues of public acceptance.

Chapter 3 uses the Qatar v. UAE/Bahrain/Saudi Arabia/Egypt dispute as an *exemplaire* to examine the use of ICJ provisional measures in a multi-*forum* litigation strategy. There are many reasons that render this dispute a fitting case-study. Arguably, Qatar instituted ICJ proceedings with a limited interest in a final judgment, but mainly in the rendering of provisional measures. Then, the ICJ's final judgment, whereby the Court dismissed the application, was delivered one month after the confrontation formally ended. What is more, the circumstances of the case highlight the different aims pursued by both litigants when requesting provisional measures from the ICJ. And finally, the indicated provisional measures had implications for States that did not appear before the ICJ. The Chapter argues that provisional measures can be instrumentalized in a twofold way based on the objectives of the requesting State: as *means* when they are utilized as strategic tools to maximize a litigant's chances of winning the main suit, or of strengthening its position in other dispute

66 For an outlook on this perception see *infra* Chapter 5.

settlement methods. And as *ends* when the one who invokes them only seeks to benefit from the advantages they provide, without any interest to how they may influence other proceedings.

Further, the Chapter highlights the limits of instrumentalization of ICJ provisional measures, especially when used in the context of such a strategy. According to the latest ICJ jurisprudence, interim protection has acquired an autonomous standing from main proceedings and fulfills purposes that go beyond those incorporated in the Court's Statute, amounting thus to an unripe dispute settlement mechanism. These peculiar features justify the heightened State interest in pursuing provisional measures and dictate their instrumentalization in a litigation strategy. When examined as standalone actions, ICJ provisional measures have limited influence on the disposition of disputing parties. States may use provisional measures to take advantage of their disruptive nature, their autonomous standing and the fast-track settlement of the dispute that accompanies it, in order to influence other non-judicial dispute settlement procedures. In particular, they maximize the pressure exercised upon a non-compliant State by creating the 'shadow of the law'. When they take center stage in a multi-*forum* litigation strategy though, ICJ provisional measures maximize strategic benefits. As was the case with the instrumentalization of main proceedings, a multi-*forum* litigation strategy that incorporates provisional measures may promote State objectives in a twofold way; by putting on the table a possible domino effect of like-minded rulings, and further, as a means of communication, as the Court's rulings effectively advance a strategic narrative.

Due to its peculiar features, ICJ interim protection is viewed by States as a way to manage international crises. The barrage of requests with respect to the Gaza conflict and the Nagorno Karabakh war testify to this. This perception on the Court's role accounts for the spike of cases at its docket. It also directs States to submit to adjudication disputes that develop on the ground in order to capitalize on provisional measures. This trend has already stretched the Court's resources. Its continuation will likely not do any favors to its legitimate authority either. For non-compliance with the Court's Orders in situations that develop on the ground is expected to spike the more this mechanism is utilized for addressing this type of disputes.

The penultimate Chapter follows the unfolding of the Chagos archipelago saga to examine the use of ICJ advisory opinions in a multi-*forum* litigation strategy. The bilateral dispute between the UK and Mauritius regarding sovereignty over the Chagos Archipelago is an ideal running example for many reasons. It has given rise to a judicial saga before domestic and international tribunals that began in 1998 and has almost come to a close. Mauritius has repeatedly sought adjudication or arbitration of that dispute and the UK has consistently refused its consent thereto. Given the UK's stance, Mauritius has been playing a 'cat and mouse' game with international courts; it has endeavored to cloth its sovereignty claim in an alternative legal garment without at the same time denying that a sovereignty dispute exists between itself and the UK. Since the UK has sturdily opposed any such determination, the turning point to promoting a settlement of the dispute has been the *Chagos* advisory opinion rendered by the ICJ on 25 February 2019.

In order to understand the limits of utilization of advisory opinions in a multi-*forum* litigation strategy, the function and nature of such opinions is scrutinized. In particular, whether they constitute a *de facto* dispute settlement mechanism. The Court is prepared to advise on any dispute, by circumventing the (lack of) consent of interested States to have their dispute determined by the Court. In this way, resort to an advisory opinion is rendered a *prima facie* attractive option for interested States. While the ICJ is using the non-binding nature of advisory opinions as the key consideration in order to entertain disputes, recent practice shows that its opinions are not perceived as such. Rather, they carry a normative weight akin to a dispute settlement mechanism. Arguably, this carrot and stick situation, exemplified in the UK-Mauritius dispute, may provoke State backlash. Especially, in view of the strong moral and political effects that ICJ advisory opinions may produce. Also, the Chapter juxtaposes the concomitant effects of advisory opinions rendered by the Inter-American Court of Human Rights which have recently been used in the context of multi-*forum* proceedings but have not yielded similar results. Contrary to the ICJ, the regional court enjoys limited legitimate authority when exercising its advisory jurisdiction. Thus, it has been more attentive to State interests and has declined to render opinions when to do so could provoke extreme State backlash.

The main contention of the Chapter is that both the nature and the function of ICJ advisory opinions have been redefined after *Chagos*. The role of a rule-maker is implanted in the Court when it delivers an advisory opinion. And when the opinion pertains to a bilateral dispute the Court is expected to act as a *de facto* legal dispute settler. This will likely give new life to ICJ advisory opinions, for it promotes compliance with their findings, it develops their potential to accelerate the resolution of international disputes and hence their capacity to be used in the context of a multi-*forum* strategy. However, in view of the severe political ramifications of its opinions, the ICJ may need to be more prudent when delivering them in order to anticipate unintended consequences.

The final Chapter concludes. The intention here is to summarise the main findings from the previous chapters and, in their synthesis, understand two things: what does the use of multi-*forum* litigation strategy signify for the authority a. of the Court as a judicial institution, and b. of international law as a system of rules with a normative claim? The continuation of the trend to resort to multi-*forum* litigation strategy may impact upon the legitimate authority of the Court as a judicial institution. In a world where inter-State multi-*forum* litigation multiplies, so does the risk of perceiving the ICJ as another diplomatic platform to air State grievances. Also, given the ICJ's instrumental role in preserving the perception of international law as a legitimate means of regulating international relations, such concerns may be generalized and affect the normative authority of international law as a normative regulator.

CHAPTER 2

Engaging the ICJ in a Multi-*forum* Litigation Strategy

The One Where an Old Map Was Used to Vindicate New Myths

1 Ukraine v. Russia as a Multi-*forum* Litigation Strategy Paradigm

On 24 February 2022, war hit Europe. It did not come knocking. Some say it was anticipated for years, many suggest it has been present in Ukrainian soil for so long.[1] It is shocking to observe that this continues to be the case almost three years later with no signs of abatement or reasonable prospect of termination in sight. An event of this magnitude needs no particular introduction to international lawyers. It was felt across the world, mobilized the international community and will be examined as a case-study on a hoist of public international law disciplines (from investment law to use of force, to environmental law, refugee law and the law of international organizations just to name a few) for quite some time.[2]

The latter holds true for international dispute settlement too. To achieve peace and justice, Ukraine put its hopes in international institutions. Especially those that operate on the basis of international law: courts, ad hoc tribunals, quasi-legal bodies, fact-finding missions, monitoring missions and commissions of inquiry. It is no accident then that a body of literature has focused on Ukraine's litigation efforts,[3] and the Ukrainian Ministry of Justice

1 The ICRC held international humanitarian law applicable in Eastern Ukraine at least since the downing of MH17 on 17 July 2014: ICRC, "Ukraine: ICRC calls on all sides to respect international humanitarian law", *ICRC-Webpage*, 23 July 2014, available at: https://blogs.icrc.org/new-delhi/2014/07/24/ukraine-icrc-calls-on-all-sides-to-respect-international-humanitarian-law/). Relatedly, the European Court of Human Rights (ECtHR) held that the Lugansk and Donetsk areas of Eastern Ukraine have been "from 11 May 2014 and subsequently, under the effective control of the Russian Federation", *Ukraine and the Netherlands vs. Russia* [GC] Decision (Application nos. 8019/16, 43800/14, 28525/20 and 11055/22), 30 November 2022, [695].

2 For an overview see M Asada and D Tamada (eds), *The War in Ukraine and International Law* (Springer, 2024).

3 J Goldenziel, 'An Alternative to Zombieing: Lawfare between Russia and Ukraine and the Future of International Law' 108 (2023) *Cornell Law Review Online* 1; M Ramsden, 'Strategic Litigation in Wartime: Judging the Russian Invasion of Ukraine through the Genocide Convention', 56 (2023) *Vanderbilt Law Review* 181; K Dzehtsiarou and V Tzevelekos, 'The Aggres-

 DOI:10.1163/9789004704565_003

has constructed a dedicated website (lawfare.gov.ua) which, as these words are written, is down. In an attempt to complement the war effort,[4] to undermine Russia's legitimacy,[5] to provide an institutional alternative to Russian storytelling[6] and to mobilize its allies to support its cause,[7] Ukraine has been committed to proving that international judicial mechanisms actually work. Having this in mind, and considering Ukraine's adamant stance in proceeding all the way before all engaged judicial fora irrespective of the financial cost, it is safe to assume that Ukraine has been interested – if not from the get go, at least for some time now – in a final ICJ judgment and not only in the indication of provisional measures.[8] What is more, no other bilateral dispute has been present before so many international judicial bodies, and this engagement of several international *fora* has been openly advertised by Ukraine as a strategic choice.[9] Ukraine has relied consistently on the multi-*forum* aspect of its legal confrontation with Russia and the ICJ has had a key role to play in it. For all the above, it is fitting to use the judicial saga over the ongoing conflict in Eastern Ukraine as a running example in the present Chapter.

In the direct aftermath of the invasion, on 26 February, Ukraine rushed to the ICJ. It was the first judicial body Ukraine resorted to and this was not by coincidence.[10] The decision to begin the post-invasion litigation campaign

---

sion Against Ukraine and the Effectiveness of Inter-state Cases in Case of War' 3 (2022) *European Convention on Human Rights Law Review* 165; D Tamada, 'War in Ukraine and the International Court of Justice: Provisional Measures and the Third-Party Right to Intervene in Proceedings' 26 (2024) *International Community Law Review* 39; A Kulick, 'Provisional Measures after Ukraine v Russia (2022)', 13 (2022) *Journal of International Dispute Settlement* 328; K Wigard, O Pomson and J McIntyre, 'Keeping score: an empirical analysis of the interventions in Ukraine v. Russia' 14 (2023) *Journal of International Dispute Settlement* 305; E Chang, *Lawfare in Ukraine: Weaponizing International Investment Law and the Law of Armed Conflict Against Russia's Invasion* (National Defense University Press, 2022).

4 Ramsden, *supra* note 3, 186.

5 Goldenziel, *supra* note 3, 5.

6 See *infra* Section 3(B).

7 M Kelly, 'The Role of International Law in the Russia-Ukraine War', 55 (2023) *Case Western Reserve Journal of International Law* 61, 86.

8 *Contra* M Milanovic, ICJ Indicates Provisional Measures Against Russia, in a Near Total Win for Ukraine; Russia Expelled from the Council of Europe, *Ejil:talk!* (Mar. 16, 2022), available at: https://www.ejiltalk.org/icj-indicates-provisionalmeasures-against-russia-in-a-near-total-win-for-ukraine-russia-expelled-from-thecouncil-of-europe/.

9 ICJ, *Allegations of Genocide under the Convention on the Prevention and Punishment of the Crime of Genocide* (*Ukraine v. Russia: 32 States Intervening*) CR 2022/5, 61[16] (Koh).

10 Ramsden lists at least eight goals underpinning Ukraine's resort to the Court, *supra* note 3, 185–192.

from the ICJ was informed by the Court's authority and its influence over the development of international law.[11] Ukraine candidly expressed its belief that a pronouncement by the Court will be "the essential spark that will inspire other competent international organs and agencies to take the further steps".[12] This statement was made with respect to a provisional measures order but it holds all the more true for an ICJ judgment. The initiation of litigation before the Court would also focus critical attention on Russia.[13] Given Ukraine's wish to draw as much international attention to the dispute as possible from the outset, a propaganda victory against the opponent is more likely if it begins from the principal judicial organ of the UN.[14] It is evident then, that the ICJ's engagement in Ukraine's multi-*forum* litigation strategy was a well-timed tactical move for the mounting of a public relations campaign and the infliction of pressure upon Russia to comply with international law.

These considerations attach to the Court's authority as such, thus they may also underpin a decision to request a provisional measures order, not necessarily a judgment.[15] However, the Ukraine-Russia saga amply demonstrates that there is added value in pursuing a judgment as part of a multi-*forum* litigation strategy for multiple reasons: first, the *de jure* authority – hence the ensuing pressure for compliance – of a judgment is not comparable to an order on provisional measures;[16] its validity is not time-constrained and it is the product of comprehensive judicial scrutiny. Hence, it is easier to capitalise upon such a pronouncement in other proceedings.[17] Particularly in disputes that involve a recalcitrant respondent who only reacts to pressure, it is worth the wait for a judgment. Testament to the different *gravitas* of the two processes is Russia's abandonment of its strategy of non-participation in provisional measures during the main proceedings. Further, by keeping the dispute open before the Court, the claimant keeps the matter in the headlines, which usually accords with its

11 M Ramsden, 'Accountability for Crimes against the Rohingya: Strategic Litigation in the International Court of Justice' 26 (2021) *Harvard Negotiation Law Review* 153, 159.

12 Koh, *supra* note 9, 61[16]. See *infra* Section 3(A).

13 A Rovine, 'The national interest and the World Court' in L Gross (ed.) *The Future of the International Court of Justice* (Oceana, 1976), 313, 324.

14 Chr. Gray, 'Why states resort to litigation in cases concerning the use of force', in N Klein (ed.), *Litigating International Law Disputes: Weighing the Options* (CUP, 2014), 305, 313. See *infra* Section 3(B)

15 On the objectives underlying a request for provisional measures, *see infra* Chapter 3.

16 On the ICJ's authority, see *infra* Section 4.

17 Ramsden, *supra* note 3, 186.

objectives, especially if the violation is ongoing. Even if in *Allegations of Genocide* the focus on the merits will be solely on Ukraine's conduct, this is allegedly important for Ukraine.[18] Because the applicant State believes that both legally and morally it is in the right side of history, it welcomes any stirring of the matter. Especially in a time when news from the front have been pushed onto the back pages.[19]

What is more, and perhaps more importantly in the context of this dispute, a favorable ICJ judgment that adopts a factual narrative conforming to the claimant's storytelling, may have a myth-debunking function.[20] Alas, such history-making cannot be adequately served by provisional measures orders. For, due to time constraints, the evidentiary rules that govern establishment of facts in such pronouncements cannot be as strict and detailed as these applicable to main proceedings.[21] It is telling that provisional measures orders have no section dedicated to establishing the dispute's factual background, as is usually the case in judgments. And while Ukraine counts on the history-producing function of international courts to debunk Russian allegations of genocide in Ukrainian territory, Russia has taken this propaganda war to another level. On 23 May 2023 the President of the Russian Constitutional court overwhelmed with enthusiasm showed President Putin a map compiled in the times of Louis XIV so as to argue that historically Ukraine never existed.[22]

Finally, main ICJ proceedings allow for the rallying of international support through the procedural tool of intervention. While it has been over-

18 After the delivery of the Preliminary Objections judgment, the leader of Ukraine's legal team told reporters that: "[i]t is important that the court will decide on the issue that Ukraine is not responsible for some mythical genocide", Associated Press, 'The UN's top court says it has jurisdiction in part of Ukraine's genocide case against Russia', 3 February 2024, available at: https://apnews.com/article/ukraine-russia-genocide-court-un-icj-c3f9cf7462cd85e73ab53aa9499093f4.

19 A Baunov, 'The Dangers of Losing Focus on Russia's War Against Ukraine' *Carnegie Politika* (17 January 2024), available at: https://carnegieendowment.org/russia-eurasia/politika/2024/01/the-dangers-of-losing-focus-on-russias-war-against-ukraine?lang=en.

20 D Guilfoyle, 'The Chagos Archipelago before International Tribunals: Strategic Litigation and the Production of Historical Knowledge' 21 (2021) *Melbourne Journal of International Law* 749, 751–2; M Hirsch, The Role of International Tribunals in the Development of Historical Narratives, 20 (2018) *Journal of the History of International Law* 391. See *infra* Section 4(c).

21 For more on ICJ fact-finding see, J Devaney, 'Fact-Finding and Expert Evidence' in C Esposito and K Parlett (eds) *The Cambridge Companion to the International Court of Justice* (CUP, 2023) 187.

22 M Gnatovskyy, 'Ukraine' in A van Aaken et al. (eds) *The Oxford Handbook of International Law in Europe* (OUP, 2023), 1–2.

looked whether intervention is possible during the provisional measures process, it seems that while it is legally possible,[23] practically it is unlikely. A State does not have time on its side should it want to organize a campaign of third-party interventions during the provisional measures phase, so it is safe to assume that, realistically, interventions are a strategic tool reserved for main proceedings. Conscious of these ramifications of a final judgment, Ukraine tactically decided to keep advocating before the ICJ, as well as before all other *fora* involved.

This Chapter fleshes out the complications, at the legal and policy level, that derive from the use of the ICJ to deliver a judgment on the merits as part of a multi-*forum* litigation strategy. And it is fitting to use Ukraine v. Russia as a running example here, because arguably, the delivery of a final judgment is the main motivation underpinning Ukraine's request.[24] The first Section will recount the way in which Ukraine engaged several international judicial mechanisms to address the post-invasion phase of the conflict. Apart from the UN's main judicial organ, also the ECtHR, the International Criminal Court and international investment tribunals formed part of Ukraine's litigation strategy. The next Section will scrutinize the legal issues arising from multi-*forum* proceedings. Legal literature has dealt extensively with such issues in the context of international disputes between private entities and States (i.e. international investment disputes). And they can be grouped in three categories: *lis pendens*, *res judicata* and abuse of process. The first two pertain to inter-institutional relationships, while the third to the ability of the parties to engage a particular judicial forum in a dispute. So, this Chapter will juxtapose the two categories of disputes (State v. State and private v. State) to understand whether they are comparable and to examine whether analogous solutions may be applicable to both.

Subsequently, the focus turns on policy issues. For the involved parties first and then for the Court. From such a perspective, utilization of the ICJ in a multi-*forum* litigation strategy may be particularly useful for States as it promotes their policy objectives in a couple of ways: first, through the exercise of pressure on the non-complaint State by the aligned pronouncements of adjudicative bodies. Multi-*forum* litigation strategy can be understood as an attempt to create a domino of judicial decisions that point

23 R Kolb, *The International Court of Justice* (Hart, 2013), 721.

24 Up to this date, the only ICJ merits judgment where this strategy was pursued has been the one on Crimea, ICJ, *Application of the International Convention for the Suppression of the Financing of Terrorism and of the International Convention on the Elimination of All Forms of Racial Discrimination (Ukraine v. Russia)* Judgment (merits), 31 January 2024.

towards the same direction. Especially, when the Court is the first tile in this line of dominoes, its power to establish an authoritative account of the factual background can precipitate this domino and thus exert a strong compliance pull. Second, as a means of gathering political support and of promoting compliance in an indirect fashion. The latest trend to stage interventions before the Court has transformed the ICJ from a dispute settler to a public platform of political advocacy. And the more judicial institutions are involved in this campaign, the more effective it becomes. In this way, applicant States aim to mount the pressure and set in motion extra-legal dispute resolution mechanisms.

For the ICJ though, that enjoys a large measure of *de jure* authority, its instrumentalization as part of this strategy can prove to be a double-edged sword. States regularly attempt to capitalize on the ICJ's influence over other judicial institutions in a multi-*forum* litigation strategy. This sends a strong signal as to which institution is perceived as the most authoritative in the constellation of international judicial *fora*. So, on the one hand, it reaffirms its central role in the international dispute settlement system. On the other, the Court must be very careful as to how it responds to such utilization because its authority is potentially at stake. Its instrumentalization for objectives that do not pertain to its judicial function could heavily impact upon its legitimate authority. Since there is no legal framework in place that regulates the political utilization of the ICJ it is impossible to put this use in check. The instrumentalization of the ICJ in the context of such a litigation strategy is a strong sign that the ICJ's perceived role as a dispute settler is changing: from a legal promoter of dispute resolution to a political one. And because of this role implanted in it, the Court risks losing its legitimacy in the eyes of its clientele (so-called sociological legitimacy).

As mentioned above, the ongoing Ukraine v. Russia dispute is used here as a multi-*forum* litigation strategy paradigm, albeit a caveat is in order from the outset. Developments are expected in this case, and they will likely run in the headlines for the next year at least (unless settlement in all pending proceedings occurs before that time, which is highly unlikely at this point in time). However, the twofold purpose of its inclusion is independent of any judicial outcome: first, to demonstrate the turn inter-State dispute resolution has taken towards multi-*forum* litigation – and hence the overt political use of judicial organs – and further, to demonstrate the characteristics of this strategy and its effects on international dispute settlement (how it is – not – analogous to a concomitant strategy in a private v. State dispute, what objectives Ukraine expects to achieve by pursuing such a strategy and how it will affect the Court's role and legitimate authority). So, the final outcome in this dispute, which, as far as the ICJ proceedings is concerned, is expected after the book's completion, will not affect the soundness of the argument put forward here.

2 War in Ukraine after 24 February 2022: International Judicial Mechanisms in the Mix

It would be futile though to recount the facts that lead up to Russia's 2022 military operation in Eastern Ukraine. One may have to go back to Louis XIV and the Rzeczpospolita to explain which factors culminated in the ongoing war. What is important to note though, is that the factual matrix underlying the judicial proceedings examined in this Chapter has a temporal starting point: 24 February 2022. At first glance, it is tempting to understand the conflict as part of a greater dispute, the Russo-Ukraine war, that arguably began on 27 February 2014 with the seizure of the Crimean parliament by Russian forces.[25] Albeit, Crimea and Eastern Ukraine have a different story to tell as to how they have become part of Russian territory. In the direct aftermath of the seizure, a referendum was held in Crimea, the peninsula declared independence and was subsequently annexed by the Russian Federation. The regions of Donetsk and Luhansk became embroiled in an armed struggle since 2014 and declared independence the same year. Russia would formally recognize the Donetsk People's Republic (DPR) and the Luhansk People's Republic (LPR) three days before its forces invaded Ukraine in 2022. Russia would go on to annex both regions in September of the same year.

Ditto, it is tempting at first glance to examine Ukraine's post-invasion litigation efforts as part of a comprehensive litigation strategy that reflects Ukraine's foreign policy since 2014. As a reaction to the annexation of the peninsula, Ukraine filed complaints before the ICJ, the WTO, an Annex VII arbitral tribunal and the International Tribunal for the Law of the Sea, engaged with the ICC and played an active role in investment disputes brought before international arbitral tribunals by Ukrainian investors.[26] However, the exclusion from the scope of examination of all facts that preceded 24 February 2022 is necessary here. It is necessary practically, as the plethora of inter-State judicial proceedings initiated by Ukraine during this whole

25 S Plokhy, *The Russo-Ukrainian War* (Penguin, 2023), xxi; V Fedorchak, *The Russia-Ukraine War: Towards Resilient Fighting Power* (Routledge, 2024) 1.

26 Goldenziel, supra note 3, 5–10; C Miles, 'Lawfare in Crimea: treaty, territory, and investor–state dispute settlement' 38 (2022) *Arbitration International* 135, 142.

period would render their examination unmanageable.[27] It is also necessary factually, for Russia post-2022 has upped the ante and launched a full-scale invasion against Ukraine that both escalated and transformed the situation on the ground. Undoubtedly, 24 February 2022 is a historic watershed and a rupture point in the Russo-Ukraine war. After the invasion, Ukraine lost no time in engaging international judicial mechanisms in the war effort.

2.1 *An Exceptional ICJ Case*

Two days later, the ICJ received Ukraine's application requesting simultaneously a provisional measures order and a judgment. The provisional measures stage of an ICJ case will be analysed in the next Chapter, but Ukraine's main application was exceptional in a twofold sense. Ukraine employed a legal maneuver when attempting to establish the Court's jurisdiction. Because no international court can decide over the violation(s) of the UN Charter committed by Russia, the respective war crimes, crimes against humanity or the crime of aggression, Ukraine invoked instead the Genocide Convention in an unprecedented way.[28] It argued that Russia's false allegations that Ukraine was engaging in genocide against members of the Russian ethnic minority in Eastern Ukraine made for a 'dispute' under the Genocide Convention.[29] Against this background, Ukraine asked the Court, *inter alia*, to declare that Ukraine was not responsible for genocide in Donetsk and Luhansk as Russia contends.[30] This reverse compliance/non-violation claim

27 The inter-State cases that pertain to the 2014–2022 events in Ukraine are, based on the geographical area of the disputed events: one ICJ case on Crimea, three ECtHR cases on Crimea, three on Eastern Ukraine and one on the Kerch Strait, two Annex VII Law of the Sea Tribunal cases on the Black Sea, Sea of Azov and Kerch Strait. For an overview see I Marchuk, 'From warfare to "lawfare"- Increased Litigation and Rise of Parallel Proceedings in International Courts', in A Kent et al. (eds) *The Future of International Courts: Regional, Institutional and Procedural Challenges* (Routledge, 2019) 217.

28 I Marchuk and A Wanigasuriya, 'Beyond the False Claim of Genocide: Preliminary Reflections on Ukraine's Prospects in Its Pursuit of Justice at the ICJ' 25 (2023) *Journal of Genocide Research* 256; M Milanovic, 'Ukraine Files ICJ Claim against Russia' *Ejil:talk!* (27 February 2022).

29 This was not the only jurisdictional basis invoked by Ukraine. It submitted in its Memorial that Russia's use of force and the recognition of the DPR/LPR violated Articles I and IV of the Convention, *Allegations of Genocide*, Ukraine Memorial, 1 July 2022, 69[117]*ff.* In its Preliminary Objections judgment, the ICJ found such arguments to fall outside the scope of the Genocide Convention, *Allegations of Genocide*, Judgment, 2 February 2024, 56[147].

30 Ukraine also asked the ICJ to declare that Russia is responsible for violating the Convention by making the false allegation of genocide against Ukraine, and then by using force against it, *Allegations of Genocide, Ukraine Memorial* 106[178](c) and (d).

kills two birds with one stone. It combats Russian propaganda about Ukraine allegedly committing genocide in Donbas and it creates a jurisdictional basis for the Court to keep hearing the case. The Court was persuaded by this interpretation and it will review on the merits whether Russia's justification for its military campaign stands, but not whether Russia's behavior on the ground is itself in accordance with the Genocide Convention.[31]

Further, Ukraine benefited from a campaign of third-State interventions of a volume the Court has never experienced in the past.[32] In the, more than a hundred year, combined PCIJ-ICJ history eight intervention requests have been granted out of 14 such declarations.[33] In *Allegations of Genocide* thirty three States intervened to support Ukraine and an international organization, the EU, furnished 'relevant information' pursuant to Article 34(2) of the ICJ Statute.[34] Third-State intervention before the ICJ is possible under two headings: under Article 62 of the ICJ Stature a State may request to intervene in an existing dispute if it has 'an interest of a legal nature which may be affected' by the ensuing judgment. Or, intervention is further permitted under Article 63 of the same text where a third State has a more general interest in the interpretation of a treaty to which it is a party, alongside the disputants. Intervention then serves a function that is informative of a third State's interest, and also protective of this interest against any possible prejudice from the ensuing decision in the case.[35] By rendering the Genocide Convention the flagship of its ICJ application, Ukraine opened the Article 63 door to all State parties to this treaty. This is so, because for such States the

31 Ibid 35[54] and 57[149].

32 J McIntyre, 'Less a Wave than a Tsunami: Procedural Implications for the ICJ of the Article 63 Interventions in *Ukraine v. Russia*', *Völkerrechtsblog* (11 October 2022)

33 A Miron and Chr. Chinkin, 'Article 62' in A Zimmermann, Chr. Tams, K Oellers-Frahm, Chr. Tomuschat (eds) *The Statute of the International Court of Justice: A Commentary* (OUP, 2019), 1686, 1691[11]; A Miron and Chr. Chinkin, 'Article 63' in *Ibid.* 1741, 1745–1746 [8]. B Bonafé, 'The collective dimension of bilateral litigation: The Ukraine v Russia case before the ICJ' 96 (2022) *Questions of International Law. Zoom-out*, 27, 28.

34 In order of filing: Latvia, Lithuania, New Zealand, UK, Germany, United States, Sweden, France, Romania, Italy, Poland, Denmark, Ireland, Finland, Estonia, Spain, Australia, Portugal, Austria, Greece, Luxembourg, Croatia, Czech Republic, Bulgaria, Malta, Norway, Belgium, Slovenia, Slovakia, Canada and the Netherlands (joint declaration), Cyprus and Liechtenstein. The declarations are all available at: https://www.icj-cij.org/en/case/182/intervention. The text of the EU's *amicus curiae* contribution was never made public, see *Allegations of Genocide,* ICJ Press Release 2022/29, available at: https://www.icj-cij.org/public/files/case-related/182/182-20220818-PRE-01-00-EN.pdf.

35 Y Ronen and Y Naggan, 'Third Parties' in C Romano, K Alter and Y Shany (eds), *The Oxford Handbook of International Adjudication* (OUP, 2014) 807.

admissibility prerequisites for an Article 63 intervention are not stringent *per* Article 82 of the Rules of Court. According to the Court's case-law, only exceptional circumstances may render the declarations of intervention inadmissible.[36] As expected, in its 5 June 2023 order, the Court dismissed only the US' declaration because it didn't conform to the Article 63(2) bindingness requirement.[37]

While it is impossible to prove Ukraine's exact involvement in its organization, the tsunami of third-State interventions formed part of Ukraine's litigation strategy. It would be strange if this was not the case since Ukraine had received extensive international support.[38] Actual proof that Ukraine coordinated the interventions, cannot be inferred. There are telling signs that the campaign was orchestrated,[39] and that Ukraine had an active role in it.[40] But even if this can be conclusively proven, it would not affect the standing of third States before the ICJ. Russia attempted to highlight this aspect of the campaign in order to strike out the interventions as not genuine and politically biased against it.[41] More specifically, the respondent State held that the motivation of all intervening States was not to assist the Court with the interpretation and construction of the Genocide convention, but rather 'to become *de facto* co-applicants and pursue a joint case with Ukraine'.[42] The Court rejected this objection without blinking; genuineness of a declaration of inter-

36 *Allegations of Genocide,* Admissibility of the Declarations of Intervention Order of 5 June 2023, 7–9[33]–[40].

37 The US was not bound by Article IX of the Genocide convention, the provision the Court had to interpret at the preliminary objections phase of the proceedings. Therefore, the ensuing ICJ judgment could not be 'binding upon it' as provided for by Article 63(2) ICJ Statute *Ibid.* 20[97].

38 E.g. over 140 States have repeatedly condemned the war in the UN General Assembly several times over, beginning with a March 2022 Resolution, UNGA, Res ES-11/1 Aggression against Ukraine, 2 March 2022, UN Doc A/RES/ES-11/1, [3].

39 Wigard, et al. *supra* note 3, 323; *Joint Statement on Ukraine's application against Russia at the International Court of Justice*, 20 May 2022, available at: https://www.auswaertiges-amt.de/en/newsroom/news/-/2532254.

40 E.g. Romania openly admitted that its intervention has been requested by Ukraine and further that it 'will coordinate with other like minded States', Ministry of Foreign Affairs of Romania, Press release, Romania Has Decided to Intervene in favour of Ukraine at the International Court of Justice in Proceedings against the Russian Federation, 18 May 2022, available at: https://www.mae.ro/en/node/58706#null.

41 *Ukraine v. Russia,* Russia's Written Observations on Admissibility of the Declarations of Intervention Submitted by France, Germany, Italy, Latvia, Lithuania, New Zealand, Poland, Sweden, the United Kingdom, and the United States, 17 October 2022, 9–19 [11]–[31].

42 Ibid. 20[31].

vention shall be judged only against its substance – i.e. whether it relates to the interpretation of the convention in question – and not against its motivation.[43] So, being aware that the international community stands beside it, Ukraine capitalized upon this support by using a procedural tool in an unprecedented way. Seen together with the reverse compliance claim, one can suggest that some good lawyering helped Ukraine keep the case alive before the ICJ.

2.2 *ECtHR, International Criminal Court, International Investment Tribunals: the Story Continues*

Ukraine has been fighting the legal war on other fronts too. At least three judicial proceedings, that have been part of Ukraine's litigation strategy since 2014, have been engaged in the post-invasion phase of the conflict. Two standing mechanisms, the ECtHR and the ICC, moved at lightning speed to address the particularities of a major conflict. And international investment tribunals, well-known both for the speedy delivery of justice and the unique enforcement mechanism that accompanies their awards, have been employed to mount extra financial pressure on Russia.

Two days after its ICJ application, Ukraine resorted to the European Court of Human Rights alleging violations of the European Convention on Human Rights and requesting the indication of interim measures.[44] This move increased the number of ECtHR inter-State applications that Ukraine has brought against Russia since the annexation of Crimea to ten.[45] And it took the President of the court a day to order Russia to refrain from military attacks against civilians and civilian objects.[46] In this way, the European Court of Human Rights was the first judicial institution to rule against Russia following its invasion, uninfluenced by the ICJ proceedings. The completed application arrived at the Court in June 2022, and it was more straightforward than the ICJ one in terms of substance. Ukraine argued that almost every substantive protection afforded by the European Convention on Human Rights was cancelled by the targeted, indiscriminate and disproportionate attacks launched by Rus-

43 *Allegations of Genocide,* Admissibility of the Declarations of Intervention Order of 5 June 2023, 10[44].

44 Press Release ECHR 220 (2022) 28 June 2022.

45 On top of these, over 8,500 individual applications are currently pending before the ECtHR concerning the events in Crimea, eastern Ukraine and the Sea of Azov, Press Release ECHR 082 (2023), 17 March 2023.

46 Press Release ECHR 073 (2022), 4 March 2022. The scope of the measures indicated has been expanded twice since (4 March and 1 April) *Press Release 28 June.*

sia against civilians and their property across Ukraine.[47] No legal maneuvers were necessary as Ukraine had already resorted to the court three times with respect to the situation in Eastern Ukraine, so it was not surprising that the ECtHR joined the application with these previous pending inter-State applications.[48] And it is expected to uphold its jurisdiction in this latest application, because before joining all four applications it had already declared the other three admissible when it ruled that "from 11 May 2014 and subsequently [the Lugansk and Donetsk areas of Eastern Ukraine have been], under the effective control of the Russian Federation".[49]

Like the ICJ, the ECtHR provided another fitting forum for States to express their solidarity with Ukraine. With the exception of the Netherlands, no ECHR State party has formally engaged with Ukraine's first nine applications against Russia. Nevertheless, post-invasion the *momentum* shifted and Ukraine capitalized upon its strategic choice to have beside it in court as many States as possible. Interestingly, the Netherlands was the first State to make public its intention to intervene in the *Ukraine v. Russia* (X) proceedings in mid-July 2022.[50] Within a time-span of a few weeks a hoist of third-party interveners followed suit, to raise the tally of intervention applications by CoE members under Article 36(2) ECHR to twenty-seven.[51] The legal nuance that symbolically differentiates intervention before the ECtHR under Article 36(2) ECHR from its ICJ Article 63 Statute counterpart, is that the former does not establish a right of intervention.[52] Rather, intervention permission is granted under

47 It alleged administrative practices in violation of Articles 2, 3, 4, 5, 8, 9, 10, 11, 13, and 14 and of Article 1 of Protocol No. 1, Article 2 of Protocol No. 1, Article 2 of Protocol No. 4 and Article 3 of Protocol No. 4, *Press Release 28 June*.

48 Press Release ECHR 055 (2023), 20 February 2023. The only Council of Europe member State that decided to join Ukraine in litigation against Russia was the Netherlands. Concerning the downing of flight MH-17, the Netherlands initially supported several individual applications as a third-party intervener, later filed its own complaint (28535/20), which was then merged by the Court with two more inter-State applications regarding the situation in Eastern Ukraine into *Ukraine and The Netherlands v. Russia.* Canada also submitted an intervention request in the MH-17 case in favor of the applicants, but it cannot lodge an application before the ECtHR, *Ukraine and the Netherlands vs. Russia* [GC] *Decision*, [21].

49 *Ukraine and the Netherlands vs. Russia* [GC] *Decision*, [695].

50 'Political Declaration of the Ministerial Ukraine Accountability Conference' (14 July 2022), available at: https://www.government.nl/ministries/ministry-of-foreign-affairs/documents/diplomatic-statements/2022/07/14/political-declaration-of-the-ministerial-ukraine-accountability-conference.

51 *Press Release 17 March.*

52 *Cf.* Rule 44(3)(b) of the Rules of Court; W Schabbas, *The European Convention on Human Rights A Commentary* (OUP, 2016) 792.

the ECtHR's discretion 'in the interest of the proper administration of justice'.[53] And it seems that the ECtHR is prepared to scrutinize the objectives underlying the interventions and not consider those that 'express support for one or the other party'.[54] In an attempt to put in check the use of the ECtHR for ulterior political purposes, the court signals that it is not the appropriate *forum* for the expression of solidarity with a party to the dispute.[55] This is so, since CoE member States are allowed to make use of the Article 33 inter-State application instead, for violations by other members as has happened in previous inter-State cases.[56] So, by choosing to intervene and not to become parties to an ECtHR case against Russia, third States 'have chosen the passenger's seat instead of the driver's in their response to the Russian invasion'.[57] This may take away from the political and symbolic significance of such interventions, nevertheless it constitutes a significant upgrade in terms of international support when considered against the lukewarm international engagement with previous Ukrainian ECtHR applications.

As international news are constantly filled up with images of war atrocities, the demands for individual accountability of political and military officials have gained centre stage in Ukraine's litigation agenda.[58] In an attempt to secure international criminal responsibility for war crimes, Ukraine has maintained an open channel of communication with the International Criminal Court after the invasion.[59] At the time of the invasion, proceedings against Russian officials for their conduct in Ukrainian soil were already underway before the International Criminal Court. Nevertheless, Ukraine has not ratified the Rome Statute. But, it accepted the ICC's jurisdiction after the annex-

53 *Sejdovic v. Italy* [GC], no. 56581/00 [8] ECHR 2006–II.

54 *Practice Direction, Third-party intervention under Article 36 § 2 of the Convention or under Article 3, second sentence, of Protocol No. 16* (13 March 2023), 1[2].

55 J Batura, 'The Objective Friends of the Court – New Insights into the Role of Third Parties before the European Court of Human Rights', *Ejil:talk!* (19 April 2023), available at: https://www.ejiltalk.org/the-objective-friends-of-the-court-new-insights-into-the-role-of-third-parties-before-the-european-court-of-human-rights/.

56 European Commission, *Denmark, Norway, Sweden and The Netherlands v. Greece* (Application nos. 3321/67, 3322/67 and 3323/67) Decision, 31 May 1968; European Commission, *France, Denmark, Norway, Sweden and the Netherlands v. Turkey* (Application nos. 9940/82, 9941/82, 9943/82 and 9944/82) Report, 7 December 1985.

57 J Batura and I Risini, 'Of Parties, Third Parties, and Treaty Interpretation: Ukraine v. Russia (x) before the European Court of Human Rights' *Ejil:talk!* (26 September 2022).

58 Ramsden, *supra* note 3, 206.

59 M Frulli, 'International Criminal Justice at the Russia-Ukraine Crossroads' 32 (2023) *Italian Yearbook of International Law* 231, 235.

ation of Crimea for an indefinite duration (a self-referral under Article 12(3) of the Statute) 'for the purpose of identifying, prosecuting and judging the perpetrators and accomplices of acts committed in the territory of Ukraine since 20 February 2014'.[60] And while a preliminary investigation was ongoing since 2014, on 28 February 2022 the court's prosecutor expressed his intention to open an active investigation into the situation in Ukraine.[61] At the same time, he invited State parties to the Rome Statute to expedite the procedure by referring the situation to the Prosecutor's Office *per* Article 14 of the Statute. Unsurprisingly, within two days 39 States answered to the prosecutor's call and on 2 March 2022 the investigation was officially open.[62] Once more, 24 February 2022 was a catalyst for the wheels of justice to start turning and for the mobilization of the international community.

Finally, Ukraine brought on board an unexpected judicial ally in its litigation efforts; international investment tribunals. Surprising though it may be, the use of such tribunals is not unprecedented. They have been employed with respect to the annexation of Crimea.[63] The government expressly encouraged Ukrainian investors to file these investment claims against Russia, it intervened in a handful of them and appears to be coordinating some of them.[64] Pursuant to Article 9 of the 1998 bilateral investment treaty between Russia and Ukraine,[65] such tribunals have examined claims by Ukrainian investors against Russia concerning the mistreatment of their investments in territories over which Russia performs a *de facto* con-

60 *Letter by P Klimkin (Minister of Foreign Affairs) to the ICC Registrar* (8 September 2015), available at: available at: <https://www.icc-cpi.int/sites/default/files/iccdocs/other/Ukraine_Art_12-3_declaration_08092015.pdf#search=ukraine.

61 *Statement of ICC Prosecutor, Karim AA Khan QC, on the Situation in Ukraine* (28 February 2022), available at: https://www.icc-cpi.int/news/statement-icc-prosecutor-karim-aa-khan-qc-situation-ukraine-i-have-decided-proceed-opening.

62 *Statement of ICC Prosecutor, Karim AA Khan QC, on the Situation in Ukraine* (2 March 2022), available at: https://www.icc-cpi.int/news/statement-icc-prosecutor-karim-aa-khan-qc-situation-ukraine-receipt-referrals-39-states. The total number of referrals amounts to 43.

63 Miles, *supra* note 26, 135; Chang, *supra* note 3, 1.

64 "Oschadbank Files Claim Worth UAH 15 Bln Against Russia for Losses Caused by Crimean Annexation – Yatseniuk," *Interfax-Ukraine*, 7 August 2015, available at https://en.interfax.com.ua/news/economic/276618.html; Miles, *supra* note 26, 145.

65 Agreement between the Government of the Russian Federation and the Cabinet of Ministers of Ukraine on the Encouragement and Mutual Protection of Investments (signed in 1998 and entered into force in 2000), available at: at: https://investmentpolicy.unctad.org/international-investment-agreements/treaties/bit/2859/russian-federation—ukraine-bit-1998-.

trol or which have been formally annexed by Russia.[66] Unlike other international courts and tribunals, such bodies may incidentally render declarations confirming the unlawful use of force or the illegal occupation of territory in a very speedy fashion.[67] With the hope that Crimean cases could be extrapolated to Eastern Ukraine, Ukrainian investors have been encouraged to continue the same strategy and at least three investment cases that pertain to the post-invasion phase of the conflict are currently pending before such bodies.[68] If these efforts are successful like their Crimean counterparts, they may end up in awards of billions (plus interest).[69] And because they can be enforced worldwide against Russian assets this could turn out to be a considerable financial harassment for the Kremlin.

The outcome of all aforementioned judicial proceedings is, at this point in time, uncertain. Their pendency though, is in itself a reason that may affect inter-institutional relations. Then, and before assessing whether Ukraine's litigation strategy has been *de facto* influential over the parties' attitude, it is important to understand under which circumstances ICJ main proceedings can be affected *de jure* by their incorporation in a multi-*forum* litigation strategy. So, the analysis will turn right away to the legal repercussions that may ensue from the employment of the ICJ to deliver a judgment in the context of a multi-*forum* litigation strategy.

3 *De jure* Complications: Analogies with Private vs State Multi-*forum* Litigation before International *fora*

More than fifteen years ago, McLachlan pointed out that '[c]onsideration of the issues arising from parallel litigation in the crucible of the litigation process is in its infancy in Public International Law'.[70] This statement holds true until today, especially when compared to the extensive case-law and com-

66 Eg. *JSC DTEK Krymenergo v. Russia*, PCA Case No. 2018–41, Award (1 November 2023). For an overview of relevant cases see D Tamada, 'War in Ukraine and Implications for International Investment Law' 26 (2024) *International Community Law Review* 187, 191–6.

67 Miles, *supra* note 26, 142.

68 *SCM Group v. Russia, Ukrhydroenergo v. Russia* and *Energoatom v. Russia (II)*. Very few details are available about these procedures. It is likely that other investment claims have been filed, but specific information is not publicly available.

69 D Pinsky and P Aboro, '"Back in the U.S.S.R." How Russia's Invasion of Ukraine May Invite Billions in Arbitration Claims' 50 (2024) *Litigation* 44.

70 C McLachlan, *Lis Pendens in International Litigation* (Brill, 2009), 300.

mentary around parallel litigation in private international law and international arbitration.[71] For present purposes, a broader question may be asked at this point: what rules may or ought to be applied, in the absence of express statutory provisions, when the ICJ is faced with parallel or consecutive litigation between the same parties arising out of the same facts in another international court or tribunal?[72] Three relevant considerations have been put forward as possible avenues to regulate inter-institutional relations in such scenarios: the related concepts of *lis pendens* and *res judicata*, and the objection of *abuse of process*. Also, it is pertinent to understand how such rules may affect the strategy of the parties in initiating, maintaining or terminating judicial proceedings.

3.1 Lis pendens*: Parallel Litigation*

It is important to clarify from the outset the meaning of *lis* (*alibi*) *pendens* or *litispendance* in public international law. Contrary to the common understanding among European scholars of *lis pendens* as a legal principle,[73] the term as understood here describes a factual phenomenon.[74] Namely, that of a claim already pending before another court or tribunal. In this way, all solutions aimed at controlling duplicative litigation through the 'jurisdictional equilibration'[75] between rival systems of adjudication – such as consolidation of proceedings, *electa una via*, *forum non-conveniens*, *anti-suit injunctions* etc, fall within the ambit of *lis pendens* as understood here.[76] In public international law, *lis pendens* arises under two circumstances:

---

71 See i.e. for commercial arbitration Fr. Ragno, 'Parallel Proceedings in International Commercial Arbitration' in St. Kröll et. al (eds) *Cambridge Compendium of International Commercial and Investment Arbitration* (CUP, 2023), 1633; for investment arbitration C McLachlan et al., International Investment Arbitration: Substantive Principles (OUP, 2017), 95; for private international law G Bermann, Parallel Jurisdiction: Is Convergence Possible? 21 (2012) *Yearbook of Private International Law*, 21.

72 Shany uses the term 'competing proceedings' to refer to cases that 'exhibit a certain degree of similarity so that the parties consider them as potential alternatives', Y Shany, *The Competing Jurisdictions of International Courts and Tribunals* (2003) OUP, 21.

73 E Gaillard, 'Parallel Proceedings: Investment Arbitration' (2019) *MPEPIL* [46]; R Brand, 'Forum non conveniens' (2019) MPEPIL [3].

74 *Lis pendens* literally translates to 'lawsuit pending', F De Ly and Au. Sheppard, 'ILA Final Report on Lis Pendens and Arbitration' 25 (2009) *Arbitration International* 3, [1.11].

75 D Holleaux, 'La litispendance', (1971–1973) *Travaux du Comité français de droit international privé* 203, 209.

76 For a more detailed list, see, McLachlan, *supra* note 70, Chapter 1 (D); Shany, *supra* note 72, Part III.

a. when the claims brought before different jurisdictions are alike – likeness to be determined by the identity of parties, subject-matter and cause of action, and b. when the nature of the jurisdictions engaged is comparable.[77] Identity of cause of action is a rare instance before international courts and tribunals considering the treaty-based jurisdiction of most such bodies, hence the phenomenon of 'disaggregation' of international disputes.[78] The ICJ's general jurisdiction renders such overlap possible, albeit infrequent. In the case-study that runs through this Chapter, Ukraine could not invoke the same cause of action in its ICJ and ECtHR claims. The same holds true for the claims filed before investment tribunals (they are based on the Ukraine-Russia BIT) and the ICC investigation (that concerns individual criminal responsibility). Further, it is debatable whether such a situation triggers the application of a legal rule that demands from the *fora* engaged a specific course of action.

All relevant judicial *dicta* from the discipline of public international law are almost a century old and do not shed great light to the applicable rule. In the *Certain German Interests* case the PCIJ examined this issue starting from the relations between proceedings held in different States and considered the applicability of a specific relevant rule in international relations.[79] That court discussed whether *lis alibi pendens* could play a role in the relations between the German–Polish Mixed Arbitral Tribunal and the PCIJ and answered in the negative, because 'the essential elements which constitute litispendance are not present'. In particular, there was 'no question of two identical actions', the parties were 'not the same' and 'the Mixed Arbitral Tribunal and the Permanent Court of International Justice [were] not courts of the same character'. While it hasn't pronounced on the legal consequences arising from the existence of *litispendance*, this judgement recognized in principle its relevance as a situation potentially affecting the exercise of jurisdiction of international judicial institutions. And the disposition of that Court was made somewhat clearer a couple of years later in *Factory at Chorzów*

77 While likeness of claims is generally accepted as a relevant prerequisite for the invocation of *lis pendens*, the like nature of the jurisdictions engaged is elaborated in PCIJ, *Case concerning Certain German Interests in Polish Upper Silesia* (*Germany v. Poland*), (1925) PCIJ Rep., Ser. A, No. 6, 20.

78 "[T]he carving up of broader disputes into discrete legal claims based on different international legal rules and subject to the jurisdiction of different international tribunals", L Hill Cawthorne, 'International Litigation and the Dissaggregation of Disputes: Ukraine/Russia as A Case-Study' 68 (2019) *International and Comparative Law Quarterly* 779.

79 Ibid.

where it was decided that the PCIJ 'cannot allow its own competency to give way unless confronted with a clause which it considers sufficiently clear to prevent the possibility of a negative conflict of jurisdiction involving the danger of a denial of justice'.[80] So, the only condition that limits a court's action when a prior pending proceeding is actually on foot before another tribunal, is the perpetration of denial of justice.

Nevertheless, absent any relevant judicial pronouncement, the normative status of a relevant principle in international law remains to this day unsettled. The United Nations Charter does not provide any relevant guidance as to the applicability of a relevant rule in disputes submitted before multiple adjudicatory mechanisms. Article 95 merely provides: "Nothing in the present Charter shall prevent Members of the United Nations from entrusting the solution of their differences to other tribunals by virtue of agreements already in existence or which may be concluded in the future." Ditto, the ICJ Statute, unlike other treaties establishing dispute settlement mechanisms,[81] makes no express provision for its inter-relationship with the jurisdictions of other courts and tribunals. In the event of parallel proceedings, the way in which they may be regulated can only be considered on the basis of relevant general principles of law applicable to international tribunals. Given the paucity of judicial practice, the controversy around the contours and normative status of the dominant way in which public international law regulates parallel proceedings persists.[82] According to the latest – albeit not recent – detailed study on the matter, the existence of *lis pendens* 'requires both courts to take account of the parallel proceedings and in the exercise of their discretion, to use their inherent powers both to protect the exercise of their jurisdiction in appropriate cases, and to suspend the exercise of their jurisdiction in the light of pending proceedings elsewhere'.[83] Which is not much after all.

80 PCIJ, *Factory at Chorzów (Germany v. Poland)*, (1927) PCIJ Rep., Ser. A, No. 9, 30.

81 *McLachlan, supra* note 70, 327–346.

82 Due to the rare occurrence of the prerequisites for its application in public international law, Pauwelyn and Salles suggest that the application of *lis pendens* is 'at best a fig leaf designed to cover cracks in the international system; at worst, it is false judicial deference or comity', J Pauwelyn and LE Salles, 'Forum Shopping before International Tribunals: (Real) Concerns, (Im)Possible Solutions' 42 (2009) *Cornell International Law Journal* 77, 110.

83 This is McLachlan's outcome after consideration of the *Mox Plant* and the *Southern Bluefin Tuna* cases, *supra* note 70, 406. According to Reinisch, the existence of a *lis pendens* rule also follows from the applicability of a *res judicata* rule ("As a matter of legal logic it would be inconsistent to permit parallel proceedings [...] up to the point where one of them has decided the case and then prevent the other ('slower') one from proceeding as a result of res judicata."), Au. Reinisch "The Use and Limits of Res Judicata

On the other hand, in the field of international treaty arbitration several tribunals have endorsed a rule in favour of the tribunal seized first in *lis pendens* situations and characterised it as a general principle of law (according to Article 38(1)(c) ICJ Statute). Before the surge of arbitration cases – especially in the discipline of investment law – in the early '00s, such a rule was considered of little relevance for the resolution of jurisdictional conflicts since these mainly arose between *fora* of a different order; arbitral tribunals and domestic courts.[84] Jurisdictional conflicts between two international tribunals (e.g. commercial and investment arbitral tribunals), both of which derive jurisdiction through the parties' agreement and benefit from their consent, proliferated in the past twenty years, hence *lis pendens* acquired new prominence.[85] As argued in the judgments of these judicial bodies, the widespread use of such a rule in domestic legislations of all legal traditions, as well as its inclusion in several international agreements militate in favor of the existence of such a legal principle.[86] Nevertheless, such determinations from arbitral tribunals have been made in private vs. State disputes and it is unlikely that the ICJ will rely upon them when adjudicating inter-State cases.

Until the *Qatar v. UAE* dispute, *lis* (*alibi*) *pendens* or *litispendance* was not raised in any dispute before the Court. Nevertheless, no relevant guidance came from the first – and only – time *lis pendens* was invoked before the Court either. Throughout the provisional measures phase of the dispute, the UAE requested that the Court orders Qatar to stay proceedings before the CERD committee due to the existence of *lis pendens*.[87] In rather dramatic terms the UAE argued that the parallel proceedings pursued by Qatar threaten "a breakdown of the legitimate institutions established by the CERD and make [...] a mockery of the systemic integrity of its dispute reso-

and Lis Pendens as Procedural Tools to Avoid Conflicting Dispute Settlement Outcomes", 3 (2004) *Law and Practice of International Courts and Tribunals* 37, 50.

84 H van Houtte, 'Parallel Proceedings before State Courts and Arbitration Tribunals' in P Karrer (ed), *Arbitral Tribunals or State Courts: Who Must Defer to Whom?* (Swiss Arbitration Association Special Series, 2001) 35.

85 H Pathak, 'Jurisdictional Conflicts between Investment Treaty and Commercial Arbitration – The Role of Lis Pendens' 12 (2020) *Journal of International Dispute Settlement* 1, 19–20.

86 J Magnaye and Au. Reinisch, 'Revisiting *Res Judicata* and *Lis Pendens* in Investor-State Arbitration' 15 (2016) *The Law and Practice of International Courts and Tribunals* 264, 270.

87 *Qatar v UAE,* Request for the Indication of Provisional Measures by the UAE (22 March 2019) 18 [41]. While the UAE did not classify its *lis pendens* objection as pertaining to either jurisdiction or admissibility, it has been argued that it relates to the latter, Kolb, *supra* note 23, 1203.

lution mechanism".[88] The ICJ's orders deferred such a pronouncement for a later stage of the proceedings,[89] a stage that never arrived since the Court finally declared itself incompetent to hear the case on the merits. Hence, it remains a mystery how the ICJ will address a relevant scenario in the future. If viewed as an admissibility issue, the disposition of the parties could be a critical factor for the Court's decision. If jurisdiction is already established 'a tribunal may then be inclined to decide the case anyway because "that is what the parties asked it to do"'.[90] Contrariwise, the consensual nature of an international court's jurisdiction may deter it from keeping a dispute despite the wishes of a party to it.[91]

Strong policy and legal considerations suggest that duplicative litigation should not be tolerated within a single legal order. And indisputably international judicial institutions that adjudicate inter-State disputes operate within the public international legal order.[92] From a policy viewpoint, the elimination of the danger for conflicting judgments and hence the enforcement of normative coherence in the system, the discouragement of a 'race to the Court' and the enforcement of comity or judicial propriety in inter-institutional relations militate in favor of a rule that addresses *lis pendens* situations. Several legal commentators have argued in favour of a general principle of law protecting international tribunals from parallel proceedings and thus granting precedence to the court seized first.[93] This is so, since most legal systems view the initiation of parallel proceedings as a litigation tactic that runs counter to due process and the rule of law.

The existence of such a general principle is not easily proven though and the ICJ will probably attempt to go around this exercise when confronted with a *lis pendens* scenario as it did in *Qatar v. UAE*. Not only because of the arduous nature of the task, but also due to the systemic repercussions the principle's

88 *Qatar v UAE*, Request for Provisional Measures 18 [43].

89 ICJ, *Application of the International Convention on the Elimination of All Forms of Racial Discrimination* (Qatar v. United Arab Emirates), Provisional Measures, Order of 23 July 2018, 420–421 [39]; ICJ, *Application of the International Convention on the Elimination of All Forms of Racial Discrimination* (Qatar v. United Arab Emirates), Provisional Measures, Order of 23 July 2019 369–370 [25].

90 Pauwelyn and Salles, *supra* note 83.

91 Shany, *supra* note 72, 163.

92 See E Benvenisti, 'The Conception of International Law as a Legal System' 50 (2007) *German Yearbook of International Law* 393.

93 G Gaja, 'Relationship of the ICJ with Other International Courts and Tribunals' in *ICJ Commentary*, *supra* note 33, 647, 656 [16]–[18]; Au. Reinisch, *supra* note 83, 50; Shany, *supra* note 72, 240 and 244; V Lowe, 'Overlapping Jurisdiction in International Tribunals', (1999) 20 *Australian Yearbook of International Law* 191, 202–3.

application may entail. Since it affects the exercise of a court's jurisdiction in favour of another, such a principle rests on deference, judicial comity and judicial propriety; notions that the ICJ is a stranger to in its inter-institutional relations. In other words, it reflects an equational perception of international courts the ICJ is not accustomed to. Testament to the Court's disinclination towards this perception was its decision to opt – in *Qatar v. UAE* – for an interpretation of Article 1(1) CERD directly at odds with that advanced by the CERD Committee.[94] While judicial propriety is utilized by the ICJ as a pertinent consideration for the rendering of an advisory opinion,[95] none of the aforementioned concepts has been invoked or *de facto* applied by the ICJ when engaging with the work of other judicial bodies.[96]

Despite the slim chances of the Court attaching legal consequences to a *litispendance* situation, respondents are incentivized to raise an objection to that effect when parallel judicial proceedings are underway. First, because the Court may, despite the legal uncertainty, suspend legal proceedings or refuse to exercise its jurisdiction if the necessary prerequisites are present. Second, and perhaps more importantly, since the respondent State will score points in a political controversy. By exposing a factual situation for which the applicant is solely responsible, the multiple seizin of international tribunals, all associated risks are attributed to the oppresive litigant: inconsistent rulings that may leave the matter unresolved and potentially undermine the legitimate authority and credibility of the international dispute settlement system, prolongation of the dispute that may put pressure in the relationships between judicial institutions and undermine the proper administration of international justice. In this way, the applicant is presented as a vexatious litigant who is not really interested in the timely and effective resolution of the dispute rather as a selfish actor, indifferent to the systemic ramifications of its strategy, who disrupts the delivery of international justice.

3.2 Res judicata*: Consecutive Litigation*

If a *litispendance* situation has so far arisen only in exceptional circumstances, considering the way the international judicial function operates, the

---

94 ICJ, *Application of the International Convention on the Elimination of All Forms of Racial Discrimination* (Qatar v. United Arab Emirates), Judgment on Preliminary Objections, ICJ Reports 2021, 105 [104].

95 A Kaczorowska-Ireland, 'Judicial Propriety: International Adjudication' (2020) *Max Planck Encyclopedia of International Procedural Law*.

96 Eg. in their study Schultz and Ridi list all the uses of comity by the ICJ and none pertains to inter-court relations, Schultz and N Ridi, 'Comity and International Courts and Tribunals' 50 (2017) *Cornell International Law Journal* 577, 600ff.

principle of *res judicata* has never been applicable in the context of a multi-*forum* litigation strategy. As the expression of a 'double *telos*',[97] this principle establishes the finality of judgments and effectively prevents re-litigation of the same issue.[98] Article 60 of the ICJ Statute ('[t]he judgment is final and without appeal') clearly pronounces the finality of ICJ judgments, so disputes settled by the Court 'cannot be reopened by the parties as regards the issues that have been determined'.[99] Nevertheless, by virtue of its normative status as a general principle of law, the applicability of *res judicata* extends to judgments rendered by all international adjudicatory mechanisms.[100] This may also be inferred from an *obiter dictum* of the Court in the *Bosnian Genocide* case whereby it held that: '[d]epriving a litigant of the benefit of a judgment it has already obtained must *in general* be seen as a breach of the principles governing the legal settlement of disputes' (emphasis added).[101] Like *litispendance, res judicata* requires identity of *persona, petitum* and *causa petendi* and further a prior judgment on the same claim by an adjudicative body. Consecutive litigation of the same claim must be in play therefore, a scenario the ICJ has faced in the past, albeit these previous cases concern claims that do not constitute relevant precedents for the cases examined here.

This is so, since in the Court's jurisprudence, examination of *res judicata* has featured with respect to previous ICJ judgments and never with those of other judicial institutions. The 2007 merits judgment in the *Bosnian Genocide* case features the most extensive examination of the principle. Thereby, it was held that the jurisdictional issues raised by the respondent after the delivery of the 1996 judgment on preliminary objections affirming jurisdiction had already been decided with the force of *res judicata*. This case verifies that the Court is indeed bound by its own decisions and cannot unilaterally change them. However, the Court's careful limitation of its reasoning to its own Statute, renders *Bosnian Genocide* of questionable usefuleness when decisions of

97 J Kammerhofer, 'Beyond the res judicata doctrine: The nomomechanics of ICJ interpretation judgments' 37 (2023) *Leiden Journal of International Law* 1, 2. First, that there must be an end to litigation and second that no one should be proceeded against twice for the same cause, *Bosnian Genocide* 90 [116].

98 A Zimmermann and T Thienel, 'Article 60', in *ICJ Commentary, supra* note 33, 1616, 1620 [3]; WS Dodge, 'Res Judicata', in R Wolfrum (ed.) *Max Planck Encyclopedia of Public International Law* (January 2006) [1].

99 *Bosnian Genocide* 91 [116].

100 C Brown, *A Common Law of International Adjudication* (OUP, 2007), 153.

101 Ibid.

other courts and tribunals are involved.[102] Further, a couple of times throughout its history the ICJ has been asked to review the validity of arbitral awards,[103] but never to re-examine the merits of a judgment. In these instances, no *res judicata* was raised since both parties recognized that the proceedings before the Court were not intended as a means of appeal from the award or as an application for its revision.

What remains to be seen then, is how the ICJ will react when it is engaged as an appellate body after another dispute settlement mechanism has pronounced on the same claim. Initially, *res judicata* does not trump the consent of the disputing parties; if, for whatever reason, both parties wish to have their dispute re-examined by the Court, no legal rule prevents them from doing so.[104] And the Rules of the Court envisage such an eventuality in Rule 87[1] which reads as follows:

> When in accordance with a treaty or convention in force a contentious case is brought before the Court concerning a matter which has been the subject of proceedings before some other international body, the provisions of the Statute and the Rules governing contentious cases shall apply.

But, is there any cogent legal reason why the Court must not exercise its established jurisdiction and hence refuse to examine the merits of a dispute that has already been decided by another dispute settlement body with the force of law?

---

102 M Ottolenghi and P Prows, 'Res Judicata in the ICJ's Genocide Case: Implications for Other Courts and Tribunals?', 21 (2009) Pace International Law Review 37, 38.

103 ICJ, *Arbitral Award made by the King of Spain on 23 December 1906* (Honduras vs Nicaragua) Judgment, ICJ Reports (1960), 198–9; ICJ, *Arbitral Award of 31 July 1989*, (Guinea Bissau vs Senegal) Judgment, ICJ Reports (1991) 62, [24]–[25]. In the latter case, the Court examined the application made under the optional clause declaration, not 'in accordance with a treaty or convention' which testifies to the overarching power of consent in setting aside jurisdictional limitations deriving from other sources.

104 A relevant clause is found in the agreements regulating Hungary's financial obligations after WWI. Article X of Agreement II provides: "a right of appeal to the Permanent Court of International Justice from all judgments on questions of jurisdiction or merits which may be given henceforth by the Mixed Arbitral Tribunals in all proceedings other than [...]", *Agreement No. II Concerning the Settlement of Questions Relating to the Agrarian Reforms and to the Mixed Arbitral Tribunals*, (Paris, 28 April 1930), Article X[1]. The ICIJ explicitly acknowledged such a possibility of review in ICIJ, *Appeal from a Judgment of Hungaro-Czechoslovak Mixed Arbitral Tribunal*, Czechoslovakia v. Hungary, 1933 P.C.I.J. (ser. A/B) No. 61 (Dec. 15), 207, 221 [54].

An intricate issue of judicial propriety underlies this question. When the due and proper administration of justice may be compromised, the Court will refuse to exercise a jurisdiction that has been conferred upon it in a regular manner.[105] Along these lines, Kolb suggests that the ICJ must refuse to adjudicate as an appellate mechanism the merits of a claim already examined by another judicial organ for two reasons: first, since such organs are perceived – by their founding instruments – as last-instance courts and further, because the possibility of an appeal by the ICJ 'would be disavowing the other tribunal, setting itself up as the other tribunal's superior, undermining its prestige, and endangering its future activities'.[106] Thus, acting as 'the guardian of [its] judicial integrity',[107] the Court must refrain from dealing with the merits of the case. Nevertheless, according to this reasoning, it is not its own judicial integrity that the Court protects, but rather that of the international dispute settlement system. And, in reality, it is not judicial integrity that is at stake, but mainly the enforcement of judicial comity. This seems far-fetched. The principle of consent should not yield to such systemic considerations. Out of respect to the States that willingly decide to bring their disputes before it, this must occur only in extreme circumstances.[108] Because such circumstances have not yet been present in inter-State adjudication and it is hard to think of an example when they will arise, there is yet no legal reason why the Court mustn't enforce its Statute *per* 87 [1] and act as an appellate body even if this is not courteous towards other *fora*.

3.3 *Abuse of Process*

Finally, a principle that underpins both aforementioned situations is that of abuse of process. A rule derived from the generic notion of abuse of right, it constitutes a general principle of international law applicable also in inter-State disputes, prohibiting the improper use of the general right to judicial

105 Cases where the determination of the legal position of a third State would necessarily have to be considered by the Court (*Monetary Gold* principle), constitute the most often-cited examples of refusal to exercise jurisdiction, *see East Timor* (Portugal v. Australia), Judgment of 30 June 1995, 104–5, [34]–[35].

106 Kolb, *supra* note 23, 874.

107 *Northern Cameroons, ICJ Reports 1963*, 29.

108 If the Court determines that a litigant does not consent to the examination of such a request for reconsideration a claim, then it should not adjudicate, not for reasons of comity but rather for lack of jurisdiction.

protection.[109] In *Immunities and Criminal Proceedings,* the Court distinguished between abuse of rights and abuse of process, clarifying that the latter "goes to the procedure before a court or tribunal and can be considered at the preliminary phase of these proceedings".[110] While the Court has often dealt with related claims in recent cases,[111] it has not yet defined the *contours* of the term which does not appear in its Statute.[112] Commentators have outlined two constitutive features though, which have made their way into ICJ jurisprudence;[113] first, the acting party must have the right to access the *forum,* so its jurisdiction must be established ('a valid title of jurisdiction') [114] and second, the delivery of justice must be distorted, due to the use of procedural rights for a purpose they are not intended for.[115] So far, the ICJ has rejected objections based on abuse of process when raised with reference either to the whole process or to single procedural rights, withholding its application 'only in exceptional circumstances'.[116] Understandably so, since exposing the rationale behind a State's application presents evidentiary diffi-

109 AD Mitchell and T Malone, 'Abuse of Process in Inter-State Dispute Resolution' in *Max Planck Encyclopedia of International Law* (2018) [2] and [16]; Y Shany, *supra* note 72, 159, 258.

110 ICJ, *Immunities, and Criminal Proceedings* (*Equatorial Guinea v. France*), Preliminary Objections, Judgment, ICJ Reports 2018, 336 [150].

111 Lemey enumerates the cases in which it has been invoked, M Lemey, 'Incidental Proceedings before the International Court of Justice: The Fine Line between "Litigation Strategy" and "Abuse of Process"' 20 (2021) *The Law and Practice of International Courts and Tribunals* 5, 8 [fn10]. For more recent case-law, see *Allegations of Genocide,* Judgment, 2 February 2024, [110]–[118].

112 Contrariwise, the UNCLOS (Art 294) and the ECHR (Art 35[3]) refer explicitly to the notion as a ground for inadmissibility of an application.

113 C Ceretelli, "Abuse of Process: An Impossible Dialogue Between ICJ and ICSID Tribunals?" 11 (2020) *Journal of International Dispute Settlement* 1, 2; R Kolb, 'General Principles of Procedural Law', in ICJ Commentary, *supra* note 33, 963, 998; ILA Committee on International Commercial Arbitration, *Interim Report: Res Judicata and Arbitration* (Berlin, 2004).

114 *Immunities and Criminal Proceedings* (*Equatorial Guinea v France*), Preliminary Objections, Judgment, I.C.J. Reports 2018 (I), 336 [150].

115 *Bosnian Genocide,* Preliminary Objections, ICJ Reports 1993, 622 [46]. Kolb provides an indicative list of abusive purposes: "use [...] for reasons that are fraudulent, or designed to cause delay, or simply frivolous; designed to harm the other side or give the abusing party an illegitimate advantage; intended to devalue other pending proceedings or deprive them of their object; intended purely for propaganda purposes [...] actions based on an intention which is malevolent", *supra* note 23, 947.

116 *Alleged Violations of the 1955 Treaty of Amity, Economic Relations, and Consular Rights* (*Islamic Republic of Iran v. United States of America*), Preliminary Objections, Judgment, ICJ Reports 2021, 36 [93].

culties, and, further, the gravity of the allegation – the Court is approached for ulterior motives and not for the pursuance of justice – justifies such heightened standard of proof.[117] The outstanding question is whether the litigation strategy of resorting to more than one international tribunals, in a parallel or consecutive fashion, could be considered abusive under this principle. This is a question the ICJ has not addressed yet, and a different one from the application of a rule in a situation of *lis pendens* or *res judicata* since, *prima facie*, abuse of process does not depend upon identity of *persona, petitum* and *causa petendi*.

Since no relevant precedent exists in ICJ case-law, in order to define the scope of the principle in international law it is pertinent to look into the practice of other international judicial mechanisms where determinations of abuse of process due to prior or parallel proceedings have been made. Parallel and consecutive litigation is a recurring phenomenon in the field of international economic law, hence the heightened interest of commentators into the application of the doctrine in WTO-related disputes,[118] and investment-related disputes.[119] Albeit, only investment tribunals have qualified the practice of jurisdictional forum shopping as an abuse of process, for international tribunals are generally reluctant to make such a finding.[120] In investment disputes the State is commonly forced to defend itself before several arbitral tribunals when the claimants' subsidiaries pursue overlapping claims. This strategy was found to be inconsistent with the doctrine of abuse of process when multiple proceedings are initiated 'in relation to the same investment, the same measures and the same harm.'[121] As applied, the doctrine overcomes the identity of

117 *Immunities and Criminal Proceedings*, Dissenting opinion of Judge Donoghue, 387, [18].

118 *See* eg ST Nguyen,' The Applicability of Comity and Abuse of Rights in World Trade Organisation Dispute Settlement' 35 (2016) *University of Tasmania Law Review* 95.

119 *See* eg E Gaillard, 'Abuse of process in international arbitration' 32 (2017) *ICSID Review* 17; T Gazzini and A Pietrobon, 'Parallel Proceedings Concerning Investment and Human Rights Claims' in *The Changing Character of International Dispute Settlement* (CUP, 2023), 45; JD Branson, 'The Abuse of Process Doctrine Extended: A Tool for Right Thinking People in International Arbitration' 38 (2021) *Journal of International Arbitration* 187.

120 Latest relevant case: *Orascom v. Algeria*, ICSID Case No ARB/12/35, Award (31 May 2017); early authorities where the doctrine was declared potentially applicable are *Grynberg v. Grenada* ICSID Case No. ARB/10/6, Award (10 December 2010) and *Ampal v. Egypt*, ICSID Case No. ARB/12/11, Decision on Jurisdiction (1 February 2016).

121 This test, formulated in *Orascom v. Algeria* [545] was confirmed explicitly by the annulment committee (Decision on Annulment, (17 Sept. 2020)) and implicitly in *Eskosol v. Italy*, ICSID Case No. ARB/15/50, Award (4 Sept. 2020).

persona requirement of *res judicata* and *lis pendens*,[122] and arguably it also goes around the identity of *causa petendi*. In this sense, the protective scope of the principle in public international law extends to proceedings that do not conform the strict prerequisites of *lis pendens* or *res judicata*, but rather pertain to the same factual matrix (same investment, same measures and same harm). While it has been argued that the ICJ should introduce such a standard for dropping claims when they the same subject matter has been presented to a more appropriate judicial forum,[123] whether the Court will in fact do so is another matter.

It seems improbable that the aforementioned perception of the principle, which is of rather broad applicability when compared to *lis pendens* or *res judicata*, will be endorsed by ICJ jurisprudence for multiple reasons. First, to appease any misgivings of its clientele; the wider the application of the doctrine, the more hesitant States may be to resort to the Court. Second, for another reason that pertains to the principle's rationale. Abuse of process in multiple proceedings is strongly connected to the avoidance of double – or multiple – recovery.[124] The latter is undoubtedly possible when two investment tribunals, competent to adjudicate monetary compensation, are dealing with connected disputes.[125] This is so, because double – or multiple – recovery relates to a State's overpayment of compensation as a result of multiple proceedings. However, it is doubtful whether it is applicable to other forms of reparation.[126] When the ICJ is requested to intervene in a dispute *in tandem* with or after another judicial *forum*, it is highly unlikely that both requests will focus on monetary compensation for the same harm. In *Allegations of Genocide* for example, Ukraine requested the Court to order full reparation 'for all harm suffered *by Ukraine* as a consequence of the Russian Federation's use of force in the territory of Ukraine that it commenced on 24 February 2022',[127] while the request before the ECtHR concerns pecuniary com-

122 G Camilla and P Maximillian, 'Abuse of Process' (2024) *Jus Mundi* [11], available at: https://jusmundi.com/en/document/publication/en-abuse-of-process.

123 Ph. Okowa, 'The International Court of Justice and the Georgia/Russia Dispute' 11 (2011) *Human Rights Law Review*, 739, 756.

124 The principle dates back to the Alabama arbitration, *Alabama Claims of the United States v. Great Britain* (Award of 14 September 1872) 29 *Reports of International Arbitral Awards* 125, 133.

125 L Bahmany, *Double Recovery in Investment Arbitration Toward a Principled Treatment of Double Compensation* (Nijhoff, 2023), 1–8.

126 *Factory at Chorzów (Germany v. Poland)*, 1928 PCIJ Series A No. 17 at pp. 29, 59.

127 Ukraine Memorial [179].

pensation for damage suffered *by individuals* on account of the same facts (emphasis added). Third, because the Court has failed to take into consideration the jurisprudence of investment tribunals over the application of the principle already twice, in *Qatar v.* UAE and in *Equatorial Guinea v. France*. And the former case pertained to the initiation of multiple proceedings by Qatar, but the Court did not engage with relevant ICSID case-law at the provisional measures phase. In fact, it did not pronounce upon the issue at all since the objection was eventually dropped by the UAE. While it has been argued that '[i]t would not seem so difficult to qualify Qatar's procedural strategy as an abuse',[128] the Court is reluctant to accuse a State of abusing its procedure hence the application of the 'only in exceptional circumstances' threshold mentioned above. The ICJ has not provided any examples as to what these circumstances may be, nevertheless, it seems that the application of abuse of process for the initiation of a multi-*forum* strategy is reserved for circumstances similar to these of *lis pendens* and *res judicata*. Therefore, the admissibility objection of abuse of process will continue to operate under a very limited scope, rendering it an almost impossible threshold to overcome in scenarios of multi-*forum* litigation.

3.3.1 A Comment on the Rhetorical Use of the Abuse of Process Admissibility Objection

At this point, one comment on the use of the admissibility objection based on abuse of process is in order. Despite the clear indication from the Court that such objections will probably fail, it has lately become a standard part of a respondent's defensive strategy.[129] And the allegation that the applicant is utilizing a judicial body, wasting its time and resources for ulterior purposes, is a grave one. Thus, States level serious accusations often as a rhetorical formula without the allegations being really serious or aiming to persuade the Court.[130] In reality, the audience to which these claims are presented is not the Court, but rather the international community at large.[131] Under this

128 Ceretelli, *supra* note 113, 67.

129 Lemey, *supra* note 111; R Kolb, *Good Faith in International Law* (Hart, 2017), 221.

130 E.g. the reference *in passim* by Colombia without pursuing it further, ICJ, *Question of the Delimitation of the Continental Shelf between Nicaragua and Colombia beyond 200 nautical miles from the Nicaraguan Coast* (*Nicaragua v. Colombia*), Oral proceedings, Verbatim record CR 2015/26, 9.

131 Perelman and Olbrechts-Tyteca would refer to the 'universal audience', C Perelman and L Olbrechts-Tyteca, *The New Rhetoric* (University of Notre Dame Press, 1969) 26–35, [6]–[7].

prism, abuse of process objections are used as a rhetorical stratagem. I submit that such a use of admissibility objections is evidence of a turn towards defense strategies within the courtroom that disorientate the discussion before the Court towards issues of no legal significance for the judicial outcome of the dispute.

In fact, abuse of process objections are a textbook example of the 28th of Schopenhauer's 'dishonest' stratagems as exposed in his 'The Art of Being Right' treatise, entitled 'Persuade the Audience, Not the Opponent'.[132] He claims that an argument *ad auditores* is 'chiefly practicable in a dispute between scholars in the presence of the unlearned'. Arguably, of all international judicial *fora,* the discussion held between the parties before the ICJ attracts the greatest publicity. It is in the States' interests then to infer arguments that sap the opponent's position, credibility or reputation. Schopenhauer explains the stratagem as follows:

> you can start some invalid objection, which, however, only an expert sees to be invalid. Now your opponent is an expert, but those who form your audience are not, and accordingly in their eyes he is defeated; particularly if the objection which you make places him in any ridiculous light.[133]

This is an accurate description of the intended use and effect of abuse of process objections. They constitute an attempt to discredit the applicant as a user of international law, a spectacular move, made mainly to impress. At the same time, it is a move that diverts the discussion towards non-legal issues which may have a bearing beyond the courtroom on the overall political debate. Since abuse of process requires a demonstration of bad faith, casting a doubt on the motivation underlying the application to the Court, presents an opportunity to discuss issues tangential to the judicial proceedings aiming to bring the opponent in disrepute.

The utilization of the ICJ as a platform for the furtherance of such objectives may impact upon the counsel's argumentation when pleading for such objections and the Court's disposition to engage with them. To the extent that law is 'a culture of argument', it establishes 'roles and relations and voices, positions from which one may speak and audiences to whom one

132 A Schopenhauer, *The Art of Being Right* (Beers and Politics, 2017), 13, 26.

133 Ibid, 27.

may speak'.[134] The strategic use of such legal tools may affect both the position and voice of a counsel in ICJ disputes. It is not just the audience she addresses that is different, but concomitantly the rhetoric narrative through which she aims to connect with the audience is not a strictly legal-technical one. Characteristic is Russia's oral argumentation in this respect; by invoking a series of self-proclaimed truths ('There could be no doubt by the virtue of the underlying proceedings Ukraine attempts to handcuff a State's right to self-defence. […] While a rally to arrange such intervention is indeed an abuse.') and characterisations ('This twisted case cannot survive on its own. […] This was […] performed in the most insolent manner') it aims to assert rather than establish that Ukraine's application has been made in an abusive manner.[135] So, unsurprisingly, when Russia invoked three arguments to support its abuse of process objection, the Court dealt with each in one paragraph in a rather hasty manner.[136] From the ICJ's viewpoint, if such a reproach towards other States for their litigation tactics is made in an imprudent manner, it might force the Court to dispense with such objections superficially, if not plainly ignore them.

All in all, multi-*forum* litigation is a strategic choice beyond legal reproach before the ICJ. The Court will preserve the jurisdiction conferred upon it as it is not willing to dispose of a dispute brought before it consensually by States. *Lis pendens* and abuse of process are practically unknown to ICJ jurisprudence, while the principle of *res judicata* operates with a much more limited scope. The aforementioned principles have been utilized in international treaty arbitration for the regulation of parallel or consecutive disputes and in this discipline they have found adequate room to influence the respective judicial outcomes. Nevertheless, given the specificities of the ICJ procedure and the context in which this procedure operates, it seems unlikely they will produce an analogous effect before the Court.

The analysis will now change viewpoint and will scrutinize whether other judicial proceedings may be affected by an ICJ judgment when they concern the same factual matrix. At the same time, it will attempt to understand the limits of such an effect in order to consider which objectives may be achieved in the context of this strategy and to what extent the ICJ is the adequate forum to pursue them.

---

134 J Boyd White, 'Law as Language: Reading Law and Reading Literature' 60 (1981–82) *Texas Law Review* 415, 441.

135 *Allegations of Genocide,* CR 2023/13 (18 September 2023), 96–98, [34]–[43].

136 *Ukraine v. Russia* 2024 Judgment [114], [115] and [117].

4 Instrumentalizing ICJ Judgments in a Multi-*forum* Litigation Strategy: the Parties' Objectives

The previous Section demonstrated the limited *de jure* impact the applicant's strategic choice to embed the ICJ in a multi-*forum* litigation strategy may exert upon the outcome or the running of ICJ main proceedings. This is testament to the uninfluenced way in which the Court comports when exercising its judicial function. The interpretations, pronouncements and lines of reasoning of international judicial decisions may have broader implications though. In international law, 'courts and tribunals routinely take into account the legal reasoning contained in the decisions of other courts and tribunals, although they are not obligated to apply them'.[137] Without constituting binding precedents, judicial decisions establish judicial givens[138] or 'reference points that others can hardly escape'.[139] They shape the understanding of international law and by clothing rules and interpretations with their authority, they legitimize them. In reality, they are not merely subsidiary means for the determination of rules of law per Article 38(1)(d) of the ICJ Statute.[140] Thus, international courts and tribunals exert influence over the work of other law-applying organs by taking advantage of their own authority. Due to its institutional prestige and the general recognition of its jurisprudence as relevant, the capacity of the Court to influence the pronouncements of other *fora* tops that of other international judicial bodies.[141] It is not surprising then, that in this power-play (for authority is a sub-category of power[142]) the ICJ dominates rather than submits, shows the way and seldom follows.

The Court asserts its pre-eminence over other bodies in the interpretation and application of international legal rules. This is so with respect to general rules. In *Bosnian Genocide* the ICJ was anxious to underline a certain prece-

137 ILC, *Report on the work of the seventy-fifth session* (2024), UN Doc A/79/10, 43[1].

138 V Rezadoost, 'Unveiling the 'author' of international law: The 'legal effect' of ICJ's advisory opinions' (2024) *Journal of International Dispute Settlement* 1, 10 (published as advance article).

139 I Venzke, 'Authoritative Interpretation' (2018) *Max Planck Encyclopedia of International Procedural Law* [76].

140 A Ross, *Textbook of International Law* (London, 1947), 8.

141 Chr. Tams, 'The ICJ as a 'Law-Formative Agency': Summary and Synthesis' in Chr. Tams and J Sloan (eds) *The Development of International Law by the International Court of Justice* (OUP, 2013), 376, 391; Gl. Hernandez, 'Interpretative Authority and the International Judiciary' in Bianchi et al. (eds) *Interpretation in International Law* (OUP, 2015), 166, 181–2.

142 P Capps and HP Olsen, 'Explaining power and authority in international courts' 34 (2021) *Leiden Journal of International Law* 533.

dence over the ICTY on issues not related to criminal liability.[143] This is apparently the case with respect to specialized rules too. While the Court stated in 2010 that it 'should ascribe great weight to the interpretation adopted by' specialized bodies in their field of expertise,[144] it did a u-turn in 2021 when it interpreted CERD convention obligations in the opposite manner than the CERD Committee.[145] This is not to say that the ICJ is not willing to cross-reference decisions by other international courts and tribunals,[146] but to infer that in reality the Court remains uninfluenced by the determinations of such organs. Hence, the reliance mainly in its own jurisprudence. So, a State does not engage the ICJ in a multi-*forum* strategy with the expectation that the Court itself will be affected in its judgment by pronouncements of other organs. Rather, the opposite.

Engagement of the Court in such a strategic choice may hold sway over other dispute resolution attempts and thus affect the attitude of disputing States. Being aware of such side-effects from the implication of the ICJ, the parties employ this strategy for two overarching reasons: a. to instrumentalize the ICJ's strong *de jure* authority in order to influence other proceedings, or b. to instrumentalize the ICJ's potential to act as a *forum* for political advocacy. This Section will focus on whether an ICJ judgment by virtue of its legal authority may impact the rulings of other courts and tribunals engaged in the context of a multi-*forum* litigation strategy. And in turn, whether a stream of coordinated judicial rulings will further compliance with judicial pronouncements. Then, the attention will shift to whether this strategy can be understood as a storytelling campaign. In this context, the ICJ may constitute an effective political advocacy platform. Such an attempt to 'set the record straight' and promote a particular narrative does not focus on securing compliance with judicial rulings, but rather on bolstering a State's reputation and legitimacy in the eyes of the international community. Before delving into the particulars of how States may utilize a court's authority to their benefit, it is important to put forward an understanding of what are the manifestations of

---

143 A Pellet and D Müller, 'Article 38' in ICJ Commentary, *supra* note 33, 819, 952[321].

144 ICJ, *Diallo* (*Guinea v. Congo*), Judgment (Merits) ICJ Reports 2010, 639, 663–4[100].

145 ICJ, *Application of the CERD* (*Qatar v. UAE*), Judgment (Preliminary Objections) ICJ Reports 2021, 71, 99[88]. This was lamented by Judges Bhandari ([21]) and Robinson ([13]) in their respective dissenting opinions.

146 Pellet and Müller, *supra* note 143, 950–2 [318]–[320]. For a comprehensive survey on the use of judicial decisions as subsidiary means in the case-law of international courts, tribunals and other judicial bodies, see ILC, *Subsidiary means for the determination of rules of international law: Memorandum of the Secretariat,* UN Doc. A/CN.4/765 (23 May 2024).

court authority and clarify how it relates to the ideas of legitimacy, compliance and effectiveness.

4.1 *The ICJ, an Authoritative Institution?*

In legal and in political philosophy authority means the right to rule.[147] This establishment of a formal hierarchy on the basis of a 'right' is what separates authority from brute force, persuasion or influence. Authority then functions as a maxim for action due to the relationship of authority it creates,[148] even in the absence of agreement with the substance of the rule itself because it provides 'content-independent reasons for action'.[149] This 'right' need not be a legal one, albeit it arguably conveys the idea that authority is contingent upon some kind of justification. Hence, the concept of justified authority.[150] When it comes to justifying the authority of institutions whenever they exercise their powers, the concept of authority is commonly treated as necessarily implying the concept of legitimacy, hence Raz's influential theory of legitimate authority.[151] According to this strand of theory, an institution may be in a position of authority only when it exercises legitimated power.[152] And a legitimate (or justified) power is understood to mean one that has the right to rule.[153] Thus, when discussing institutional authority the ideas of authority and legitimacy get fused.[154] All the above have been contested by theorists who attempt to understand and explain the authority of international courts as institutions.[155] For present purposes though, they provide a *de minimis*

147 The list of relevant works is too long to make a selection here, so I shall cite three relatively recent works on the authority of international courts that refer to previous scholarship; K Gorobets, (2022) *Contemplating an Uneven Landscape: The Authority of International Law* (PhD Thesis, University of Groningen); K Alter, L Helfer and M Rask Madsen (eds) *International Court Authority*, (OUP, 2018); HGr Cohen, A Follesdal N Grossman and G Ulfstein *Legitimacy and International Courts* (CUP, 2018).

148 M Weber, *Economy and Society: An Outline of Interpretative Sociology* (University of California Press, 1978), 217.

149 HLA Hart, *Essays on Bentham* (OUP, 1983), 254–5.

150 HGr Cohen, A Follesdal, N Grossman and G Ulfstein, 'Legitimacy and International Courts: A Framework' in Cohen *et al. supra* note 147, 1, 5,

151 J Raz, *The Authority of Law: Essays on Law and Morality* (OUP, 2009), 2.

152 I Hurd, *After Anarchy: Legitimacy and Power in the United Nations Security Council* (Princeton University Press, 2007) 3; N Grossman, 'The Normative Legitimacy of International Courts' 86 (2013) *Temple Law Review* 61, 80.

153 Cohen Follesdal, Grossman and Ulfstein *supra* note 150, 4.

154 Ibid. describe legitimacy as "justified authority", *supra* note 150, 5.

155 Eg. Alter, Helfer and Rask Madsen contest the idea of authority as only a question of legitimated power, K Alter, L Helfer and M Rask Madsen, 'International Court Authority in a Complex World' in Alter et al. *supra* note 147, 1, 11. They concede though that

starting point in order to understand the authority of international courts and the ICJ in particular.

The authority of any court may arguably be broken down into two components; *de jure* and *de facto*. *De jure* authority denotes the court's power to rule on disputes that fall within its jurisdiction.[156] From this feature derives the court's power to engage in authoritative interpretations of the law,[157] and its justifiable right to issue pronouncements which those normatively addressed must obey, or at least consider with due care. So, with respect to these institutions, *de jure* authority coincides with legitimate authority.[158] This authority is justified by a range of factors.[159] For international courts specifically, it is primarily an act of delegation that creates both a right to rule and a defined scope of competence.[160] But apart from such predetermined standards, the subjective beliefs of interested actors may affect a court's *de jure* authority too (or its sociological legitimacy).[161] According to the most commonly shared view, the ICJ enjoys *de jure* authority because it is both believed to be an authoritative institution by the users of its products, and because it exercises its judicial function within the confines of State consent.[162] By capitalising on its *de jure* authority, the Court benefits from

'authority that is perceived to be illegitimate will likely wane', *K Alter, L Helfer and M Rask Madsen*, 'International Court Authority in Question: Introduction to Part III', in Ibid, 365, 373.

156 I Venzke, *supra* note 139[3].

157 A Orakhelashvili, *The Interpretation of Acts and Rules in Public International Law* (OUP, 2008) 515.

158 To be used interchangeably throughout the book.

159 Cohen Follesdal, Grossman and Ulfstein identify four categories of such factors: normative goals, design features, audiences, and environments, *supra* note 150, 22 table 1.1.

160 C Bradley and J Kelley, The Concept of Delegation, 71 (2008) *Law and Contemporary Problems* 1. For certain legal sociologists this stems from Courts being reflective of society, M Rask Madsen, 'Explaining the Power of International Courts in Their Context: From Legitimacy to Legitimization' in A de Klor, M Maduro and A Vauchez (eds) *Courts, Social Change and Judicial Independence* (European University Institute, 2012), 23.

161 This view is shared by judges themselves, see *Allegations of Genocide*, 2 February 2024, Joint Advisory Opinion by Judges Sebutinde and Robinson, 11[52]; A Buchanan and RO Keohane, 'The Legitimacy of Global Governance Institutions' 20 (2006) *Ethics and International Affairs* 405; D Bodansky, 'The Legitimacy of International Governance: A Coming Challenge for International Environmental Law?' 93 (1999) *American Journal of International Law* 596.

162 N Grossman, 'Solomonic Judgments and the Legitimacy of the International Court of Justice' in Cohen et al. *supra* note 147, 43, Grossman argues that the Court often detracts from its adjudicatory function when it tries to accommodate the interests of both parties, and in this way harms its sociological legitimacy.

rulings with a strong normative weight (hence their precedential impact noted *supra* and analysed in the next Section), betters the record of achievement of its goals[163] and renders non-compliance with its judgments cumbersome.

However, even if a court acts upon its *de jure* authority, this does not mean that its rulings will in fact result in a change in the behaviour of engaged audiences. How actors respond to an institution's activities and outputs is a matter of empirical or sociological observation and may be termed its *de facto* authority.[164] The latter targets a court's power to cast its shadow; e.g. its capacity to actually exercise authority by producing commands that are obeyed by their addressees or by mobilising non-parties to the dispute. Then, it is strongly connected to the question of compliance with judicial decisions.[165] And it is also tied to the notion of effectiveness of judicial institutions, since the latter is commonly understood as a broader concept that incorporates compliance with court outputs.[166] All three notions – *de facto* authority, compliance and effectiveness – to the extent that they pertain to judicial institutions, have a common core; they attempt to measure their real-life impact.[167] For present purposes, it is not important to delve into a deeper analysis of how each should be measured, rather to underscore that they may be conceptualized as concentric circles. The ICJ, has traditionally enjoyed a good measure of

163 Y Shany, 'Stronger Together? Legitimacy and Effectiveness of International Courts as Mutually Reinforcing or Undermining Notions' in Cohen et al. *supra* note 147, 354, 370.

164 Alter Helfer and Rask Madsen, *supra* note 155, 28.

165 D Kapiszewski and M Taylor, 'Compliance: Conceptualizing, Measuring, and Explaining Adherence to Judicial Rulings', 38 (2013) *Law and Social Inquiry* 803, 829–30; Judge Oda refers to the 'court's dignity' which may be affected due to limited compliance with its pronouncememts, ICJ, *Armed Activities on the Territory of the Congo* (*DRC v. Uganda*) Order of 1 July 2000, Declaration of Judge Oda, 131, 132[6].

166 Y Shany, 'Compliance with Decisions of International Courts as Indicative of their Effectiveness: A Goal-based Analysis' in J Crawford and S Nouwen (eds) *Select Proceedings of the European Society of International Law* (Hart, 2012) 229; G Navarro, 'Effectiveness of International Courts: From Compliance to Transformative Impact' in A von Bogdandy et al. (eds) *The Impact of the Inter-American Human Rights System: Transformations on the Ground* (OUP, 2024) 138, 143; Y Shany, 'Effectiveness of International Adjudication' (2019) *Max Planck Encyclopedia of International Law.*

167 I am aware of the so-called 'system resources' approach that links effectiveness to an organization's longevity and not to its *lato sensu* impact, but I agree with Giladi and Shany that it is 'ill-suited for a normative evaluation of judicial effectiveness', R Giladi and Y Shany, 'Assessing the Effectiveness of the International Court of Justice' in C Esposito and K Parlett, *The Cambridge Companion to the International Court of Justice* (CUP, 2023), 101, 104. For more on the methodology of measuring effectiveness, see *infra* Chapter 3, Section 3.

all three since its judgments were generally complied with, and they arguably have the capacity to modify the behavior of actors.[168] Lately however, commentators have been more skeptical as to the Court's *de facto* authority over specific constituencies.[169]

De jure and *de facto* authority capture the capacity of courts to generate power, but they are not the two sides of the same coin. They do not necessarily go hand-in-hand. The rulings of an otherwise *de jure* authoritative court may be ignored by the litigants.[170] Nevertheless, the opposite is not observed since "justifications of authority, which make it legitimate, play a role in what practical reasons a court is capable of generating. Legitimacy outlines the boundaries in which *de facto* authority is likely to be achieved".[171] This is why, courts with strong *de facto* authority, such as national courts, enjoy an equally strong legitimate authority.

It is uncontested that, when compared to national courts, international judicial institutions fall short in *de facto* authority. And on the contrary, there are usually fewer concerns about their *de jure* authority.[172] This is accentuated with respect to the ICJ. States and other actors have a strong moral and political justification to follow the Court's rulings, but its pronouncements sometimes have little to no impact on the practical reasoning of the subjects it addresses. In instances of multi-*forum* litigation, the issue of limited impact of judicial pronouncements is particularly acute. *Ukraine v. Russia* exemplifies this. This observation, is not made in order to suggest that this strategy may negatively affect the *de facto* authority of international courts. Rather, it is made in order to assess whether and how their *de jure* authority may be affected by the way they are utilized in such a strategy. This is an important inquiry '[f]or failing to understand and respond to legitimacy concerns endangers both the international courts and the law they interpret and apply. If international courts lack justified authority, so too will their interpretations

168 H Jones, 'Why Comply? An Analysis of Trends in Compliance with Judgments of the International Court of Justice Since Nicaragua', 12 (2012) *Chicago-Kent Journal of International and Comparative Law* 57; C Schutze, *Compliance with Decisions of the International Court of Justice* (OUP, 2004).

169 EJ Powell, 'The International Court of Justice and Islamic Law States Territory and Diplomatic Immunity' in Alter et al. *supra* note 147, 277; Giladi and Shany, *supra* note 167, 116.

170 The East African Court of Justice falls in this category according to JT Gathii, 'The East African Court of Justice: Human Rights and Business Actors Compared' in Alter et al. *supra* note 147, 59, 80.

171 Gorobets, *supra* note 147, 93.

172 Ibid, 85.

of international law'.[173] Before making such an assessment though, it is important to understand the two basic ways in which the Court is utilized in the context of a multi-*forum* litigation strategy. The discussion turns to this right away.

As noted in Chapter 1, the distinction between instrumentalization of the Court for its legitimate authority and instrumentalization for its potential to act as a *forum* for public advocacy is important for all aspects of the ICJ's jurisdiction. Whenever the discussion focuses on judgments, this will be done explicitly.

4.2 *Instrumentalizing the Court's Legitimate Authority*

When engaging the ICJ in a multi-*forum* litigation strategy, applicant States aim to benefit from its legitimate authority. In particular, from the capacity of the Court to generate normative commands and the potential of its rulings to transcend the particular case, to offer general guidance and to affect the determinations of other *fora*. By capitalizing on this feature of the ICJ, the States resort to the Court to create a domino of like-minded rulings and to use the 'shadow of the law' in order to create favorable bargaining conditions.

In order to delimit the Court's potential to influence other proceedings, it is important to highlight what has been extensively portrayed in literature as its law-development function. Understood as the midway between the classic dispute settlement role the Court embraces and the legislative role the Court consistently and vehemently rejects,[174] legal development is a task ascribed primarily to another UN organ, the International Law Commission.[175] It is impossible to carve out here a clear-cut distinction between interpretation of the law (what the Court can do), development of the law (what the Court often does do) and legislation (what the Court cannot do). It is only fitting to observe that, mindful of its judicial function and its mandate per Articles 38

173 Cohen *et al.* supra note 147, 2–3.

174 ICJ, *Nuclear Weapons* Advisory Opinion, ICJ Reports, 226, 237[18]. The development of legal rules is the primary reason why ICJ advisory opinions are utilized in a multi-*forum* litigation strategy, *see* Chapter 4.

175 Article 1 ILC Statute, *Statute of the International Law Commission,* UN General Assembly Resolution 174 (II) of 21 November 1947, as amended by resolutions 485 (V) of 12 December 1950, 984 (X) of 3 December 1955, 985 (X) of 3 December 1955 and 36/39 of 18 November 1981. On the distinction between legal development and legislation, see N Voulgaris, 'The ILC and Politics: Taking the Science Out of International Law's Progressive Development' 33 (2022) *European Journal of International Law* 761.

and 65 of its Statute, the Court is careful not to state that it straddles the fence and transgresses the boundaries set by its judicial character.[176]

Albeit, the Court is considered the most important judicial agent of legal development in international law. When international judicial organs face legal problems akin to the ones the Court has tackled – likely pertaining to general international law, such as jurisdiction and admissibility issues or the application of general customary rules – the ICJ is the prime candidate for the application of *mutatis mutandis* solutions. In *Ukraine v. Russia* (*re: Crimea*) the ECtHR referred to the *2005 Armed Activities* judgment in order to the establish the general principles on the relationship between human rights law and international humanitarian law.[177] In *Cyprus v. Turkey,* the same court drew inspiration from the *Namibia* opinion to assert whether the exhaustion of domestic remedies rule was applicable in unrecognized entities.[178] The ICJ had declared in 1971 that official acts performed by the government of South Africa on behalf of or concerning Namibia after the termination of the mandate were illegal and invalid, however, this invalidity could not be extended to those acts, the effects of which could be ignored only to the detriment of the inhabitants of that territory. Following the same logic, the ECtHR decided in 2001 that remedies available in the unrecognized Turkish Republic of Northern Cyprus must be exhausted, provided that they existed to the advantage of individuals and offered them reasonable prospects of success. While here is no place to list the fields of international law the Court has in fact shaped,[179] it must be stressed that ICJ judgments constitute a source of clarity and predictability as to the content and applicability of international rules.[180]

Numerous factors suggest that the Court is an authoritative moulder of international legal rules. Its general competence, its geographically diversified and numerous composition, its permanence and its status as the principal judicial organ of a global organization, are all testament to this.[181] And

176 ICJ, *Interpretation of Peace Treaties*, Advisory Opinion, ICJ Reports 1950, 221, 229; ICJ, *Fisheries Jurisdiction* (*UK v Iceland*), Judgment (Merits), ICJ Reports 1974, 3, 23–4[53].

177 [914].

178 ECtHR, Cyprus v. Turkey, *Judgment of 10 May 2001* (Application no. 25781/94) [93]–[96].

179 For an overview, see *The Development of International Law by the ICJ*, *supra* note.

180 In this way, the Court also acts as a legitimizing agent for international norms, Y Shany, 'Assessing the Effectiveness of International Courts: A Goal-Based Approach', 106 (2012) *American Journal of International Law* 225, 244–47 (2012).

181 For these reasons the Court is especially mentioned by the ILC in Draft Conclusion 4(1) in the latest report on 'Subsidiary means for the determination of rules of international law' which reads: 'Decisions of international courts and tribunals, in particular of the

due to their law-development faculty, ICJ judgments have acquired an idiosyncratic precedential impact. They have significant weight beyond any concrete dispute in the broader struggles over what the law *means*.[182] In other words, the interpretive authority of ICJ judgments projects legal interpretations beyond the parties to the case by virtue of the power of *res interpretata*.[183] And, since the line separating legal interpretation from law-creation is nowhere to be found, ICJ judgments in practice have also significant weight over what the law *is*.[184] The Court has for example been instrumental in shaping the law of the sea and its relevant case-law is followed by all tribunals that apply the UN Convention on the Law of the Sea.[185] Careful as it may be in its own decisions not to enter the realm of legislation, the ICJ cannot control how its interpretations, pronouncements and lines of reasoning may be perceived by third parties.[186] In this way, absent any *stare decisis*, the Court has acquired by the international community a *de facto* law-making power. As Shahabuddeen eloquently put it: '[i]t is not then a question whether the decision per se applies as a binding precedent, but whether the law which it lays down is *regarded* as part of international law (emphasis added)'.[187] By stabilizing and developing normative expectations

---

International Court of Justice, are a subsidiary means for the determination of the existence and content of rules of international law', *ILC 2024 Report*, *supra* note 137, 33–5[7]–[10].

182 S Besson, 'Legal Philosophical Issues of International Adjudication: Getting Over the Amour Impossible between International Law and Adjudication' in *Oxford Handbook of International Adjudication, supra* note 35, 414, 422.

183 Similar definition of *res interpretata* by: OM Arnardóttir. 'Res *interpretata, erga omnes* effect and the role of the margin of appreciation in giving domestic effect to the judgments of the European Court of Human Rights' (2017) 28 *European Journal of International Law* 819, 822. I find the definition by Gerards and Fleuren restrictive for present purposes, because they do not extend *res interpretata* to other judicial organs; 'the normative consequence or implications or 'force of interpretation' of a ruling *against third party states* that were not party to the case on which the ruling in question was made' (emphasis added), J Gerards and J Fleuren 'Comparative analysis' in J Gerards and J Fleuren (eds) *Implementation of the European Convention of Human Rights and of the judgments of the ECtHR in national case law: A comparative analysis* (2014), 248.

184 M Shahabuddeen, *Precedent in the World Court* (CUP, 2010), 76–80.

185 E De Brabandere, 'The Use of Precedent and External Case-Law by the International Court of Justice and the International Tribunal for the Law of the Sea', 15 (2016) *The Law and Practice of International Courts and Tribunals*, 24, 31–3.

186 Sir Fr. Berman, 'The International Court of Justice as an 'Agent' of Legal Development?' in Tams and Sloan, *supra* note 141, 7, 17.

187 M Shahabuddeen, *supra* note 184, 109.

then, ICJ judgments are understood as coordination points between the users of international law.[188]

If the Court 'speaks the law', how can this be utilized in a multi-*forum* litigation strategy? Arguably, it would be of relevance for the infliction of political pressure in ongoing non-judicial proceedings (e.g. negotiations); on account of the rulings themselves who create the so-called 'shadow of the law'.[189] Given the timeframe for the rendering of a final judgment by an international court though, it is unlikely that this type of political pressure is the prime factor animating resort to judicial institutions in such occasions.[190] Further, this attribute is of marginal relevance in an attempt to influence other judicial proceedings. Since claims before different *fora* are usually based on distinct normative bases, even in the context of a multi-*forum* litigation strategy the legal issues to be resolved by different judicial bodies are seldom the same. There are however striking exceptions to this, such as the *Qatar v. UAE* claims before the ICJ and the CERD committee.[191] Further, ICJ main proceedings are notoriously protracted. Few States, no matter how certain they may be of a favorable ICJ legal pronouncement and of the latter's usefulness for subsequent proceedings, have the luxury to devise a litigation strategy that spans until a final ICJ judgment is rendered. In the case of election-run States, the executive power and hence State policy will likely be exercised by different people at that time. So, the decision to sue may not be chiefly animated by so forward-looking considerations. Of course, the subject-matter of the dispute will be crucial in this respect. A long-standing border dispute may be amenable to such a long-term strategy while an ongoing military conflict may be not.

Beyond 'speaking the law', I submit that the Court's judgments and the accompanying authority with which they are clothed may be of considerable importance for another reason when other judicial *fora* are engaged. And this concerns the establishment of the factual background. 'Speaking the facts' is no less important than the establishment of the law for the

188 HG Kohen, 'Theorizing Precedent in International Law' in *Interpretation in International Law*, supra note 141, 268, 286.

189 According to this idea, the outcome of any dispute settlement process will be influenced by the result of any relevant litigation and the presence and behavior of a third-party adjudicator, R Mnookin and L Kornhauser, 'Bargaining in the Shadow of the Law: The Case of Divorce' 88 (1979) *Yale Law Journal* 950.

190 This is more prevalent in requests for provisional measures, *see infra* Chapter 3, Section 3(B).

191 In this case, the ICJ ruled after the CERD Committee, therefore Qatar did not profit from the ICJ's influence over the CERD Committee.

outcome of a case. The recent ECtHR judgment in *Ukraine v. Russia* (*re: Crimea*) provides a good example on how an ICJ judgment may impact fact-finding by other international judicial organs in the context of a multi-*forum* litigation strategy. The European court adopted *verbatim* the conclusions of the respective ICJ *Crimea* judgment (in [370]) as an authoritative account of "the way in which it [nb Russia] has implemented its educational system in Crimea after 2014 with regard to school education in the Ukrainian language".[192] Of course, in its fact-finding exercise the ECtHR made reference also to the work of other institutions on the same issue, however this was done to corroborate the ICJ findings. To the extent that the claims before different *fora* are based on the same factual matrix, the importance of this inter-institutional dialogue – that goes beyond mere cross-referencing for the purpose of establishing the content of rules – cannot be stressed enough. In this way, the Court's factual pronouncements provided for the ECtHR the most authoritative account of the relevant facts. Due to the high-level fact-finding process adopted by the Court, its conclusions as to the establishment of facts function as a documentary shortcut for other judicial organs. In this sense, ICJ judgments act as coordination points also beyond the legal level, at the fact-finding level.

Turning to the running example in this Chapter, it is worth asking: how likely is it for the ICC or the ECtHR to rely on relevant ICJ factual *dicta* as to the situation in Eastern Ukraine? Not very, given the limited jurisdictional scope of the ICJ case, which will only focus on an assessment of Ukraine's conduct. After the ICJ preliminary objections judgment, there is little overlap as to the essential facts underpinning these cases and no heavy – if none at all – reliance on a future ICJ judgment by other judicial bodies is expected. Further, the ICC has taken evidence and fact-finding in its own hands,[193] which is not surprising since it is establishing a different type of responsibility, that is individual criminal responsibility. This lack of influence by the ICJ over factual determination in other *fora* renders the domino of like-minded rulings slightly less probable in the pending judicial proceedings on Eastern Ukraine. Also, the pressure exerted by all cases seen together is not that great since the ICJ claim is merely declaratory without any finding of Russian responsi-

192 ECtHR, *Ukraine v. Russia (re Crimea)*, Judgment [Grand Chamber], 25 June 2024, Applications nos. 20958/14 and 38334/18, [1160].

193 The mobilisation of the Office of the Prosecutor has been monumental in this respect, see T Mariniello, 'The ICC Prosecutor's Double Standards in the Time of an Unfolding Genocide' *OpinioJuris* (3 January 2024).

bility. It is not wonder then that for some the ICJ judgment was disappointing,[194] and calls for another ICJ case on a different basis altogether were put forward.[195]

It may be that in the particular dispute examined here, the instrumentalization of the ICJ's legitimate authority in this sense did not bear fruit. Albeit, this does not negate the general point; from a litigation strategy perspective such an insight is invaluable for applicant States. It is not hard to fathom how such States may take advantage of the Court's capacity to act as a coordination mechanism at the legal and the factual level. If acceptance of international law is a requirement of membership in the international community, "international law discourse may be understood as having an ideological function in international politics", that of framing and determining State legitimacy.[196] Rulings that point to the same direction, mount the pressure of non-compliance as they expose the disobedient State as a social pariah in the international community. For it is one thing to oppose the ruling of one *forum* and quite another to defy a series of decisions rendered by judicial *fora* of an international reach. Then, the situation is portrayed under a different light: the recalcitrant State is seen as not recognizing the legitimate authority not just of a court, but of international law and its institutions generally.[197] So, international law – a system of rules with normative weight[198] – defends the position of one party to a dispute and the counter-position becomes hard to sustain.[199] And when one of these *fora* is the Court, that carries with it the label of the 'principal judicial organ of the UN' this symbolism is heightened.

194 M Milanovic, 'ICJ Delivers Preliminary Objections Judgment in the Ukraine v. Russia Genocide Case, Ukraine Loses on the Most Important Aspects' *Ejil:talk!* (2 February 2024).

195 I Marchuk and A Wanigasuriya, 'The Curious Fate of the False Claim of Genocide: On the ICJ's Preliminary Objections Judgment in Ukraine v. Russia and Beyond', *Verfassungsblog* (24 February 2024).

196 D Giulfoyle, 'Litigation as Statecraft: Small States and the Law of the Sea' (2023) *British Yearbook of International Law* 1, 18.

197 On the legitimate authority of international law, see D Lefkowitz, *Philosophy and International Law: A Critical Introduction* (OUP, 2010) Chapter 6; S Besson, 'The Authority of International Law: Lifting the State Veil' 31 (2009) *Sydney Law Review* 343.

198 Chr. Chinkin, 'Normative Development in the International Legal System' in D Shelton (ed) *Commitment and Compliance: The Role of Non-Binding Norms in the International Legal System,* 21.

199 Chr. Borgen, 'The Crimea, Compliance, and the Constraint of International Law' *Opinio-Juris* (3 March 2014).

This is not the end of the story though. International courts may be instrumentalized in the context of a multi-*forum* litigation strategy as a means to mount political pressure via their non-legal attributes.

4.3 *Instrumentalizing the Court as a Forum for Political Advocacy*[200]

Judicial rhetoric is distinct from political rhetoric in form and appeal, and so it should be. This however does not necessitate that it is stripped from political significance. It is also trite to observe that inter-State adjudication has been used for political ends since 'all courts are political institutions' and the same can be said for States.[201] The motive and the decision behind the initiation of a judicial process may be political, but the court is engaged in order to deal with an issue from a legal standpoint. The judicial outcome is expected to be based on the law, and the whole process before the court is expected to circle around legal argumentation. The added value from the engagement of a court and not another institution (e.g. the Security Council) to have a saying on a dispute is closely tied to its legal function, and consequently its dispute settlement role.

In cases when compliance with court rulings is not expected, as happens with respect to most disputes where multi-*forum* litigation strategy is pursued, the applicant's main motives for engaging judicial institutions do not revolve around their dispute settlement role. Rather, international courts are chiefly being used as agents for the application of political pressure. Courts offer litigants a medium to pursue policy goals by constituting an effective platform for political communication, hence a means of public diplomacy.[202]

Such an attempt to communicate politically and to promote a particular narrative focuses on bolstering a State's reputation and on legitimizing its course of action in the eyes of the international community. Judge Robinson considered Russian allegations of alleged Ukrainian genocide to be the 'real issue' in the case at hand and not use of force.[203] Ukraine's reverse compliance claim that kept the case alive before the Court demonstrates in an exemplary

---

200 I owe this term ('political advocacy') to Prof. Yuval Shany.

201 M Reisman, 'International Politics and International Law: Reflections on the So-Called "Politicization" of the International Court' in W Heere (ed) *International Law and Its Sources: Liber Amicorum Maarten Bos* (Kluwer, 1989), 77.

202 Public diplomacy is understood here as "a government's process of communicating with foreign publics in an attempt to bring about understanding of its nation's ideas, its institutions and culture, as well as its national goals and policies", H Tuch, *Communicating with the World: US Public Diplomacy Overseas* (St. Martin's Press, 1990), 3.

203 *Allegations of Genocide*, 16 March 2022, Separate Opinion of Judge Robinson, 242, 246[13].

way that even judicial-historical pronouncements forming part of a State's narrative 'are of importance for the litigating parties, often more than traditional judicial remedies'.[204] According to Judge Tomka, this myth-debunking function of a judicial pronouncement justifies Ukraine's legal interest in pursuing a declaratory judgment against Russia.[205] And arguably only in main proceedings the fact-finding scrutiny of the Court is such that can produce factual pronouncements with a strong legitimizing capacity. Compliance is thus promoted in an indirect fashion; through the exercise of mounting political pressure which in turn impacts on non-judicial dispute settlement methods, such as ongoing negotiations or the imposition of sanctions. So, this Section argues that the Court is increasingly sought, not for the delivery of normative commands, but rather for its capacity to act as a platform for political advocacy.

In general, international judicial mechanisms constitute effective platforms of political communication. According to communication theory, channel or medium effectiveness to transport a message is the combined measure of reach (exposure) and effects (changes in behavior and knowledge).[206] International courts offer both. All the more the ICJ that is constantly in the public eye. Such institutions are then used as "fast media" of public diplomacy; channels that attempt to influence attitudes of foreign audiences through persuasion and propaganda.[207] The communicative dimension of international justice has been prevalent in literature on international criminal justice, albeit from an institutional or a systemic perspective.[208] Evidently, it is important from a strategic point of view in inter-State litigation also. For example, Russia's abandonment of its non-appearance policy testifies to the Court's potential to act as an effective platform of communication. Russia's strategy has been probably animated by the potential to further before the Court its "'creative reworking' of the humanitarian intervention doctrine and possibly even score points in the

204 Hirsch, supra note 20, 421.

205 *Allegations of Genocide*, 2 February 2024, Declaration of Judge Tomka, 4[13].

206 R Hornik, 'Channel effectiveness in development communication programs' in R Rice, and C Atkin, (eds) *Public information Campaigns*, (SAGE, 1989) 309.

207 As opposed to 'slow media' that transmit messages about lifestyles, political and economic systems, artistic achievements etc., Sv. Windahl and B Signitzer, *Using Communication Theory* (SAGE, 2009), 191.

208 C Stahn, *Justice as Message: Expressivist Foundations of International Criminal Justice* (OUP, 2020); J Bens, *The Sentimental Court: The Affective Life of International Criminal Justice* (CUP, 2022).

wider battle for legal hegemony between Russia and the West".[209] In a pioneering study from 2004, Spill Solberg and Heberlig argued that members of the US Congress are filing *amicus curiae* briefs to the Supreme Court in order to communicate their views to multiple potential audiences.[210] By publicly displaying key positions to all those watching the court, congressmen signal their beliefs to constituents, colleagues, organized interests, and the court. As they explain though, their target audience is not the court and 'communicating their preferences to the justices is simply an added benefit'.[211] Such a method of communication is more credible than giving a committee or floor speech because filing a brief requires more effort. And signalling issue commitment, which is often the overring goal of the congressmen, is served by the filing alone without any interest in the judicial outcome.

States are utilizing international courts in a similar way. Not necessarily to reach a national electorate as congressmen do, but to speak to audiences beyond the court itself such as third-States, other litigants and the general public. In particular with respect to the ICJ, the dynamic of appealing to a wide audience should not be underestimated as Russia's appearance in the preliminary objections phase demonstrates. Even if it is not sufficient to reverse the, lately fashionable, strategy of non-participation in Court proceedings, the communicative potential of Court proceedings gives States a reason to think twice before going down this road.[212] In order to speak to non-specialised audiences however, States must engage in story-telling and thus adapt their court rhetoric to this objective.[213] And the more audiences are reached, the more effective political communication becomes, as expo-

209 J McIntyre, 'Lyophilization and lawfare in Ukraine v. Russia' 34 (2023) *ANSZIL Perspective*, 4, 6. Also, non-participation would only accentuate the perception that Russia is but a pariah in the international community.

210 R Spill Solberg and E Heberlig, 'Communicating to the Courts and Beyond: Why Members of Congress Participate as Amici Curiae' 24 (2004) *Legislative Studies Quarterly* 591.

211 Ibid, 594.

212 For a recent account of this practice, see Y Sun, 'Why states refuse to participate in judicial proceedings: uncovering key reasons and historical evolution', 14 (2023) *Journal of International Dispute Settlement*, 451. Nevertheless, non-appearance before the ICJ has "rarely served the cause of the recalcitrant State", Fr. Mégret 'Russia's Non-Appearance Before the ICJ Against Ukraine: Of Not So Vanishing Vanishing Acts and their Vanishingly Thin Justification' *Ejil:talk!* (12 March 2022).

213 Same argument on the utilization of the provisional measures' hearings in *South Africa v. Israel*: 'both parties to the case appeared cognisant of the fact that they were speaking not only to the Court, but to those watching at home', J McIntyre, 'Telling Stories at the International Court of Justice: The Provisional Measures Hearings in South Africa v. Israel', *Völkerrechtsblog* (16 January 2024).

sure is enlarged exponentially. Should the applicant State believe that both legally and morally it is in the right side of history, it welcomes any stirring of the matter. The planned recourse to many channels of communication in order to get a message across, transforms an act of communication to a campaign.[214] Ukraine for example has given a public airing to its claims against Russia in courts, political *fora*[215] and the mass media.[216] So, a multi-*forum* litigation strategy more often than not forms part of a bigger diplomatic effort, where judicial institutions are engaged as parts of a campaign with a preponderant communicative objective and not a dispute settlement one.

Be that as it may, in and of itself the recourse to many judicial *fora* instills pressure upon the recalcitrant State when understood as a judicial storytelling campaign. The pressure is maximized when this storytelling is endorsed and backed by other members of the international community. In the context of ICJ main proceedings in particular, the judicial procedure accommodates third-party participation via the mechanism of interventions. Then, it is important to understand what value may be added to the applicant's litigation strategy by staging an intervention campaign.

Third-party participation is not a novel phenomenon in inter-State litigation. States have traditionally been particularly active as third-parties in WTO disputes. Lately, before other international tribunals too. As noted earlier, the ECtHR *Ukraine and the Netherlands v. Russia* case attracted an unusually large number of third-party interventions. Also, participation of third States used to be a rarity in ICJ proceedings before *Ukraine v. Russia.* Now it is transforming into a trend.[217] As of October 2024, already fourteen

214 J Mahoney, *The Nature of Strategic Communication* (Routledge, 2023), 21.

215 A recent example is the Summit on Peace in Ukraine, *Joint Communiqué on a Peace Framework* (Bürgenstock, Switzerland, 16 June 2024), available at: https://www.eda.admin.ch/eda/en/fdfa/fdfa/aktuell/dossiers/konferenz-zum-frieden-ukraine/Summit-on-Peace-in-ukraine-joint-communique-on-a-peace-framework.html.

216 J Marinho, J Ventura and L Ribeiro, 'Peace, Public Diplomacy and Media Diplomacy – Examining the Ongoing Armed Conflict in Ukraine' (11 July 2024) *Marinho Media Analysis*, available at: http://www.marinho-mediaanalysis.org/articles/peace-public-diplomacy-and-media-diplomacy-examining-the-ongoing-armed-conflict-in-ukraine; M Karalis, 'The Information War: Russia-Ukraine Conflict Through the Eyes Of Social Media' (2 February 2024) *Georgetown Journal of International Affairs* (*online edition*), available at: https://gjia.georgetown.edu/2024/02/02/russia-ukraine-through-the-eyes-of-social-media/.

217 Judge Cançado Trindade prophetically advocated the *resurrectio* of intervention proceedings in disputes of a multilateral nature in 2013, ICJ, *Whaling in the Antarctic* (*Australia v. Japan: New Zealand intervening*) Order of 6 February 2013, 14, 36–7[64]–[68].

countries either formally intervened in *South Africa v. Israel*[218] or announced their intention to do so.[219] Also, on 4 July 2024, the Court declared admissible seven declarations of intervention in *Gambia v Myanmar* that were filed in November 2023.[220] The reason why third-party interventions at the ICJ are *a la mode* now is heavily dependent upon the nature of the cases on the Court's docket. The jurisdictional basis in disputes that attract third-party participation is a multilateral treaty, as happens in cases where multi-*forum* litigation is pursued. And intervention is mostly done 'as of right' (according to Article 63 ICJ Statute) because third-parties have a general interest in the treaty's construction. The shcehorning and salami-slicing of disputes that, as explained in the previous Chapter, has been possible due to the utilization of dispute settlement clauses in multilateral treaties, has opened the door to intervention under Article 63. In this sense, third-party participation is connected to multi-*forum* litigation strategy.

Up to now, third States may have been reluctant to use Article 63 interventions due to the binding effect of the Court's interpretative findings for all States taking part in the proceedings.[221] In the case examined here, most States that have submitted requests to intervene have explicitly stated that they accept this binding effect. With this in mind, interventions may be seen as a means of promoting compliance with ICJ pronouncements – especially these touching upon core values protected by international law; if interveners accept to be bound by the construction of the relevant multilateral convention, they may also seek compliance therewith, under the law of State responsibility.[222] Lately, States are also pursuing interventions under Article 62 in disputes that allegedly pertain to *erga omnes* obligations.[223] Whether an *erga omnes* obligation provides a sufficient legal interest to justify intervention

218 ICJ, *Press Release no.2024/67*, 9 October 2024;

219 UN Regional Information Centre for Western Europe, 'South Africa vs Israel: 13 other countries intend to join the ICJ case', 10 June 2024, available at: https://unric.org/en/south-africa-vs-israel-12-other-countries-intend-to-join-the-icj-case/.

220 *Gambia v. Myanmar,* Order of 3 July 2024 on the Admissibility of the Declarations of Intervention, General list No. 178.

221 Bonafé, *supra* note 33, 28.

222 Forlati and Almeida argue that States intervening under Article 63 may adopt countermeasures under Articles 42 and/or 49 ARSIWA, should the respondent refuse to comply with the judgment, S Forlati and PW Almeida, 'Is There a Role for Intervener States in Inducing Compliance with Decisions of the International Court of Justice?' 26 (2023) *Max Planck Yearbook of United Nations Law Online* 145, 167.

223 Poland is requesting permission to intervene as a non-party in *Ukraine v. Russia* (*Ukraine v. Russia,* Application for Permission to Intervene by Poland, 23 July 2024) and Nicaragua as a party in *South Africa v. Israel,* (ICJ, *Application of the Convention on the Prevention*

under Article 62 of the ICJ's statute remains to be seen.[224] What is important to note however, is that States are increasingly willing to participate as third-parties in judicial proceedings. But this, I argue, is not because of the legal potential they open for inducing compliance, rather because interventions constitute an effective means to exercise public diplomacy.

Third-party participation in general, and interventions more specifically, may be impactful and hence amenable to strategic utilization.[225] Irrespective of their motivation, interventions constitute a move of heightened political symbolism because they consist in 'taking position on a legal matter, in a solemn and highly publicized manner'.[226] And they may be used for different objectives, albeit not all are relevant for the purposes of the present analysis. Interventions may be used to put forward the legal development of rules by a court, by virtue of its authority to 'speak the law'. Likely, intervening States in *Gambia v. Myanmar* proposed a broad construction of Article II of the genocide convention, while squinting to *Ukraine v. Russia* where the same provision would potentially be applicable.[227] Or, third party participants in *Ukraine and the Netherlands v. Russia* before the ECtHR hastened to express their views on the interaction of international humanitarian law and human rights law in view of the upcoming judgment in *Georgia v. Russia (II)*.[228] As noted previously though, in the framework of a multi-*forum* litigation strategy a court is not employed with a view to taking advantage of its legal development function. Since claims before different *fora* are usually based on distinct normative bases, altering the understanding of a legal provision is, more often than not, inconsequential in a multi-*forum* litigation strategy.

---

and Punishment of the Crime of Genocide in the Gaza Strip (*South Africa v. Israel*), Application for Permission to Intervene by Nicaragua, 23 January 2024).

224 Against, Br. McGarry, 'A Rush to Judgment? The Wobbly Bridge from Judicial Standing to Intervention in ICJ Proceedings' 100 (2023) *Questions of International Law, Zoom-in* 5. In favor, Cr. Eggett and S Thin, 'Third-Party Intervention before the International Court of Justice: A Tool for Litigation in the Public Interest?' in J Bendel and Y Suedi (eds) *Public Interest Litigation in International Law*, 75.

225 L Johns and Kr. Pelc, 'Who Gets to be in the Room? Manipulating Participation in WTO Disputes' 68 (2015) *International Organization* 663. Not necessarily by the applicant, e.g. Germany promised to intervene 'on Israel's behalf' in *South Africa v. Israel*, St. Talmon, 'Germany Rushes to Declare Intention to Intervene in the Genocide Case brought by South Africa Against Israel Before the International Court of Justice' *German Practice in International Law* (15 January 2024).

226 A Miron and Chr. Chinkin, 'Article 62' in *ICJ Commentary* 1686, 1740.

227 W Schabbas, 'The Damp Squib of Third Party Intervention in Ukraine v. Russia' *Ejil:talk*!, (5 February 2024).

228 Batura and Risini, *supra* note 57.

The WTO experience – where participation in the dispute settlement process has been long-standing – suggests that third-party participation may affect the attitude of litigants (e.g. it lowers the prospects for early settlement[229]) and of courts (e.g. information furnished by third parties reflects community preferences and courts take such preferences into consideration when ruling[230]). Whether this effect on the court's attitude will in fact materialize, depends upon several factors. The motivation underlying third-party participation is the factor that arguably weighs the most. Motivations for participation are either case-related when a State is interested in supporting a certain party in a dispute, or driven by systemic considerations when the intervening State is motivated by the substantive issues underpinning the case. And arguably, when interventions are politically biased – as Russia tried to demonstrate before the ICJ – this may not be legally significant as to their admissibility, but it certainly affects their credibility and their potential to have an impact upon the court's ruling.[231]

Unsurprisingly, the main factor animating interventions in disputes where multi-*forum* litigation strategy is pursued has been the signaling of political support towards a party to the case (the staging party). So, the information third parties furnish to the court is tainted by the stain of bias. In *Ukraine v. Russia* third-party interventions were not influential as an analysis of the preliminary objections judgment demonstrates.[232] When interventions recycle the same arguments, they are not important for the legal value of the arguments inferred by third parties. In fact, this may be in the detriment of the State in whose favor they are made.[233] Rather, they publicly demonstrate political beliefs,[234] and disincentivize third States to offer their support to the State that adopts a counter-position. Likely, in *Ukraine v. Russia* their

229 ML Busch, and E Reinhardt, 'Three's a crowd: third parties and WTO dispute settlement' 58 (2006) *World Politics* 446; the network of states surrounding the ICJ facilitates the circulation of misinformation, says Dothan, hence the Court is an ineffective *forum* for multilateral pressure on one rogue state, Sh. Dothan, 'Staging an Intervention for Rogue States' 50 (2025) *North Carolina Journal of International Law* (forthcoming), available at https://papers.ssrn.com/sol3/papers.cfm?abstract_id=4947481, 29.

230 Cl. Carrubba, M Gabel and Ch. Hankla, 'Judicial Behavior Under Political Constraints: Evidence from the European Court of Justice', 102 (2008) *American Political Science Review* 435.

231 J Ryu, 'How Do the Third Parties Contribute to WTO Dispute Resolution?' 56 (2022) *Journal of World Trade* 587, 595.

232 Schabbas, *supra* note 227.

233 Wigard, et al. *supra* note 3, 324.

234 Russia views the declarations of intervention in *Ukraine v. Russia* 'as part of a collective political strategy', Russia's Written Observations, *supra* note 41, 7[8].

main addressee was the international community and not the Court. In this sense, mass Article 63 interventions are understood here as a tool of political advocacy. By communicating publicly its alliances, Ukraine capitalized on this campaign of interventions in order to legitimize a particular strategic narrative.

Likely we have not seen the better part of multi-party or multi-State proceedings before international courts and tribunals. Recent practice indicates that States will continue to utilize judicial institutions as platforms of public advocacy in inter-State proceedings. Whether the advocate is the State itself when it uses the courtroom to address audiences beyond the court, or advocacy is done by proxy when the State stages third-party participation is not important for present purposes. For both are evidence of a new path international judicial dispute settlement has taken. A path that puts center stage non-conventional ways to promote State objectives via recourse to international courts. This Section examined how litigants may pursue such objectives when utilizing the ICJ in the context of a multi-*forum* litigation strategy. The next will turn to the Court itself and inquire whether its utilization in the ways described above may impact upon its authority.

5 The Court as a Political Agent of Dispute Resolution

Russia's first argument in its attempt to have the applications for intervention declared as inadmissible targeted their political motivation. In essence, Russia suggested that a line should be drawn as to how overtly the Court may be used for political purposes rather than for pursuing justice through the normative force of judicial pronouncements. As noted above, the Court will not delve into the 'near impossible task' of exposing the rationale behind a State's application;[235] thus, it distances itself from the political realm and justifiably focuses on the legal one. For the same reason, the Court will not declare its instrumentalization for ulterior motives as abusive.[236] The political factor the Court ignores when delivering justice is part and parcel of judicial life though. And its stance does not second-guess how attentive the ICJ is to its utilization for political ends. This Section suggests that the Court should be alarmed by the role implanted in it by litigants when they pursue a multi-*forum* litigation

235 *Supra* Section 3(C); Lemey, *supra* note 111, 20.

236 *Contra Allegations of Genocide*, Judgment, 2 February 2024, Dissenting Opinion of Vice-President Kirill Gevorgian, 6[17].

strategy. For this role is not in tune with the Court's overarching dispute settlement role and puts pressure on its legitimate authority.

The general point being that functions are different from roles. The former pertain to the exercise of a court's powers as usually provided in its constitutive instrument. They are limited and courts are careful not to push the envelope and exceed them or usurp functions they don't otherwise possess. Roles on the other hand are usually attached to the impact ensuing from the exercise of a court's functions. They are formed by the expectations of different constituencies and are malleable.[237] For example, within the UN system the Court has the role of the 'principal judicial organ' of the organization and that of a promoter of peaceful dispute settlement. Ditto, the next Chapters will demonstrate that when it is asked to deliver an Order on provisional measures the Court is expected to act as a crisis manager,[238] and when it is sought for the rendering of an advisory opinion the ICJ is expected to perform the role of a rule maker.[239] This Chapter argues that by engaging in multi-*forum* litigation, litigants are lately attempting to implant in the Court another role, that of a political dispute settler. And because the ICJ is a place for legal dispute settlement, not for other kinds of dispute resolution, this attempt will likely impact the Court's legitimate authority.

The UN Charter and the Court's Statute establish the Court as a judicial organ and prescribe the limits of its *de jure* authority. By virtue of its judicial nature, the Court has been tasked by States to fulfil two functions: according to Article 38 of its Statute, to decide legal disputes on the basis of international law and *per* Article 65 to render advisory opinions on legal questions. Nevertheless, institutions set up for the achievement of definite purposes grow to fulfil tasks not wholly identical with those in the minds of their authors at the time of their creation.[240] *In casu*, an ancillary function deriv-

237 The functions/roles divide, resembles Shapiro's task of the judge/social function of a court distinction, M Shapiro, *Courts: A Comparative and Political Analysis* (University of Chicago Press, 1981). Shapiro based the distinction on the functioning of domestic courts. It was Caron who suggested that Shapiro's theory can be meaningfully applied to international courts too, see D Caron, 'Fifth Annual Charles N Brower Lecture on International Dispute Resolution: The Multiple Functions of International Courts and the Singular Task of the Adjudicator,' 111 (2017) *American Society of International Law Proceedings* 231.

238 See *infra* Chapter 3; Sh Rosenne, *Provisional Measures in International Law, The International Court of Justice and the International Tribunal for the Law of the Sea* (OUP, 2005), 218.

239 See *infra* Chapter 4.

240 H Lauterpacht, *The Development of International Law by the International Court* (Stevens and Sons, 1958) 5.

ing from the exercise of the Court's core functions is the contribution to the development and clarification of legal rules (outlined above as 'law-development function').[241] This function is inextricably linked to the ICJ's judicial nature and indisputably forms part of its advisory function since advisory opinions have no binding force.[242] Albeit, it does not sit easily with the Court's judicial function per Article 38 since it could be perceived as judicial law-making. As explained above however (Section 3(A)), due to its strong legitimate authority, the international community perceives the Court as the ultimate authority speaking 'eternal truth' on questions of general international law. In this sense, the international community has implanted in the ICJ the role of a *de facto* legislator.[243] So, sociological perceptions about the Court's ancillary law-development function have provoked tension with the Court's core judicial function. Overall, States charged the Court with a core judicial function, hence they understood the ICJ's overarching role to be that of a legal dispute settler as distinguished from political or other roles.[244]

That States perceive the ICJ as a political agent of dispute resolution when they engage in multi-*forum* litigation is evident from the previous Section. Their objectives are telling as to their expectations when instrumentalizing the Court. When direct compliance is not on the table, the exercise of political pressure is the main factor animating recourse to the ICJ. And this pressure may accumulate either because of the creation of the 'shadow of the law' or via public advocacy. In the first case, States intend to capitalize on the normative value of an ICJ ruling to influence other procedures (instrumentalization of legitimate authority). So, they perceive the Court as a generator of normative commands. In the latter case though, ICJ proceedings are utilized for ulterior purposes unconnected to international law's role as a normative regulator (instrumentalization as a forum for political advocacy). In such occasions,

241 J Crawford, Fr. Baetens and R Cameron, 'Functions of the International Court of Justice' in K Parlett and C Esposito (eds), *The Cambridge Companion to the International Court of Justice* (CUP, 2023) 13, 32.

242 *Legality of the Threat or Use of Nuclear Weapons*, Advisory Opinion, ICJ Reports 1996, 226 [18].

243 Fr. Messineo, 'The functions of the International Court of Justice: tending to the law while settling disputes?' in Kent et al. *supra* note 27, 109, 111.

244 ICIJ, *Competence of the International Labour Organization to Regulate, Incidentally the Personal Work of the Employer,* Advisory Opinion (23 July 1926), Series B, no. 13, 23; C Romano, K Alter and Y Shany, 'Mapping International Adjudicative Bodies, the Issues, and Players', in *Oxford Handbook of International Adjudication, supra* note 35, 1, 4–5.

the Court is utilized for objectives that are unconnected to its judicial function. As a political *forum* rather than as a judicial body.

If States use the Court solely as a political *forum* though, they will gradually perceive the Court as one too. Put differently, States will expect the ICJ to promote resolution of disputes because of its potential to play the role of an advocacy platform or a *medium* of communication. This new implanted role of a political dispute-settler will likely affect in the future how the Court is viewed by the international community. Like any judicial institution, the ICJ's legitimate authority is firmly entangled with its judicial functions.[245] In the same sense that the legitimate authority of the law is a moral duty to obey the law not because it is morally correct but *qua* law,[246] legitimate authority of judicial institutions depends upon their ability to exercise their law-applying functions and to generate power because of their nature as institutions that generate legal – normative – commands. Otherwise said by Venzke, it is '[t]he dynamics of the legal discourse [that] stabilize authority and account for its further growth'.[247] Instrumentalization of judicial institutions for the by-products of their authority, for power that does not ensue directly from the exercise of their judicial function (e.g. their ability to reach a wide audience, their legitimizing potential, the ensuing political pressure) is potentially detrimental to their *de jure* authority.

Inevitably, a judicial body that is perceived by engaged audiences as a political battlefield will end up facing issues of public acceptance. In turn, the erosion of a court's sociological legitimacy impacts upon its capacity to justify compliance with its rulings. For example, the US Supreme Court is amidst a legitimacy crisis due to a lack of public trust in it performing its judicial function.[248] This court is criticized for destroying its own legitimate authority due to the political considerations underpinning its rulings (e.g. overturn of established case-law) and the use of its procedures (e.g. increasing use of the shadow docket).[249] It is not the utilization of the court then, but rather the exercise of

245 Grossman, supra note 162.

246 J Raz, *Ethics in the Public Domain* (OUP, 1995), 342–3.

247 I Venzke, 'Understanding the Authority of International Courts and Tribunals: On Delegation and Discursive Construction', 14 (2013) *Theoretical Inquiries in Law* 381.

248 J Jones, 'Supreme Court Approval Holds at Record Low', *GALLUP* (2 August 2023), available at: https://news.gallup.com/poll/509234/supreme-court-approval-holds-record-low.aspx; R Fallon, *Law and Legitimacy in the Supreme Court* (Harvard University Press, 2018).

249 M Levendusky et al., 'Has the Supreme Court become just another political branch? Public perceptions of court approval and legitimacy in a post-Dobbs world' 10 (2024) *Science Advances*, 1; special issue 73 vol. 2 (2023) *Emory Law Journal*.

its powers that has triggered a legitimacy crisis. Despite this difference in the underlying cause, the outcome is the same. Especially for the ICJ that has built its reputation on the basis of a strong sociological legitimacy, the most important factor as to why it remains highly influential until today may wane.

Nevertheless, such a change in State perception can be seen in a positive light. It corroborates the belief that the Court remains a politically influential institution, hence an authoritative one. The spike in the number of multi-*forum* litigation cases where the ICJ is called to exert its political influence suggests that States have faith in the part that the ICJ can potentially play in advancing the international justice agenda.[250] Also, the coordinating role the Court is asked to play in such disputes testifies to its pivotal position in the international dispute settlement system. And at present, the sociological legitimacy of the ICJ appears to be strong. Should this trend continue though, there is a cause for concern as explained above.

It falls beyond the scope of this book to suggest how the court should react to its political utilization in multi-*forum* litigation scenarios. It would be overly speculative to assess how alert is the ICJ to its political use by States. There are signs that the Court is indeed wary of it and that it possesses the tools to resist it. The summary rejection of South Africa's second request for provisional measures 45 days after the first one without the holding of an oral round via a decision testifies to this.[251] Likewise, the removal from the docket of two – out of ten – applications of Yugoslavia for the 1999 NATO bombings with respective provisional measures Orders, is another sign of Court resistance to its instrumentalization.[252] Given the Court's overfilled docket, it is not unimaginable that the ICJ will relax the criteria for removal of cases from the docket as a pressure mechanism towards States that attempt to ulitize it by pursuing far-fetched claims. One comment is in order though. Since the ICJ has nothing to do with the imposition of this new role that potentially erodes its *de jure* authority does not necessarily mean it is helpless in defending itself. States cannot be openly discouraged from engaging in such a strategy, but the Court may remind States of its judicial function; by rendering rulings that are firmly rooted in law, by managing its procedure according to the sound

250 I Marchuk, 'Unfulfilled Promises of the ICJ Litigation for Ukraine: Analysis of the ICJ Judgment in Ukraine v Russia (CERD and ICSFT)' *Ejil:talk!* (22 February 2024).

251 *South Africa v. Israel*, 'Decision of the Court on South Africa's request for additional provisional measures', Decision No. 2024/16 (16 February 2024).

252 ICJ, *Case Concerning the Legality of Use of Force* (*Yugoslavia v. USA*), Order of 2 June 1999, 926[34]; ICJ, *Case Concerning the Legality of Use of Force* (*Yugoslavia v. USA*), Order of 2 June 1999, 774[40].

administration of justice (e.g. the accommodation of mass interventions in *Ukraine v. Russia* to uphold the equality of parties) and by resisting temptation to make pronouncements that sit uneasily with its judicial character. And this is no easy task.

6 Legitimacy Concerns from the Employment of Multi-*forum* Litigation Strategies

After 24 February 2022, the effort to portray Russia as an international community outcast has been impressive. International institutions where Russia has been a member (e.g. expulsion from the Council of Europe and suspension from the Human Rights Council), others that do not include Russia as a member (e.g. 11 rounds of EU sanctions since 2014) and third States (e.g. exercise of universal jurisdiction by domestic courts) have been mobilized to this end. Of course, such mobilization is not automatic.[253] It depends on the political will of States. Ukraine in its turn has continued a diplomatic campaign that was put in place after the Crimean invasion. And international law features prominently in it. As a substantive benchmark against which to evaluate Russian behavior, but also as a normative language that frames the political will of States and provides the necessary context to assess international consensus.[254] Claims based on international law rhetoric were presented before many platforms such as mass media, diplomatic channels and international judicial institutions. Claims before the latter, with greater emphasis those before the ICJ, were examined in this Chapter. In particular, the requests that pertain to the rendering of a final ruling by these organs.

International courts, it is no secret, are reactive organs. They have no agenda of their own, but they exist to handle such cases as they are submitted by applicants. In other words, they perform their functions against the agenda of their users. While the ICJ has been accused of producing politically-animated judgments that 'split the baby' in order to secure compliance,[255] typically it is agnostic as to the objectives and aspirations of the parties appear-

253 Russia's attitude of open defiance towards international judicial institutions provides excuses for such mobilization; e.g. the visit by the Russian President in Mongolia, a State party to the Rome Statute, despite the existence of an ICC warrant ordering his arrest.

254 Borgen, *supra* note 199.

255 Grossman, supra note 162, 44ff; L Damrosch, 'The Impact of the Nicaragua Case on the Court and Its Role: Harmful, Helpful or in Between?' 25 (2012) *Leiden Journal of International Law* 135, 144; V Dimitrijevic and M Milanovic, 'The Strange Story of the Bosnian Genocide Case' 21 (2008) *Leiden Journal of International Law* 65, 85.

ing before it. Engaging with subjective considerations sits uncomfortably with the exercise of its core judicial function. The Court's jurisprudence testifies to this. This Chapter showcased how this non-committal attitude may be manipulated by litigants in the course of a multi-*forum* litigation strategy. Provided that consent can be established, the ICJ's doors are open to States that can dress their claims in a legal garment. And the procedure before the Court provides a publicized way of garnering international support and delegitimizing the opponent. When such instrumentalization is coupled with a respective stance before other judicial institutions, as Ukraine did with the staging of ECtHR interventions, the strong cooperation with the ICC prosecutor and the encouragement of Ukrainian investors to seek multi-million investment awards, such a judicial campaign constitutes an effective means for the promotion of policy objectives.

Especially for States that are engaged in disputes with intransigent opponents and do not count on the capacity of judicial institutions to foster compliance, the pursuance of a multi-*forum* litigation strategy may accommodate an array of policy objectives. Ukraine's judicial campaign complemented the war effort by slowly chipping away Russia's legitimacy and by mobilizing its allies to support its cause. The application of political pressure towards friends (to participate) and foe (to comply) has been part of Ukraine's judicial agenda. Albeit, it required some skillful lawyering and also a handful of proceedings. The Court's coordinating role in it cannot be stressed enough, and neither the hopes the international community has placed in the ICJ for a 'spark that will inspire other competent international organs and agencies to take the further steps'.[256] Seen together with the recent turn towards public interest litigation,[257] it looks as if the international legal community entrusts the Court with a central role in advancing international justice. The latest example being the announcement by Canada, Australia, Germany and the Netherlands to bring joint action against Afghanistan for violations of the UN Convention on the Elimination of All Forms of Discrimination against Women.[258] And the ICJ cherishes the opportunity to influence global affairs, but not at the expense of its judicial function. While the Court is careful not to push the envelope, in other words to engage in policy-making or law-making, its utilization by litigants solely as a political instrument, may impact on its legitimate authority and its sociological legitimacy in particular.

256 *Supra* note 12.

257 Bendel and Suedi, *supra* note 224.

258 S Hasar, 'Representation of Afghanistan before the International Court of Justice' *Ejil: talk!*, (16 October 2024).

CHAPTER 3

Provisional Measures: Unripe Dispute Settlement

The One Where Isolation Was Not Good for Anyone

1 Introduction

The struggle for power and dominance in the Middle East has generated a series of inter-State disputes in the UN era of great drama and controversy, the Gulf and Iraq War being the biggest in scale amongst them. The 2017–2021 diplomatic crisis between Qatar and a Saudi Arabia-led coalition was the latest part in this series. While it will not be remembered for its lasting effects or its magnitude, it is one of the few disputes in the region, the only one after the *Qatar/Bahrain* delimitation dispute,[1] that made its way before a judicial forum. Testament to the limited recourse of Arab States to judicial dispute settlement is the prioritization by the Charter of the Arab League of mediation as a dispute resolution mechanism and the concomitant practice of those States.[2] In sharp contrast to this dispute settlement culture, Qatar engaged not only one, but four standing international judicial and quasi-judicial mechanisms (the ICJ, the PCA, the Committee of the International Convention on the Elimination of All Forms of Racial Discrimination (CERD Committee) and WTO Panels) on top of arbitral tribunals[3] and the ICAO Council – a political organ with dispute settlement competences,[4] in order to bring the dispute to a close. Finally, Kuwait's mediation efforts were required to ease the tensions between the disputing States in early 2021. Nevertheless, this diplomatic rift goes back to the 2011 Arab Spring and includes many peculiar incidents such

1 ICJ, *Maritime Delimitation and Territorial Questions between Qatar and Bahrain*, Merits, Judgment, *ICJ Reports* 2001, 40.

2 See Article 5, Charter of the Arab League (22 March 1945); H Youssef, 'Mediation and Conflict Resolution in the Arab World: The Role of the Arab League', 19 (2013) *OSCE Yearbook* 299.

3 Qatar Airways, Press Release, 22 July 2020, available at: https://www.qatarairways.com/en/press-releases/2020/July/qatarairwaysarbitrations.html?activeTag=Press-releases.

4 *Decision of the Council of the ICAO on the Preliminary Objection in the Matter: The State of Qatar and the Arab Republic of Egypt, the Kingdom of Bahrain, the Kingdom of Saudi Arabia and the United Arab Emirates* (2017) – Application (A), 29 June 2018, as it appears in ICJ, Joint Application Instituting Proceedings, *Appeal Relating to the Jurisdiction of the ICAO Council Under Article 84 of the Convention on International Civil Aviation* (*Bahrain, Egypt, Saudi Arabia and United Arab Emirates v. Qatar*) 4 July 2018, Annex 1.

 | DOI:10.1163/9789004704565_004

as the kidnapping of 28 Qatari falcon hunters in Iraq and the deportation of tens of thousands of Qatari camels and sheep from Saudi Arabia.[5]

In 2013, Saudi Arabia, the United Arab Emirates (UAE), Egypt, and Bahrain (the Quartet) charged neighboring Qatar with meddling in their internal affairs and with other infractions to their sovereignty. In November of the same year, members of the Gulf Cooperation Council (GCC) met in Riyadh to discuss this issue.[6] That summit produced the First Riyadh Agreement with two more such agreements concluded under the aegis of the GCC within a one-year time span.[7] All three were concluded in order to cement regional cooperation. Nevertheless, the main concern among GCC members was Qatar's pro-Arab Spring agenda and the policies it implemented in pursuance of it. This was made explicit in the 2014 Supplementary Riyadh Agreement where the Qatari-funded and controlled *Al-Jazeera* was mentioned as a media that broadcasted offences against Egypt, a non-GCC member State. After the 2013 *coup d' etat* that overthrew the democratically elected president, Egypt has been opposing democratization of Islam alongside all GCC States except Qatar.[8] It is therefore not surprising that Qatar pledged in the Riyadh Agreements, along with other similar regional security guarantees, no interference in the internal affairs of the GCC member States and of Egypt.

Despite the rapprochement on paper, the two sides were not in good terms. In early 2017, Qatar considered the Riyadh Agreements 'overtaken by events at the international and regional levels'[9] and soon thereafter things got out of

---

5 For a detailed timeline of the crisis see, M Zweiri, M Rahman and A Kamal, 'The 2017 Gulf Crisis: An Introduction' in M Zweiri, M Rahman and A Kamal (eds) *The 2017 Gulf Crisis* (Springer, 2021) 1–18.

6 The GCC is a regional integration organization in the Gulf area and its members are: Saudi Arabia, Qatar, the United Arab Emirates, Bahrain, Kuwait and Oman.

7 The three agreements were: a. the Riyadh Agreement (with Endorsement Agreement) of 23 and 24 November 2013, b. the Mechanism Implementing the Riyadh Agreement of 17 April 2014 and c. the Supplementary Riyadh Agreement of 16 November 2014 (hereinafter the "Riyadh Agreements"), Originally known only within the GCC, the full content of the Riyadh agreements was disclosed to the press in 2017 and registered with the UN Secretariat by Saudi Arabia on 9 October 2018 in view of the upcoming ICJ case, for more see Cr. Gaver, 'What Are the Riyadh Agreements' Ejil:Talk! (1 July 2020).

8 S Al-Thani, 'The Qatari-Saudi-Egyptian Triangle After the Arab Spring', in R Mason (ed.) *Egypt and the Gulf: A Renewed Regional Policy Alliance* (Gerlach, 2017), 62.

9 In a letter to the Secretary General of the GCC, Qatar claimed that "the subject of this agreement has been exhausted" and called upon the GCC countries to "agree to terminate the Riyadh Agreement", *Letter of 19 February 2017 from the Minister of Foreign Affairs of Qatar to the Secretary-General of the GCC* as it appears in ICJ, Memorial of Bahrain, Egypt and the UAE, *Appeal Relating to the Jurisdiction of the ICAO Council Under Article 84 of the Convention*

hand. On 21 May 2017, during his first official trip abroad, US President Donald Trump coalesced with President Abdel Fattah el-Sisi of Egypt and King Salman of Saudi Arabia to open a new Global Center for Combating Extremist Ideology, based in Riyadh.[10] This move, along with the arms deal between the US and Saudi Arabia concluded the previous day, were signs that the US was picking sides on the so-called New Arab Cold War.[11] That is, the fight for leadership in the Arab world among regional powers such as Qatar, Saudi Arabia and the UAE.[12] A couple of days later, Qatari governmental media published statements attributed to Qatar's Emir whereby he expressed support for Iran, Hamas, Hezbollah and Israel. This hacking incident, escalated matters rapidly into a full-blown diplomatic row between Qatar and the Quartet.[13]

In a coordinated move, the Quartet accused Qatar of supporting and harboring terrorism and implemented a series of sanctioning measures against the small State.[14] In a time span of 24 hours, from the 5th to the 6th of June 2017, the four allies severed diplomatic relations, expelled all Qatari diplomats, and ordered all Qatari nationals inside their countries to leave their territory within 14 days. Further, they closed their borders to all land, air and sea traffic with Qatar, a peninsular nation in the Persian Gulf whose only land connection is with Saudi Arabia. Pursuant to these restrictions, all Qatar-registered aircraft were barred by the Quartet from landing at or departing from their airports and were denied the right to overfly their respective terri-

---

on International Civil Aviation (Bahrain, Egypt, Saudi Arabia and United Arab Emirates v. Qatar), 27 December 2018, Annex 72.

10 In a move of heightened symbolism, the triumvirate of world leaders placed their hands atop a translucent globe that bathed them in light, 'What Was That Glowing Orb Trump Touched in Saudi Arabia', *New York Times* 22 May 2017.

11 M Valbjorn and A Bank, 'The New Arab Cold War: rediscovering the Arab dimension of Middle East regional politics' 38 (2011) *Review of International Studies* 3. The term was coined by H Khasan in his article, 'The New Arab Cold War' 159 (1997) *World Affairs* 158.

12 St. Cook, J Stokes and A Brock, 'The New Arab Cold War', *Foreign Policy* 28 August 2014.

13 K DeYoung and E Nakashima, 'UAE orchestrated hacking of Qatari government sites, sparking regional upheaval, according to U.S. intelligence officials' *The Washington Post* 16 July 2017.

14 The analysis of the factual background to the dispute relies heavily on the following documents; ICJ, *Application of the International Convention on the Elimination of All Forms of Racial Discrimination (Qatar v. United Arab Emirates)*, Preliminary Objections, Judgment, *ICJ Reports* 2021, 71; ICJ, *Appeal relating to the Jurisdiction of the ICAO Council under Article 84 of the Convention on International Civil Aviation (Bahrain, Egypt, Saudi Arabia and United Arab Emirates v. Qatar)*, Judgment, ICJ Reports 2020, 81; Committee on the Elimination of Racial Discrimination, 'Jurisdiction of the Inter-State Communication submitted by Qatar against the Kingdom of Saudi Arabia', *UN Doc CERD/C/99/5*, 30 August 2019.

tories, including the territorial seas within the relevant flight information regions. Certain restrictions also applied to non-Qatar-registered aircrafts flying to and from Qatar, which were required to obtain prior approval from the respective civil aviation authorities. In addition, all broadcasts of Qatari media within their borders were terminated, including the Qatari-funded Al Jazeera satellite network, the most watched in the Arab world. Expression of sympathy with Qatar was criminalized and postal services with Qatar were suspended. Finally, on 9 June all four States imposed targeted sanctions on individuals and groups, most of them Qataris or with links to Qatar, and accused them of having ties to terrorism. In this isolation game, the joint effect of these measures has been an economic and diplomatic blockade with humanitarian and financial side-effects.[15]

Shortly afterwards, on 23 June, the Saudi-led Quartet sent via Kuwait a list of 13 demands that Qatar was to implement within ten days.[16] They included, *inter alia*, stipulations that Doha close the broadcaster *Al-Jazeera* and other media funded by Qatar directly or indirectly, drastically scale back cooperation with Iran, remove Turkish troops from Qatar's soil, cease all communication with opposition parties in the Quartet, end contact with – what are considered by Arab States – terrorist groups and submit to monthly external compliance checks. The consequences in case of non-compliance were left unspecified, but, according to the Qatari minister of Foreign Affairs acceptance of the demands would represent an effective end to Qatar's independent foreign policy.[17] As expected, Qatar denied the allegations and refused to accede to the demands that were perceived as an attempt to curb its sovereignty.

---

15 On the humanitarian effects see Human Rights Council, 'Visit to Qatar: Report of the Special Rapporteur on the negative impact of unilateral coercive measures on the enjoyment of human rights, Alena Douhan', *UN Doc. A/HRC/48/59/Add.1* (5 July 2021). On the financial effects see G Collins, "Anti-Qatar embargo grinds toward strategic failure" (2018) *Rice University's Baker Institute for Public Policy Issue Brief*. Being a food-import-dependent economy, Qatar relies heavily on imports coming from or through Saudi Arabia and the UAE. The crippling in the supplies of essential daily products meant that the country faced an imminent political and logistical crisis.

16 The content of the demands was leaked to the press, but the original document was not made public: P Wintour, 'Qatar Given 10 Days to Meet 13 Sweeping Demands by Saudi Arabia' *The Guardian* 23 June 2017.

17 W Maclean et al., *Arab states issue ultimatum to Qatar: close Jazeera, curb ties with Iran*, Reuters, 23 June 2017, https://www.reuters.com/article/us-gulf-qatar-demands-idUSKBN19E0BB; 'Saudi-led demands not 'reasonable nor actionable': Qatar', *AlJazeera*, 24 June 2017, available at: https://www.aljazeera.com/news/2017/6/19/qatar-fm-we-wont-negotiate-until-blockade-is-lifted.

Since then, a legal battle before multiple *fora* would commence on the legality of the imposed measures. That battle was fought not only before judicial and quasi-judicial mechanisms. While this study focuses on such organs, it is worth noting that in 2020 Qatar invited the UN Special Rapporteur on Unilateral Sanctions to undertake a country visit,[18] after which she called for a termination of the measures and reported that 'the basic legal requirements for the imposition of unilateral measures were not respected in the case of Qatar'.[19] So, a UN political organ was involved in Qatar's name-and-shame campaign, furthered its cause and pressured the Quartet to alter its course of action. However, it was international institutions with law-making powers that took center stage in Qatar's efforts to challenge the imposed sanctions. For present purposes, it is not important to refer extensively to the substantive argumentation invoked before each of these institutions. Somewhat oversimplifying, both sides relied on concepts and principles rooted firmly in general public international law; the sanctioning States claimed the measures were justified countermeasures because Qatar violated the Riyadh Agreements.[20] The violation consisted in interference in these States' internal affairs and in the support of terrorist groups, thereby contributing to the region's destabilization. Qatar denied any wrongdoing and returned the allegation on intervention accusing the sanctioning States of coercive interference in its *domaine réservé*.[21] Nevertheless, in view of the limited jurisdiction of international judicial mechanisms, and since no judicial body was competent to receive a claim based on the principle of non-intervention, this reasoning could not have been brought before a single judicial *forum* with respect to all adopted measures and towards all States involved.[22] In fact, the legality of

18 Human Rights Council, 'Negative impact of unilateral coercive measures: priorities and road map Report of the Special Rapporteur on the negative impact of unilateral coercive measures on the enjoyment of human rights' *UN Doc. A/HRC/45/7* (21 July 2020), 4 [22].

19 *Supra* note 15, 7 [27].

20 In fact, the possibility for such measures was expressly provided for in the Mechanism Implementing the Riyadh Agreement, whereby if 'any country of the GCC Countries fail to comply with this mechanism, the other GCC Countries shall have the right to take any appropriate action to protect their security and stability'.

21 A Hofer and L Ferro, 'Sanctioning Qatar: Coercive interference in the State's domaine réservé?' *Ejil:talk!* (30 June 2017).

22 The broader context in which every judicial proceeding took place was brought up by the disputants on every occasion. E.g. during the ICJ oral proceedings on the cases regarding the jurisdiction of the ICAO Council, the Appellants characterized as 'the real dispute' Qatar's harboring of extremism and terrorist groups (particularly the Muslim Brotherhood in Egypt) and the dissemination of hate speech by Al-Jazeera. Qatar on the other hand, argued that what the Appellants 'call terrorism and intervention in

three such measures has been challenged before different international judicial institutions; namely, the repatriation of Qatari nationals from their territories (and in some cases the recall of their nationals from Qatar), the suspension of postal services and the closure of airspace to Qatari civil aviation. The fragmentation of claims across several proceedings illustrates how a wide range of international legal proceedings may be brought to bear in a diplomatic rift.[23]

The ICJ was engaged in the course of two separate proceedings. First, on 11 June 2018, Qatar instituted contentious proceedings against the UAE, alleging violations of multiple CERD provisions.[24] On the basis of Article 22 CERD, Qatar challenged the conformity with the Convention of the discriminatory measures directed against Qatari nationals, residents, and visitors in the UAE, as well as towards Qatari-owned media companies. Qatar had already launched proceedings before the CERD Committee in March 2018 against the UAE and Saudi Arabia, claiming the same violations.[25] In the context of the ICJ proceedings, both States requested the indication of provisional measures, albeit at different points in time. Qatar did so simultaneously with the filing of its original application, and the UAE a year later.[26] Second, upon request of the Quartet on 4 July 2018, the UN Court was asked to review, as an appellate body, the correctness of the ICAO Council decision of 29 June 2018.[27] The ICJ affirmed the ICAO Council's juris-

---

internal affairs by Al Jazeera is actually free expression', ICJ, *Appeal Relating to the Jurisdiction of the ICAO Council Under Article II, Section 2, of the 1944 International Air Services Transit Agreement (Bahrain, Egypt and U.A.E. v. Qatar)*, Verbatim Record, CR 2019/13, (2 December 2019), [2], [7]–[10] and Verbatim Record, CR 2019/15, (3 December 2019), [21]–[22].

23 Cr. Gaver, 'Lingering Gulf Dispute Gives Rise to Multi-*Forum* Legal Proceedings' 24 (2020) *ASIL Insights*.

24 ICJ, *Application of the International Convention on the Elimination of All Forms of Racial Discrimination (Qatar v. United Arab Emirates)*, Application Instituting Proceedings, 11 June 2018.

25 CERD, *Jurisdiction of the Inter-State communication submitted by Qatar against the Kingdom of Saudi Arabia*, UN Doc. CERD/C/99/5 (30 August 2019); CERD, *Jurisdiction of the Inter-State communication submitted by Qatar against the United Arab Emirates*, UN Doc. CERD/C/99/3 (30 August 2019).

26 ICJ, *Application of the International Convention on the Elimination of All Forms of Racial Discrimination (Qatar v. United Arab Emirates)*, Request for the Indication of Provisional Measures of Protection, 11 June 2018 and 22 March 2019.

27 ICJ, *Appeal relating to the Jurisdiction of the ICAO Council under Article 84 of the Convention on International Civil Aviation (Bahrain, Egypt, Saudi Arabia and United Arab Emirates v. Qatar)*, Joint Application Instituting Proceedings, 4 July 2018; ICJ, *Appeal relating to the Jurisdiction of the ICAO Council under Article II, Section 2, of the 1944 International*

diction to adjudicate Qatar's claims regarding the aviation restrictions on the basis of two conventions, the Chicago Convention and the International Air Services Transit Agreement. It is no coincidence then, that the two – nearly identical – ICJ judgments were delivered the same day. Engaging the ICJ in this extraordinary way did not form part of the Quartet's litigation strategy since it was dependent upon Qatar resorting to the ICAO Council in the first place. What is more, the scope of the ICJ's appellate function is in general limited, the standard of review so low, that it is rather unlikely that the ICJ will reverse any decision under appeal.[28] According to the identical judgments reviewing the 2018 decision for example, the complete absence of reasoning in the ICAO Council's decision was inconsequential and 'did not prejudice in any fundamental way the requirements of a just procedure'.[29] The Court expressed its disappointment with the ICAO Council's practice not to justify its decisions, but only as part of its supervisory function over the ICAO Council.[30] Therefore, due to its limited scope and its extraordinary nature, this form of ICJ jurisdiction did not play a decisive – if any – role in influencing the outcome of the dispute and since it cannot be part of the applicant State's litigation strategy *ab initio*, it will not be examined further.

This Chapter will focus on the other set of proceedings before the ICJ and will use *Qatar v. UAE* as an *exemplaire* to examine the use of ICJ provisional measures in a multi-*forum* litigation strategy. There are many reasons that render *Qatar v. UAE* a fitting case-study. First, the ICJ's judgment, whereby the Court dismissed the application, was delivered on 4 February 2021, that is one month after the confrontation formally ended. By signing the legally binding Al-Ula declaration[31] the Quartet terminated the blockade and in

Air Services Transit Agreement (*Bahrain, Egypt and United Arab Emirates v. Qatar*), Joint Application Instituting Proceedings, 4 July 2018.

28 Apart from the twin cases against Qatar, the ICJ has functioned as an appellate body only in a dispute between Indian and Pakistan, ICJ, *Appeal Relating to the Jurisdiction of the ICAO Council*, Judgment, *ICJ Reports* 1972, 46.

29 *Appeal ICAO Council, Chicago Convention* [123].

30 C Rose, 'Appeal Relating to the Jurisdiction of the ICAO Council' 115 (2021) *AJIL* 301, 307–8.

31 *Al-Ula Declaration*, 5 January 2021, UN Registration no. 56786 It is a matter of evaluation whether the dispute has been effectively resolved. Since the Al-Ula declaration, Qatari-Saudi dialogue has moved fast, but dialogue between Qatar and Bahrain is almost non-existent, International Crisis Group, *Watch List 2023-January 2023*, 45. Qatari-Emirati relations initially improved but lately remain frosty due to the latter's alleged involvement in corruption cases of EU Parliament officials to launch a campaign against Qatar, Emirates Leaks, 'Revealed: UAE Involved In the So-Called Qatar Corruption Scandal In the EU', 14 December 2022.

return, Doha dropped pending lawsuits brought before WTO panels, discontinued the conciliation proceedings under CERD and suspended the adjudication of any claims pending before the ICAO Council and the PCA.[32] Due to the scarcity of disclosed information, the status of the arbitral investment cases brought by Qatar's national carrier Qatar Airways against the Quartet (whereby it seeks at least $5 billion in compensation) remains unclear.[33] It is a matter of interpretation whether the investment arbitrations initiated by Qatar Airways are covered by Article II of the Al-'Ula declaration that requires the termination of 'all claims, complaints, measures, protests, objections or disputes of any sort' since formally Qatar Airways is a separate entity from the State of Qatar.[34] Of course, the likely outcome of such processes – running in parallel with the ICJ one – has affected the bargaining power of disputing States,[35] and Qatar used them as a negotiating tool. But since none

---

32 While the suspension of all cases was not effectuated in the time-frame provided in the Al-Ula declaration, they were dropped before reaching a closure, ICAO, *ICAO Council concludes 222nd Session with important new progress for international aviation*, 22 March 2021; WTO, *Saudi Arabia – Measures Concerning the Protection of Intellectual Property Rights*, WTO Doc. WT/DS567/11 (25 April 2022); WTO, *UAE – Measures Relating to Trade in Goods and Services, and Trade-Related Aspects of Intellectual Property Rights*, WTO Doc, WT/DS526/6 (19 January 2021); CERD, *Decision of the ad hoc Conciliation Commission on the termination of the proceedings concerning the interstate communication Qatar v. the Kingdom of Saudi Arabia*, available at: https://www.ohchr.org/en/treaty-bodies/cerd/inter-state-communications. The PCA cases have different termination dates, the case against Saudi Arabia was terminated on 15 February 2022 (*Arbitration pursuant to Article 32 of the Universal Postal Union* (*Qatar v. Saudi Arabia*), case no. 2020–27, https://pca-cpa.org/en/cases/252/), the one against Egypt on 6 October 2021 (*Arbitration pursuant to Article 32 of the Universal Postal Union* (*Qatar v. Egypt*), case no. 2020–26, https://pca-cpa.org/en/cases/251/), while it is unknown when the case against the UAE was concluded (*Arbitration pursuant to Article 32 of the Universal Postal Union* (*Qatar v. UAE*), case no. 2020–28, https://pca-cpa.org/en/cases/253/). In the tribunal's website the proceedings against Bahrain are still shown as pending, *Arbitration pursuant to Article 32 of the Universal Postal Union* (*Qatar v. Bahrain*), case no. 2020–25 https://pca-cpa.org/en/cases/250/.

33 *Qatar Airways v. United Arab Emirates*, (all other data remain confidential), https://investmentpolicy.unctad.org/investment-dispute-settlement/cases/1058/qatar-airways-v-united-arab-emirates. According to a different source, investment arbitration proceedings are not pending, but settled: https://jusmundi.com/en/document/decision/en-qatar-airways-group-q-c-s-c-v-united-arab-emirates-wednesday-1st-january-2020.

34 It must be noted that the all-encompassing wording of Article II militates in favor of a broad interpretation: [...] each of them [nb the signatory States] is committed to bringing an end to *any* claims, complaints, measures, protests, objections or disputes of *any* sort against any other State party to the Declaration [...].

35 See *infra* Section 3.B. The argument that States bargain in the shadow of any international litigation process, was first made in E Leonhardsen, 'Trials of Ordeal in the

of these mechanisms has pronounced definitively on the dispute and the ICJ main ruling was delivered *ex posto facto*, it is easier to assess the contribution of the ICJ provisional measures towards the reaching of a binding agreement terminating the dispute.

Second, the circumstances of the case highlight the different aims pursued by States when requesting provisional measures from the ICJ. It is likely that Qatar instituted contentious proceedings before the ICJ only because it is a *sine qua non* for a provisional measures request. Further, provisional measures were resorted to, not only by Qatar, but also from the UAE and, in fact, with a different aim and at a different time, that is, not merely as a response to the applicant's request. Thus, it is pertinent to examine how this mechanism can be used and perhaps abused by litigants.

Finally, the indicated provisional measures had implications for States that did not appear before the ICJ. The proceedings were instituted solely against the UAE due to jurisdictional limitations, however, given the identical nature of the sanctioning measures adopted by all four States, any ruling against the UAE implied that the same findings as to the legality of the measures were applicable towards other Quartet members too. By using the *Qatar v. UAE* case as a vehicle then, this Chapter will highlight the features that render this mechanism appealing or off-putting for States. In this way, this case will bring to the forefront the limits of instrumentalization of such procedures, especially when used in a multi-*forum* litigation strategy.

The avenue of provisional measures is open solely through an application to the Court for main proceedings. The present Chapter will deal with cases where the request for ICJ provisional measures is made in order to instrumentalize primarily them – and not the accompanying request for a merits judgment – in the context of a multi-*forum* litigation strategy. Of course, this requires a degree of speculation on the motivation behind the request (otherwise called 'the decision to sue'), nevertheless, this Chapter will attempt to systematize it. Despite provisional measures forming part of a litigation strategy for quite some time, the ICJ offers no guidance on States' goals when requesting them,[36] and few commentators have attempted to understand

International Court of Justice: Why States Seek Provisional Measures when Non-Compliance Is to Be Expected' 5 (2015) *Journal of International Dispute Settlement* 306, 330. In a domestic context this was raised many years ago, R Mnookin and L Kornhauser, 'Bargaining in the Shadow of the Law: The Case of Divorce' 88 (1979) *Yale Law Journal* 950.

36 As per its standard phrasing, the Court "cannot concern itself with the political motivation which may lead a State at a particular time, or in particular circumstances, to choose judicial settlement", see e.g. ICJ, *Alleged Violations of the 1955 Treaty of Amity, Economic*

State objectives in such requests. Ramsden has touched upon this issue when examining two specific disputes as case-studies.[37] Leonhardsen with respect to use of force disputes.[38] While Miles' integrated study must be considered slightly outdated as the conditions for the indication of provisional measures have changed since.[39]

As a preliminary remark, it is important to note that provisional measures can be instrumentalized in a twofold way based on the principal objective of the requesting State.[40] First, as *means* when they are utilized as strategic tools to maximize a litigant's chances of winning the main suit, or of strengthening its position in other dispute settlement methods (e.g. parallel proceedings before another judicial/non-judicial *forum* or negotiations running in parallel). Or, second, as *ends* when the State that invokes them only seeks to benefit from the advantages they provide, without any interest as to how they may influence other proceedings, be they the main proceedings or a different dispute settlement method.[41] In contrast, the use of advisory opinions in the course of a multi-*forum* litigation strategy is rather clear: to supplement the use of other dispute settlement mechanisms. Advisory opinions serve to clarify the state of existing international law, send coordinating signals to all other adjudicators and to stakeholders on how the existing tools must be wielded, and offer clarity to negotiations as to where the existing tools may be lacking. Therefore, they are quintessentially utilized as *means*. This is not the case with provisional measures which may serve a variety of purposes when incorpo-

---

Relations and Consular Rights (*Iran v. United States of America*), Judgment, 3 February 2021, 37 [95].

37 M Ramsden, 'Strategic Litigation in Wartime: Judging the Russian Invasion of Ukraine through the Genocide Convention', 56 (2023) *Vanderbilt Law Review* 181; M Ramsden, 'Strategic Litigation Before the International Court of Justice: Evaluating Impact in the Campaign for Rohingya Rights', 33 (2022) *European Journal of International Law* 441.

38 Leonhardsen, *supra* note 35.

39 C Miles, Provisional Measures Before International Courts and Tribunals (CUP, 2017), Chapter 9.

40 The distinction on the instrumentalization either as *ends* or as *means* is taken from: M Lemey, 'Incidental Proceedings before the International Court of Justice: the Fine Line between "Litigation Strategy" and "Abuse of Process"' 20 (2021) *The Law and Practice of International Courts and Tribunals*, 5.

41 Miles attempted a systematization of the situations 'in which provisional measures become the primary focus of the proceedings' and came up with two categories of cases: first, time-sensitive situations and second, cases pertaining to custody of persons or moveable property, *supra* note 39, 459–461. For more on this use of provisional measures *see* T Treves, 'The Political Use of Unilateral Applications and Provisional Measures Proceedings', in J Frowein et al. (eds), *Negotiating for peace: Liber Amicorum Tono Eitel* (Springer, 2003), 463.

rated in a multi-*forum* litigation strategy; they could be used both as *ends* (e.g. when the requesting State intends to benefit from their provisional dispute settlement role) and/or as *means* (e.g. when the requesting State intends to capitalize on their strategic benefits). Hence, the *means* vs *ends* distinction is not an absolute one and it is highly likely that a plenitude of motives may underlie a State's decision to request provisional measures from the ICJ.[42] This Chapter claims that, based on the circumstances of every case and its aftermath, it is possible to infer the different motives behind a request for the indication of provisional measures.

Against this background, the second Section will expose the peculiar features of ICJ provisional measures jurisdiction. The measures ordered before the final ruling of the Court are 'provisional' in a twofold sense. First, they constitute a holding operation, a court-appointed standstill to avoid any compromise of the parties' rights before the court can rule definitively. But further, they are a temporary determination of certain facts and the law of the case. To match these goals the ICJ undertakes a *prima facie* determination of the main claim with respect to jurisdiction and merits, establishes a link of the requested measures to the main case and requests proof of irreparability of harm and urgency regarding their indication. Once satisfied that the aforementioned prerequisites are in place, the ICJ will dictate 'preservatory' measures and, if necessary, non-aggravation/non-extension measures the combination of which may reach the point of provisionally settling the dispute. The application of these jurisprudential prerequisites demonstrates that ICJ interim protection has acquired an autonomous standing from main proceedings and fulfills purposes that go beyond those incorporated in the Court's Statute, amounting thus to an unripe dispute settlement mechanism.

The peculiar features of this mechanism, the third Section will argue, dictate its instrumentalization in a multi-*forum* litigation strategy. First, when examined as standalone actions, ICJ provisional measures have limited influence on the disposition of disputing parties. They are not particularly impactful when used as *ends* because they possess a finite capacity to promote in fact the resolution of the dispute. Testament to that is the low compliance rate with interim protection Orders.[43] Neither the Court's *de jure* authority, that

42 Ramsden (2023), *supra* note 37, 186.

43 While there exist no extensive recent empirical studies on the record of compliance with provisional measures (Schulte's book should be considered outdated, C Schulte, *Compliance with Decisions of the International Court of Justice* (OUP, 2004)) most commentators (Miles, Lando, Leonhardsen) adopt this as the default position. Sole recent survey, albeit brief, by M Alexianu, 'Provisional, but Not (Always) Pointless: Compliance with ICJ

is the court's right to rule on a dispute, nor the binding nature of provisional measures seem to affect the disposition of the parties towards norm compliance. Nevertheless, provisional measures offer certain strategic benefits when used as *means*, because States make use of this swift determination and exploit the so-called 'shadow of the law' mainly for an out-of-court settlement. Second, when they take center stage in a multi-*forum* litigation strategy – as was the case in *Qatar v. UAE*, ICJ provisional measures maximize these strategic benefits. In such a context, States may use provisional measures to take advantage of their autonomous standing and the fast-track settlement of the dispute that accompanies it, in order to influence other parallel procedures and capitalize on the pressure exercised upon a non-compliant State. Therefore, when combined with other procedures, their impact is maximized for they promote dispute resolution in a twofold way; first, they put on the table a possible domino effect of like-minded rulings, and further, as a means of communication, they effectively advance a strategic narrative that can be projected to the international community.

2 A *Quasi*-autonomous Dispute Settlement Mechanism

Provisiognal measures of protection (interim measures or provisional measures), along with preliminary objections, form part of a court's incidental jurisdiction.[44] Such measures may only be requested when connected to the main proceedings since they were not conceived to form a self-standing judicial mechanism. In recent decades, not only has there been an increasing recourse to international courts and tribunals, but there is also an increasing tendency of parties to request the indication of provisional measures. The practice of States when making an application to the ICJ is testament to that. Until 2001, thirty-one applications were accompanied with a request for interim protection for a total of thirty-four requests.[45] But after the 2001 *LaGrand* case and the resounding acknowledgement therein of the binging nature of provisional measures, forty such requests have been made in the context of twenty-six

---

Provisional Measures' *Ejil:talk!* (3 November 2023), who measured an overall compliance rate of 53% since 2001, but with a clear decreasing trend in recent years.

44 P Tzeng, 'Incidental Jurisdiction' (2022) *Max Planck Encyclopedia of International Procedural Law* [1].

45 K Oellers-Frahm and A Zimmermann, 'Article 41' in A Zimmernmann et al., *The Statute of the International Court of Justice* (OUP, 2019) Annex, 964–6. It is worth noting that Yugoslavia made 10 identical requests in the *Legality of Use of Force* cases, and likewise Libya made two requests in the *Lockerbie* cases.

disputes.[46] So, it is not only the sheer number of requests that has spiked, it is also the number of requests per application that has increased dramatically. A procedure of incidental nature, to be resorted to only in limited circumstances, provisional measures have become standardized and all the more often part of a State's litigation strategy. The latest trend in this respect being a barrage of such requests for the management of a situation that develops on the ground; three requests by Armenia in the dispute over Nagorno Karabakh, four by South Africa in the dispute over Gaza, and three by Costa Rica in *Certain Activities* testify to this.[47] The recent proliferation of requests for provisional measures cannot be attributed solely to a heightened confidence that States place in the Court.[48] Rather, it mainly derives from an interest in utilizing this particular mechanism which often constitutes the very reason animating the decision to sue before the ICJ.

2.1 *The Normative Context: a Few Sketchy Rules*

The extensive use of interim protection has generated some practical issues as to the functioning of the Court because all its activity stops once a request for provisional measures arrives, according to Art. 74(1) of the Rules of the Court. In her 2022 and 2023 speeches before the UNGA, the ICJ's former President questioned the ability of the Court with its current resources to deal effectively with 'one of the most dynamic periods of its history'[49] and in particular 'with complex and time-sensitive incidental proceedings, notably requests for the indication of provisional measures'.[50] Leaving such practical issues aside, this Section will demonstrate that despite the initial understanding on the nature of provisional measures, the judge-made law on provisional measures has attributed to this mechanism a quasi-autonomous standing. The *LaGrand* pro-

46 An exhaustive list of all requests is available at: https://www.icj-cij.org/cases-by-phase/provisional-measures?language=en.

47 Pre-2001, the only case were the applicant utilized the Court by filing multiple requests was the *Bosnian Genocide* case.

48 N Panagis, 'Jurisdictional Entanglement: the Relationship between the Jurisdiction over a Dispute and the Jurisdiction to Assess Compliance with Provisional Measures' 23 (2024) *The Law and Practice of International Courts and Tribunals* 7, 8.

49 Speech of HE Judge Joan E Donoghue, President of the International Court of Justice, On the Occasion of the Seventy-Eighth Session of the United Nations General Assembly, (26 October 2023), available at: https://www.icj-cij.org/sites/default/files/press-releases/0/000-20231026-sta-01-00-en.pdf, 10.

50 Speech of HE Judge Joan E Donoghue, President of the International Court of Justice, to the Sixth Committee of the General Assembly, (28 October 2022), 'A view of the International Court of Justice from within', available at: https://www.icj-cij.org/sites/default/files/press-releases/0/000-20221028-STA-01-00-EN.pdf, 8.

visional measures order – the only order that was rendered by the ICJ *proprio motu* – has been a watershed in this respect and the ICJ jurisprudence developed thereafter has shaped the specific attributes of this judicial mechanism.

Resorting to relevant case-law to understand the special features of interim protection is inevitable, as the normative framework outlining the ICJ's interim jurisdiction consists of a few sketchy provisions. Article 41 of the ICJ Statute, the basis of the ICJ's jurisdiction in granting interim relief, is essentially a replica of the respective Article of the PCIJ Statute.[51] The provision reads:

> 1. The Court shall have the power to indicate, if it considers that circumstances so require, any provisional measures which ought to be taken to preserve the respective rights of either party. 2. Pending the final decision, notice of the measures suggested shall forthwith be given to the parties and to the Security Council.

The laconic statement in the first paragraph sparked a decades-long debate on the binding nature of ICJ provisional measures[52] and left judges a wide discretion to determine the necessary prerequisites underpinning interim protection. The second paragraph regarding the notification of the Security Council does not give rise to interpretative difficulties, but the engagement of the Security Council in a legal dispute could prove decisive in view of the political nature of this body. The Security Council may be seized of a matter irrespective of the way via which it became aware of it and it is not under a duty to act when notified according to Article 41(2).[53] Should it do so however, the *Lockerbie* precedent demonstrates that the ICJ is prepared to give way to any determinations made by the Security Council and cease any action.[54] And should

---

51 For a detailed account of the drafting history behind Article 41 ICJ Statute see, Miles, *supra* note 39, 86ff.

52 E Dumbauld, *Interim Measures of Protection in International Controversies* (Martinus Nijhoff, 1932) 168ff; J Elkind, *Interim Protection: A Functional Approach* (Kluwer, 1981) ch 6; J Sztucki, *Interim Measures in the Hague Court: An Attempt at a Scrutiny* (Kluwer, 1983) 260ff.

53 R Kolb, The International Court of Justice (Hart, 2013), 656; Oellers-Frahm and Zimermann, supra note 45, 1195.

54 ICJ, *Questions of Interpretation and Application of the 1971 Montreal Convention arising from the Aerial Incident at Lockerbie* (*Libyan Arab Jamahiriya v. United States of America*), Provisional Measures, Order of 14 April 1992, *ICJ Reports* 1992, 114, 126 [40]. In *Lockerbie*, a Chapter VII resolution imposing sanctions against Libya was adopted by the Security Council while the Court was deliberating the indication of provisional measures against the US and the UK. The Court did not make use of its *proprio motu* power to indicate

any conflict arise between the two main UN organs, the Security Council's primary responsibility for the maintenance of international peace and security militates in favor of giving priority to this political body.[55] What is more, due to the latter's central role within the UN Charter's collective security system[56] and the operation of Article 103 of the UN Charter it is likely that other judicial bodies that may be engaged in parallel will not contradict the determinations made by the Security Council. Be that as it may, a State will not request provisional measures from the ICJ in order to engage the Security Council, thus it is not appropriate to push the matter further.

The procedural aspects of such a request are outlined in Articles 73–78 of the Rules of the Court. Drafted in order to complement Article 41, these provisions 'do not do much more than articulate the capacity of the Court to award provisional measures'.[57] Of particular importance for present purposes are Articles 75 and 76 (the latter amended in 2019) which empower the Court at the request of either party or *proprio motu* to award, revoke and modify provisional measures any time before the final judgment. As legal devices ordered in response to specific circumstances,[58] provisional measures are temporarily limited[59] and address situations that are in constant flux. This is why no written procedure takes place (Article 74(3)) and the ICJ swiftly delivers its Order, usually within three months from the request. During the *Bosnian Genocide* case for example, two sets of provisional measures were ordered at the request of Bosnia in a five-month time span.[60] The dynamic

measures that would prevent aggravation of the dispute as proposed by five dissenting judges, see Dissenting Opinion Judge Bedjaoui, [31].

55 G Gaja, 'Preventing Conflicts between the Court's Orders on Provisional Measures and Security Council Resolutions' in G Gaja and J Stoutenburg (eds) *Enhancing the Rule of Law Through the International Court of Justice* (Brill, 2014), 87, 88; A Pellet, 'The International Court of Justice and the Political Organs of the United Nations: Some Further but Cursory Remarks' in Fr. Salerno (ed) *Il ruolo del giudice internazionale nell'evoluzione del diritto internazionale e comunitario*, (CEDAM, 1995), 115, 119

56 M Wood and E Sthoeger 'Introduction' in M Wood and E Sthoeger (eds), *The UN Security Council and International Law* (CUP, 2022), 1, 3.

57 Miles, *supra* note 39, 91.

58 PCIJ, *Sino-Belgian Treaty (Belgium v. China)*, Order of 15 February 1927 (1927) PCIJ Ser A No 8, 9.

59 H Thirlway, 'Provisional Measures: How "Provisional" Is "Provisional"?' in FM Palombino, R Virzo and G Zarra (eds), *Provisional Measures Issued by International Courts and Tribunals* (Asser, 2021) 9.

60 ICJ, *Application of the Convention on the Prevention and Punishment of the Crime of Genocide (Bosnia and Herzegovina v Yugoslavia (Serbia and Montenegro))*, Provisional Measures, Order of 8 April1993, *ICJ Reports* 1993, 3 and ICJ, *Application of the Convention on the Prevention and Punishment of the Crime of Genocide (Bosnia and Herzegovina v*

character of interim protection renders it an appealing mechanism for States pursuing multi-*forum* litigation, especially when they count in using such ICJ rulings before other *fora*. Qatar sought a statement from the Court in its July 2018 Order that the definition of racial discrimination in Article 1(1) of the CERD encompasses discrimination on the basis of present nationality.[61] The Court deferred the decision on this issue until the merits stage of the proceedings,[62] however Qatar clearly intended to use a relevant pronouncement in the procedure before the CERD Committee that was running in parallel.

The fact that provisional measures may be requested by the respondent too, is another factor to be weighed in by the applicant when making the application initiating ICJ proceedings. In the context of a multi-*forum* litigation strategy, the ICJ is often engaged on the basis of compulsory jurisdiction (e.g. compromissory clause in CERD or Genocide Convention) because the respondent objects to the exercise of the Court's jurisdiction ('defective consent'). In such cases, it is expected that the respondent will attempt 'to do some harm or prejudice to the subject of the dispute'.[63] In *Qatar v. UAE*, the UAE filed a request for interim protection nine months after Qatar's concomitant request, alleging that Qatar has aggravated and extended the dispute between the parties. It has done so in three ways according to the UAE: first, by initiating parallel proceedings against the UAE before the CERD Committee and the ICJ, second, by hampering the UAE's attempts to comply with the ICJ's provisional measures Order of 23 July 2018 and third, by disseminating false accusations regarding the UAE, in relation to the issues in dispute.[64] The ICJ did not oblige, but the UAE was given an opportunity to put forward a counter-narrative, to request from the Court to check Qatar's compliance with the 2018 Order and to attempt to influence the CERD proceedings that were running in parallel.

The last provision of interest is Article 78, that gives the Court the power to 'request information from the parties on any matter connected with the implementation of any provisional measures'. Such information is not a monitoring proceeding though.[65] It is rather an affirmation that the Court

---

Yugoslavia (*Serbia and Montenegro*), Provisional Measures, Order of 13 September 1993, *ICJ Reports* 1993, 325.

61 ICJ, *Verbatim Record 2018/13*, 39 [21].

62 *Qatar v. UAE 2018 Order*, 417 [27].

63 Kolb, *supra* note 53, 633.

64 *Qatar v. UAE*, Request of 22 March 2019, 10–11 [23]

65 P Patarroyo, 'Monitoring provisional measures at the International Court of Justice: the recent amendment to the Internal Judicial Practice' *Ejil:talk!* (22 January 2021).

may keep matters under review until the delivery of the judgment.[66] On the basis of this provision, any assessment of compliance with a provisional measures Order is made *in casu* in the Court's judgment.[67] In an attempt to further entrench the autonomous character of interim protection, the Court adopted a new Article 11 of the Resolution concerning the Internal Judicial Practice of the Court in December 2020.[68] According to this provision, which is yet to be tested in practice, a new implementation mechanism of provisional measures is put in place; the Court will decide *sua sponte* on any subsequent action, upon the recommendations of a three-member *ad hoc* committee comprised of ICJ judges. This is of acute importance when the ICJ intends to remain actively involved in the implementation of an Order as it did in *Jadhav*,[69] in the *Rohingua Genocide* case,[70] or in the *Israel genocide* case.[71] In view of the number of ICJ cases that result in provisional measures and the low compliance rate with respective Orders, this change will likely render this judicial mechanism even more appealing for applicants. It is nevertheless questionable whether it accords with State responsibility rules[72] or with the limited purposes of provisional measures which will be scrutinized in the next Section.

2.2 *The Jurisprudential Prerequisites*

The overarching aim pursued by the ICJ with the indication of provisional measures is the preservation of rights *pendente lite* as expressly stated in Article 41. This per force requires the protection of the rights of either party while

---

66 ICJ, *Request for Interpretation of the Judgment of 15 June 1962 in the Case concerning the Temple of Preah Vihear (Cambodia v. Thailand)*, Provisional Measures, Order of 18 July 2011, *ICJ Reports* 2011, 537, 556 [69 (4c)]; The 2018 *Qatar v. UAE* Order did not involve such a requirement.

67 See e.g. *LaGrand,* 508 [115]; *Bosnian Genocide,* 231 [456].

68 ICJ, Press Release no. 2020/38, 21 December 2020.

69 ICJ, *Jadhav (India v. Pakistan)*, Provisional Measures, Order of 18 May 2017, *ICJ Reports* 2017, 231, 246 [61].

70 ICJ, *Application of the Convention on the Prevention and Punishment of the Crime of Genocide (The Gambia v. Myanmar)*, Provisional Measures, Order of 23 January 2020, *ICJ Reports* 2020, 3, 31 [4].

71 ICJ, *Application of the Convention on the Prevention and Punishment of the Crime of Genocide in the Gaza Strip (South Africa v. Israel)*, Provisional Measures, Order of 26 January 2024, General List no. 192, 26 [86 (6)].

72 Miles, *supra* note 39, 329. Due to the requirements for the invocation of State responsibility, he argues, a *proprio motu* determination of a breach of provisional measures from the Court would run counter to the *ne ultra petita* principle, lest the measures were requested by the parties.

their conclusive determination in a judgment is still pending.[73] But, it is also connected to the execution of a future judgment on the merits which must not be frustrated by the actions of one party *pendente lite*.[74] So, the open-ended phrase 'preservation of rights *pendente lite*' conceals within it a number of measures that may be understood as expressions of the wider general purpose.[75] The subjective interest of avoiding irreparable damage to the parties' rights is entangled with the objective interest that none of the parties is put at a disadvantage while the Court is seized of the matter.[76] The subjective interest is guaranteed through an assessment of the strength of the applicant's rights on the merits ('plausibility' test)[77] and the establishment of a connection between the measures requested and the rights subject to litigation ('link' test).[78] And the objective one via a call towards both parties to prevent any aggravation or extension of the dispute.[79] For present purposes, it is important to understand how these institutional interests have shaped the ICJ jurisprudence regarding the indication of provisional measures. And also, how they accord or discord with the objectives of the parties when requesting interim protection in the course of a multi-*forum* litigation strategy. Such a juxtaposition will dictate the limits of their instrumentalization in the context of such a strategy.

---

73 ICJ, *Fisheries Jurisdiction* (*UK v Iceland*), Provisional Measures Order of, ICJ Reports 1972, 12, 16 [20].

74 ICJ, *Aegean Sea Continental Shelf* (*Greece v Turkey*), Provisional Measures, ICJ Reports 1976 3, 15–16.

75 Miles, *supra* note 39, 176.

76 Kolb, *supra* note 53, 616.

77 Introduced in ICJ, *Pulp Mills on the River Uruguay* (*Argentina v. Uruguay*), Provisional Measures, Order of 13 July 2006, Separate Opinion Judge Abraham, ICJ Reports 2006, 113, 140–1 [10]. Adopted by the majority in ICJ, *Questions relating to the Obligation to Prosecute or Extradite* (*Belgium v. Senegal*), Provisional Measures, Order of 28 May 2009, ICJ Rep 2009, 139, 151 [57].

78 Introduced as an independent prerequisite in ICJ, *Request for Interpretation of the Judgment of 31 March 2004 in the Case concerning Avena and Other Mexican Nationals* (*Mexico v. United States of America*), Provisional Measures, Order of 16 July 2008, ICJ Reports 2008, 311, 326–7 [58].

79 ICJ, *Application of the International Convention for the Suppression of the Financing of Terrorism and of the International Convention on the Elimination of All Forms of Racial Discrimination* (*Ukraine v. Russian Federation*), Provisional Measures, Order of 19 April 2017, ICJ Reports 2017, 139 [103].

2.2.1 Prerequisites Aimed at Securing Protected Interests: a Purpose Overreach

2.2.1.1 *Plausibility of Rights*

The ICJ has been constantly refining its thinking on the requirements of provisional measures, and the standardized approach it now follows has been finalized in the past five years.[80] According to this approach, the ICJ examines under a common heading both the plausibility and the link tests, in this order. These two are connected as they serve the same purpose (the preservation of rights), however they are analyzed separately. The assessment of the strength of the applicant's rights on the merits has oscillated greatly throughout the ICJ's jurisprudence, until it took the formula of a 'plausibility test'.[81] In the Court's own words:

> the Court, [...] is not called upon to determine definitively whether the rights which [the State requesting interim protection] wishes to see protected exist; it need only decide whether the rights claimed by [the State requesting interim protection] on the merits, and for which it is seeking protection, are plausible.[82]

Yet, the exact level of scrutiny in this respect remains unsettled because the Court must balance two competing considerations. One the one hand, the ICJ wants to avoid any prejudgment or anticipation of the merits and consequently its assessment should be confined to the legal level; whether the rights sought to be protected are grounded in a possible interpretation of the law.[83] On the other hand, the Court is also concerned with countering clearly frivo-

80 These Orders are: *Alleged Violation of the 1955 Treaty* (*Iran v. US*); *Application of the Genocide Convention* (*Gambia v. Myanmar*); *Allegations of Genocide* (*Ukraine v. Russia*); *Application of the CERD* (*Armenia v. Azerbaijan*) *General list no. 180*, (*Armenia v. Azerbaijan*) *General List no. 181; Application of the Convention Against Torture and Other Cruel, Inhuman and Degrading Treatment or Punishment* (*Canada and the Netherlands v. Syrian Arab Republic*), *General List no. 188; Application of the Convention on the Prevention and Punishment of the Crime of Genocide in the Gaza Strip* (*South Africa v. Israel*) *General List no. 192.*

81 R Virzo, 'Introduction' in *Provisional Measures 2021, supra* note 59, 3; M Lando, 'Plausibility in the Provisional Measures Jurisprudence of the International Court of Justice' 31 (2018) *Leiden Journal of International Law* 641, 644; C Miles, 'Provisional Measures and the "New" Plausibility in the Jurisprudence of the International Court of Justice' (2018) *British Yearbook of International Law* 1.

82 *Qatar v. UAE*, 422 [44].

83 This low threshold is the position advocated by the State requesting interim protection, see eg. *Ukraine v. Russia, Genocide*, [55].

lous claims, therefore the examination should extend to factual matters; whether tangible evidence adequately support the claims.[84] The middling position embraced by the ICJ is a mix-and-match of both, which does not completely detach the plausibility test from the inference of evidence.[85] But, what is the required threshold of proof is case-specific. Note the difference between the *Ukraine v. Russia* 2017 Order where the ICJ demanded that Ukraine satisfy the subjective elements of Article 2(1)(b) of the Convention for the Suppression of the Financing of Terrorism and the *Gambia v. Maynmar* 2020 Order where the Court held the determination of genocidal intent, as provided in Article II of the Genocide Convention, to be unnecessary.[86] Arguably then, the Court expects that the State requesting interim protection will demonstrate a *prima facie* existence of the rights, but when the ICJ is satisfied that this has taken place is far from clear.

The uncertainty regarding this prerequisite affects the way litigants present their arguments on plausibility to the Court. This was evident in the context of *Qatar v. UAE* – even exacerbated when compared to other cases – as the request was made in the aftermath of the *Ukraine v. Russia* 2017 Order and the high factual threshold enunciated therein.[87] Qatar's application had been quite detailed. The Applicant stressed the effects of the June 2017 measures on Qatari nationals living in the *UAE*; separation of UAE-Qatari mixed families, suspension of medical care services, deprivation of the right to education of Qatari students, unequal treatment before domestic courts and blocking of transmissions by Qatari media outlets.[88] Overall, Qatar accused the UAE of interfering with basic human rights of its citizens as these rights are protected in Articles 2 and 5 of CERD.[89] The UAE countered that the request fails on both fronts, legally and factually. It argued

84 A rather high threshold was applied in the *Ukraine v. Russia* Order of 19 April 2017. For a criticism see, E Rieter, 'The ICJ and Provisional Measures Involving the Fate of Persons' in S Kadelbach, T Rensmann and E Rieter (eds) *Judging International Human Rights. Courts of General Jurisdiction as Human Rights Courts* (Springer, 2019) 127, 151–7.

85 E.g. *Gambia v. Myanmar,* [56] "all the facts and circumstances mentioned above are sufficient to conclude"; *Ukraine v. Russia,* [59] "the Court is not in possession of evidence substantiating the allegation of the Russian Federation that genocide has been committed on Ukrainian territory".

86 *Ukraine v. Russia 2017 Order,* [75] and *Gambia v. Myanmar 2020 Order,* [55].

87 E Rieter, 'Autonomy of Provisional Measures' in *Provisional Measures 2021, supra* note 59, 69.

88 *Qatar v. UAE 2018 Order,* [26].

89 Qatar also invoked the violation of Articles 4, 6 and 7 of the same convention, see Ibid. [21]. However, they are tangential to the main claim and the ICJ did not engage with these provisions in its Order.

that the rights claimed were not plausible for legal reasons as the interpretation of Article 1 CERD did not comprise discrimination based on active nationality and further that the evidence furnished in support of Qatar's claims was inadequate.[90] Thus, the circumstantial nature of the ICJ's pronouncement in this respect forces litigant States to open their cards, reveal a big part of their case and expose their argumentation to the other party.

Nevertheless, this risk of exposing one's legal strategy is counter-balanced by the potential of extracting information from the Court at such an early stage of the case. And the importance of such information cannot be overemphasized.[91] First, a factual assessment of Qatari claims would provide a first, primitive and incomplete 'crash test' of their soundness and hence outline the prospects of fruition of the forthcoming ICJ judgment on the merits. And a sign that Qatar's claims (do not) have a grounding in law, could be used as basis for negotiations between the Parties.[92] This has arguably been the case in *Certain Documents and Data*.[93] The ICJ determination that Timor-Leste's property rights over certain documents seized by Australia are indeed plausible, precipitated bilateral negotiations and was the catalyst in finally settling the case.[94] Second, a 'sneak peek' on the ICJ's disposition towards the applicant's case could determine the evolution of the dispute before other *fora*. With respect to the *Qatar v. UAE* case, where CERD, WTO and arbitral proceedings were running in parallel, the stakes were particularly high for Qatar. A legal assessment whether the disputed measures fall within the scope of CERD *rationae materiae* could have influenced directly the concomitant determination of the CERD Committee or incidentally the assessment of WTO panels and investment tribunals.[95] It is readily apparent that the ruling on 'plausibility' in the context of a multi-*forum* strategy is a

90 Ibid. [48]–[49].

91 Obtaining such information is a top priority for litigants since resolution of the dispute has been effectively placed in the hands of a neutral third party over whom they have no control, Miles, *supra* note 39, 445.

92 B Kempen and Z He, 'The Practice of the International Court of Justice on Provisional Measures: The Recent Development' 69 (2009) *Zeitschrift für ausländisches öffentliches Recht und Völkerrecht* 919.

93 ICJ, *Questions relating to the Seizure and Detention of Certain Documents and Data* (*Timor-Leste v. Australia*), Provisional Measures, Order of 3 March 2014, I.C.J. Reports 2014, 147. For an analysis, see Miles, *supra* note 39, 447.

94 P Tzeng, 'The State's Right to Property in International Law' 125 (2016) *The Yale Law Journal* 1805, 1807.

95 See *infra* Section 3 B II.

two-edged sword. Given the ICJ's authority and its concomitant influence, it may create a domino effect on other *fora* or favor the early settlement of a dispute.

2.2.1.2 *Link between Rights and Measures*

The other prerequisite developed from case-law that aims to 'secure' the parties' rights *pendente lite* and to insulate the Court from vexatious claims is the link requirement. Introduced as an independent requirement in the *Avena (Interpretation)* 2008 Order,[96] it requires a connection between the rights which a State seeks to protect by way of provisional measures and the rights which may be subsequently adjudged in the main judgment to belong to that State. While examination of plausibility is centered around the rights claimed, the link requirement revolves around the requested measures. In particular, it is examined by assessing the causal relationship between the aim of the measures sought and the plausible rights that the State seeks to protect.[97] As clear-cut as this may seem, it has proved rather impressible, for the ICJ has room for maneuver when examining the necessity of the requested measures. In its 2023 Order on *Armenia v. Azerbaijan* for example, the ICJ considered plausible that Article 5 CERD guaranteeing freedom of movement was violated 'through the interruption of movement along the Lachin Corridor'.[98] Being the only route connecting the landlocked oblast of Nagorno-Karabakh and Armenia, the Court granted Armenia's measure requesting 'uninterrupted free movement [...] along the Lachin Corridor'.[99] At the same time, the Court held unwarranted the measure that Azerbaijan cease its orchestration and support of the alleged 'protests' blocking the Lachin Corridor. Even if it targeted the same objective with the indicated measure and in this way it was linked with a plausible right, this measure would have been awarded *ex abundanti* and was thus unnecessary in order to preserve Armenia's right under

96 ICJ, *Request for Interpretation of the Judgment of 31 March 2004 in the Case concerning Avena and Other Mexican Nationals (Mexico v. United States of America)*, Provisional Measures, Order of 16 July 2008, ICJ Reports 2008, 311, 326–7 [58].

97 See *Gambia vs. Myanmar*, 24 [61]. This makes clear why the link and plausibility requirements are examined by the ICJ under a common heading. Lando argues that not only are these two connected, but the link requirement is in fact sometimes subsumed into the plausibility test, M Lando, 'Provisional Measures and the Link Requirement' 19 (2020) *The Law and Practice of International Courts and Tribunals* 177, 182.

98 ICJ, *Application of the International Convention on the Elimination of All Forms of Racial Discrimination (Armenia v. Azerbaijan)*, Provisional Measures, Order of 22 February 2023, General List no. 180, 9 [39]

99 Ibid. 14 [67].

Article 5 CERD.[100] Nevertheless, when considering the wider circumstances of the case, especially when a humanitarian catastrophe is looming, the Court has ruled in the opposite direction of the *Armenia v. Azerbaijan* case; rather than discarding requested measures as unwarranted, it has imposed *proprio motu* wider measures by stretching the link requirement to its limits.[101] Characteristic example in this respect is the *Temple (Interpretation)* 2011 Order where the ICJ was requested to interpret the geographic scope of an area that it had previously adjudged to belong to Cambodia. While it had not been requested by either party, the Court ordered the imposition of a demilitarized zone, a measure the ICJ could not determine under the jurisdictional mandate granted by Article 60 of the ICJ Statute.[102] So, the link requirement is in essence a 'reality check' of the provisional measures requested. It ensures that they are aimed at safeguarding only plausible rights, and further that they are necessary in the given circumstances.

This requirement functions as a reminder that any request should be attached to the main claim and also as a scanner of the purposes pursued by the requested measures. As to the connection to the main claim, this is examined via the plausible character of the rights sought to be protected with the provisional measures. When the UAE approached the ICJ to request, *inter alia*, that Qatar desists from creating obstacles to the implementation of the 2018 Order, the Court denied the request.[103] The reason was that the measure was not sufficiently linked to the protection of a plausible right since '[t]he judgment on the merits is the appropriate place for the Court to assess compliance with the provisional measures'.[104] The ICJ then found the particular measure to be targeting a right that did not need protection while the case was pending and consequently to be unconnected to the UAE's main claim. Being so strongly connected to plausibility, the link requirement does not uncover further information to the parties regarding the Court's disposition towards the main claim than the plausibility requirement does. Due to its impressible

100 Ibid. 13 [63].

101 Miles, *supra* note 39, 183–4.

102 *Temple Interpretation 2011 Order*, 537, 547–8 [44]. Similarly, the Orders in the consular rights cases *Breard, LaGrand, Avena* and *Jadhav* included a plea for the halting of pending executions while this was outside the legal purview of the cases, eg ICJ, *Vienna Convention on Consular Relations (Paraguay v. USA)*, ICJ Reports 1998 248, 261 [5] (Declaration of Judge Oda).

103 *Qatar v. UAE 2019 Order* 370 [26]–[27].

104 Ibid. It is interesting to see whether the ICJ will adopt the same stance in a future case, after the new Article 11 implementation mechanism of provisional measures is put in place, see *supra* note 68 and accompanying text.

character though, it may guide States to direct their pleadings towards the humanitarian aspects of a dispute.[105]

As to the scanning of the aims fulfilled by the requested measures, the link requirement gives the ICJ the possibility to discard any excessive or unnecessary measures and to distinguish between measures targeting the protection of party rights and non-aggravation measures aimed at ensuring that none of the parties is put at a disadvantage while the Court is seized of the matter. The link requirement is inapplicable with respect to the latter type of measures and in this context the ICJ has the power to grant any measure, no matter how unrelated to the parties' rights. However, non-aggravation measures are add-ons; it is not possible to order provisional measures independently aiming at non-aggravation.[106] On this basis, in the *Qatar v. UAE* 2019 Order, the Court refused to consider the indication of concomitant UAE measures (e.g. to immediately stop Qatari-owned, controlled and funded media outlets [*Al Jazeera* network] from aggravating the dispute via disseminating false accusations) since no measures protecting UAE's rights were awarded.[107] *A contrario,* in its 2018 Order in the context of the same dispute, the ICJ requested from both parties to ensure non-aggravation of their dispute once it had indicated other measures pertaining to the preservation of Qatar's rights under CERD.[108] The link requirement then, is stretched with respect to measures aimed at protecting the parties' rights and is inapplicable with respect to non-aggravation measures. It is no wonder then, it has been suggested that it must be dropped altogether[109] and further, that States do not devote much of their pleadings to it. For present purposes, the link requirement is of marginal importance for a State's litigation strategy as it scarcely impacts the measures that States may request from the Court.

105 The prioritization of human vulnerability in provisional measures had been consistently advocated by Judge Au. Cançado Trindade since the *Ukraine v. Russia 2017 Order,* Separate Opinion of Judge Cançado Trindade, 641–3 [44]–[51], *see* also T Sparks and M Somos, 'The Humanisation of Provisional Measures? Plausibility and the Interim Protection of Rights Before the ICJ' in *Provisional Measures 2021, supra* note 59 77.

106 *Pulp Mills 2007 Order* [49]–[51]; *Treaty of Amity,* 651 [99]; P Palchetti, 'The Power of the International Court of Justice to Indicate Provisional Measures to Prevent the Aggravation of a Dispute', 21 (2008) *Leiden Journal of International Law* 623, 633.

107 *Qatar v. UAE 2019 Order,* 370–1 [28].

108 *Qatar v. UAE 2018 Order,* 432–3 [76]. With the thinnest of margins (8 judges to 7), of Qatar's nine requests the Court granted three; reunification of mixed families, continuation of studies for Qatari students, and access to UAE courts, Ibid 433–4 [79].

109 Lando, *supra* note 97, 195ff.

On the other end of the spectrum, rather important strategically is the scenario where the ICJ itself indicates measures in the absence of any link requirement; usually, these measures being different from those requested (Article 75 of the Rules of the Court). The Court is at liberty to indicate, without any further justification and without the restriction of the *ne ultra petita* rule, non-aggravation measures which may be different from those requested by the parties. Different types of measures may guarantee non-aggravation, e.g. measures concerning the preservation of evidence[110] or measures establishing a reporting obligation to the Court.[111] Such measures testify to the willingness of the Court to achieve purposes beyond the preservation of the parties rights in the context of interim protection. Relatedly, it has been questioned whether non-aggravation is a purpose encapsulated within Article 41 of the ICJ Statute.[112] Or, rather, it is a measure of general prevention closer to action under Chapter VII of the UN Charter, which accordingly is not restricted to the preservation of rights.[113] Further, due to the relaxation of the link requirement explained *supra*, measures allegedly targeting the parties' rights have been pursuing purposes marginally covered by the wording of Article 41. For example, the measures indicated in the *Maynmar Genocide* case – to take actions pursuant to the Genocide Convention and to prevent the destruction and ensure the preservation of evidence – instead of preserving a right or the *status quo*, sought to prevent the perpetration of international crimes and the disappearance of relevant evidence.[114] Judge Cançado Trindade had advocated in several opinions that the purpose of provisional measures in cases that are based on the application and interpretation of human rights treaties lies in putting an end to the alleged vulnerability of the affected persons.[115] Whether this consideration has underpinned ICJ rulings in the

110 ICJ, *Questions relating to the Seizure and Detention of Certain Documents and Data (Timor-Leste v. Australia)*, Provisional Measures, Order of 3 March 2014, ICJ Reports 2014, 147, 161 [55].

111 *Temple Interpretation 2011 Order*, 556 [69, (4)C].

112 Oellers-Frahm and Zimermann, *supra* note 45, 1145–1148.

113 J Sztucki, 'Case Concerning the Land and Maritime Boundary (Cameroon v. Nigeria): Provisional Measures Order of 15 March 1996' 10 (1997) *Leiden Journal of International Law* 341, 357–8;

114 Patarroyo, *supra* note 65; similar criticism could be made with respect to the 2022 *Ukraine v. Russia* Order, see A Kulick, 'Provisional Measures after Ukraine v Russia (2022)', 13 (2022) *Journal of International Dispute Settlement* 323, 334–5.

115 *Qatar v. UAE 2018 Order*, Dissenting Opinion Cançado Trindade, 459 [69]. Cerna argues that the ICJ modifies at will the prerequisites for the indication of provisional measures when individuals are confronted with urgent and serious risk of irreparable harm, Chr. Cerna, 'Provisional Measures: How International Human Rights Law is Changing Inter-

consular rights cases, in *Myanmar Genocide, Qatar v. UAE, 1955 Treaty of Amity, Ukraine v. Russia* and *Israel Genocide* cannot be definitely determined.[116]

What stands out from the above is the overall effect of such a purpose overreach effectuated with the Court's latest Orders. The ICJ comes closer to an integrated arrangement of the dispute from the interim protection stage, which is testament to the developing autonomous nature of provisional measures. Put another way, the ICJ uses provisional measures as a – provisional – dispute settlement tool. The Court's proactiveness in this respect could offer insights to the parties as to how far it is prepared to go in the final determination of the dispute.[117] Nevertheless, this must not be exaggerated as the Court is mindful not to anticipate the main judgment with an interim protection Order.[118]

More importantly though, this expansion of the purposes fulfilled by provisional measures, and hence of the measures indicated, may dictate the instrumentalization of this mechanism by States. Qatar would have surely welcomed an interim protection Order reversing all the effects of the measures taken by the UAE and thus *de facto* restoring the *status quo ante* until the delivery of the ICJ's judgment. All along, Qatar's main objective before all *fora* has been to challenge the legality of the Quartet's measures in order to apply pressure on the sanctioning States. Achieving this objective within the limited framework of ICJ provisional measures, required an expansive interpretation of CERD rights – an aspect mentioned by the UAE in the oral pleadings

national Law (Inspired by Gambia v. Myanmar)' 11 (2021) *Notre Dame Journal of International and Comparative Law* 34.

116 In favor of this view, Somos and Sparks, *supra* note 105, 98–9. A strong indication that this has been a critical factor in *Israel Genocide* is the wording in [70] of that Order whereby the Court justifies urgency on the basis that "the civilian population in the Gaza Strip remains extremely vulnerable."

117 This was Wolfrum's main point in the concomitant discussion at the Institut de Droit International, 'Provisional Measures (Rapporteur: Lord Collins of Mapesbury)' 78 (2017) *Yearbook of Institute of International Law*, 99, 108.

118 It is standard practice for the Court to include a non-prejudice disclaimer in a provisional measures Order, e.g. *Armenia v. Azerbaijan 2023 Order, General list no. 181*, 7 [26]: 'the decision given in the present proceedings in no way prejudges the question of the jurisdiction of the Court to deal with the merits of the case or any questions relating to the admissibility of the Application or to the merits themselves'. Rieter argues that the authority and persuasiveness of a provisional measures Order depends, *inter alia*, on whether provisional measures anticipate the judgment on the merits. So, the high plausibility threshold in the *Ukraine v. Russia 2017 Order* undermined the credibility and the effectiveness of provisional measures as it prejudged the merits to an unacceptable level, *supra* note 87, 67–9.

phase[119] – and perhaps a broadening of this mechanism's protective scope. Another prominent example whereby the Court expanded the umbrella of measures justified on the basis of the stated purpose of Article 41, is the *Ukraine v. Russia* 2022 Order. Ukraine requested and was awarded an Order on the general suspension of hostilities until delivery of the final judgment, a measure that arguably went beyond the purpose of securing Ukraine's rights as they are guaranteed in the Genocide Convention.[120] With respect to use of force disputes in particular, applicant States will all the more often attempt to engage the ICJ to deliver provisional measures, as 'general non-aggravation measures lay at the borderline with the function of preserving international peace and security'.[121] Arguably, the ICJ's choice to adjudicate measures beyond what could be justified according to the stated purpose of this mechanism, does not favor the Court's legitimate authority, and the future compliance with such orders.

This feature of provisional measures – i.e. the integrated settling of a dispute – renders this mechanism particularly appealing in situations that develop on the ground while the dispute is pending before the Court. Either through the imposition of new measures per Article 75 of the Rules of the Court, or via the modification of previous ones per Article 76, the possibility to request such measures time and again is open to States. This is particularly relevant with respect to developing circumstances and provides States with the opportunity to engage the ICJ at will as the situation goes. The barrage of requests in the two cases over Nagorno-Karabakh (five in two years, three by Armenia and two by Azerbaijan) and *South Africa v. Israel* (four in five months) testify to this.[122] Armenia and South Africa keep the pressure on, in an attempt to 'enforce the Court's earlier provisional measures decision[s] in the face of Israel's [and Azerbaijan's] apparent non-compliance'.[123] Be that as

119 *Qatar v. UAE*, *Verbatim Record of the Oral Hearings 2018/13*, (June 28, 2018), 51–3.

120 *Ukraine v. Russia 2022 Order*, 19 [86 (1)]. Kulick, *supra* note 114, 340; O Pomson, "The ICJ's Provisional Measures Order: Unprecedented" *Articles of War* 17 March 2022.

121 Oellers-Frahm and Zimermann, *supra* note 45, 1148.

122 Relatedly, Israel's ad hoc Judge suggested that South Africa is instrumentalizing provisional measures in order to have the ICJ 'micromanage' an armed conflict, *South Africa v. Israel* Provisional Measures Order (28 March 2024) Separate opinion of Judge ad hoc Barak, 1[6]. In subsequent proceedings this was picked up by Israel, *South Africa v. Israel*, CR 2024/28 (17 May 2024), 13[31] and by Judge Sebutinde, ICJ, *Alleged Breaches of Certain International Obligations in respect of the Occupied Palestinian Territory* (*Nicaragua v. Germany*), Order of 30 April 2024, Separate Opinion of Vice-President Sebutinde, 1[1].

123 M Becker, 'Desperate Times, Desperate (Provisional) Measures: Rafah and South Africa's Latest Action at the ICJ', *VerfassungsBlog* (14 February 2024).

it may, it is a sign that a golden era of ICJ provisional measures is likely upon us, especially considering the formulation of the other jurisprudential prerequisites underpinning provisional measures, i.e. jurisdiction *prima facie* and risk of irreparable prejudice and urgency to which the attention turns right away.

2.2.2 Prerequisites Aimed at Securing the Integrity of the Proceedings: beyond the Interests of the Parties

2.2.2.1 Prima facie *Jurisdiction*

Perhaps the most well-settled aspect of the Court's jurisprudence on provisional measures is the test of *prima facie* jurisdiction. Championed by Judge Lauterpacht in *Interhandel*, it was adopted by the Court in the *Fisheries Jurisdiction* cases, some 15 years later. The idea behind the introduction of such a precondition for the indication of provisional measures is the necessity to anticipate any occasion of institutional overreach and to guarantee the proper administration of international justice. However, Article 36 of the Court's Statute that establishes the consensual nature of ICJ jurisdiction deals with the merits and not with the Court's jurisdiction to order provisional measures. The latter derives from the combination of Articles 35 and 41 which do not stipulate a clear jurisdictional standard. Nevertheless, the consensual character of judicial dispute resolution in international law demands that some form of jurisdictional review is required prior to the awarding of interim relief. Absent such a requirement, the ICJ's incidental power to award interim protection would be converted into an unlimited grant of jurisdiction. In the meantime, measures under Article 41 are an urgent matter which calls for swift action.[124] An exhaustive scrutiny of all matters related to the Court's jurisdiction would frequently undermine such necessity for rapid determination. This is why, the scrutiny of *prima facie* jurisdiction being an autonomous jurisdictional standard represents a compromise between the urgency of the judicial action and respect for the sovereignty of States.[125]

According to the modern elaboration of this test, the ICJ examines its jurisdiction *in toto*, considering not only the putative jurisdictional title and the existence of a dispute, but also any legal complications that may arise, as specified by the respondent.[126] Despite its width, the jurisdictional review at this stage remains skin-deep. The ICJ need only establish at this stage that it

---

124 Kolb, *supra* note 53, 623.

125 G Pascale, 'Provisional Measures Under the African Human Rights System' in *Provisional Measures 2021*, *supra* note 59, 253, 259.

126 Miles, *supra* note 39, 152–3.

might have jurisdiction over the merits. Of course, it may reverse its position and reject the main application on jurisdictional grounds, as it did in *Qatar v. UAE*.[127] Such instances are relatively uncommon, yet they testify to the separate and autonomous nature of the two levels of review.[128] Therefore, the threshold is set quite low and the benefit of the doubt when assessing jurisdiction vis-à-vis provisional measures is given to the claimant. But, the possibility of awarding interim protection in cases where the respondent would object to the exercise of the Court's jurisdiction ('defective consent') is what renders this mechanism pertinent in the context of a multi-*forum* litigation strategy. As explained *supra,* the necessity of accessing multiple jurisdictions on the basis of the same factual matrix arises in cases of defective consent.[129] So, any jurisdictional mechanism that awards legal protection without a full review of this foundational element of international dispute resolution, becomes automatically relevant for present purposes.

When determining *prima facie* jurisdiction in *Qatar v.* UAE the ICJ had to juggle two hot potatoes. First, whether the expression 'national [...] origin' mentioned in Article 1(1) of CERD encompasses discrimination based on the individual's present nationality. If not, the UAE measures targeting solely Qatari nationals are not capable of falling within the scope of CERD *rationae materiae*. Second, whether negotiations and recourse to the procedures referred to in Article 22 of CERD constitute alternative or cumulative preconditions to be fulfilled before the seisin of the Court. If the latter was the case, this precondition was not fulfilled. The Court dodged both bullets, by arguing that it was not necessary to determine such questions at this stage. The threshold for *prima facie* jurisdiction was met since both interpretations to those questions were possible.[130] This echoes the threshold adopted with respect to the 'plausibility' test. The common approach adopted is only logical since the two tests target, *inter alia*, the same objectives: to counter clearly frivolous claims and at the same time to avoid any prejudgment or anticipation of the merits.

Strategically, the low *prima facie* jurisdictional standard, if established, may confer a psychological advantage to the applicant.[131] The reversal of the deter-

127 Such reversal also occurred in *Anglo-Iranian Oil co* UK v. Iran (1952); *Application of* CERD Georgia v. Russia (2011) and *Avena* (*Request for Interpretation*) Mexico v. USA (2009).

128 G le Floch, 'Requirements for the Issuance of Provisional Measures' in *Provisional Measures 2021, supra* note 59, 19, 33.

129 See *supra* Chapter 1 Section 1.

130 *Qatar v.* UAE *2018 Order*, 417 [27] and 420–1 [39].

131 A Pellet and T Barsac 'Litigation Strategy' (2019) *Max Planck Encyclopedia of International Procedural Law* [66].

mination on jurisdiction in the main proceedings has occurred only in four occasions throughout the ICJ's history, so *prima facie* jurisdiction may function as a litmus test to ascertain whether the main application will surpass the jurisdictional obstacle. This is exacerbated when provisional measures are used as *means*, that is as strategic tools to maximize a litigant's chances of winning the main suit. Especially, in the modern era of dispute settlement where jurisdictional challenges have become standard practice and applicant States devote substantial resources in defending the Court's jurisdiction, the establishment of *prima facie* jurisdiction acquires new significance.

When utilized as *ends* though, they are invoked only for the advantages they provide, even a failure to establish *prima facie* jurisdiction may sometimes be insignificant for the applicant's cause. This will be the case when the hearing of the request itself by a public *forum*, such as the ICJ, is all the applicant intends to achieve. Interim protection was arguably utilized in this sense in the *Legality of Use of Force* cases where Yugoslavia initiated proceedings against ten NATO member States in order to politically de-legitimize NATO's 1999 intervention in that State.[132] Due to its manifest lack of jurisdiction, the Court ordered two such cases to be removed from its General List already from the interim protection phase.[133] But, at the same time, expressed its concern with respect to the humanitarian situation in Kosovo,[134] and stated *obiter* that the parties must act in compliance with the Charter, and not aggravate or extend the dispute.[135] Similar considerations animated DRC's applications against Burundi and Rwanda – alongside Uganda – for armed aggression during the second Congo war.[136] Due to the apparent lack of ICJ jurisdiction with respect to the two first States and for fear that the Court's disposition towards the ongoing application against Uganda would be affected, the DRC discon-

132 K Oellers-Frahm, 'Uses and Abuses of Interim Protection Before International Courts and Tribunals', in H Hestermeyer et al. *Coexistence, cooperation and solidarity: Liber Amicorum Rüdiger Wolfrum* (Brill, 2012), 1685, 1688; G le Floch, *L'urgence devant les juridictions internationales* (Pedone, 2008), 289.

133 ICJ, *Legality of Use of Force* (*Yugoslavia v. Spain*), Provisional Measures, Order of 2 June 1999, ICJ Reports 1999, 761, 774 [40(2)]; ICJ, *Legality of Use of Force* (Yugoslavia v. United States of America), Provisional Measures, Order of 2 June 1999, ICJ Reports 1999, 916, 926 [34(2)].

134 *Legality of Use of Force* (*v. Spain*), 1999 Order, 768 [15].

135 Ibid. 773 [37]–[39].

136 ICJ, *Armed Activities on the Territory of the Congo* (*Democratic Republic of the Congo v. Uganda, Rwanda and Burundi*) Application Instituting Proceedings (23 June 1999), 1999 General List no. 117.

tinued proceedings before any public hearing took place.[137] Similarly, the instrumentalization of the ICJ as a public *forum* was put forward by the UAE during the oral proceedings. Its agent suggested that Qatar requested interim protection from the ICJ 'to distract attention away from its own unlawful conduct and for the purpose of mounting a public relations campaign against those States that have been most critical of its policies'.[138] Even if this was Qatar's main motivation behind its request, the risk of striking the application out of the Court's list prematurely was minimal given its grounding in both law and facts.[139] Then, Qatar would obtain with minimal risk as much information as possible as to which way the ICJ was leaning with respect to jurisdiction prior to its final decision.

2.2.2.2 *Irreparable Prejudice and Urgency*

Inherent to the nature of interim protection, the last precondition to be fulfilled before such an application is granted is that of irreparable prejudice and urgency. Analytically, the two components of this precondition can be separated but they are examined jointly by the Court, even conflated in certain cases to the extent that they form an integrated whole.[140] The ICJ grounds irreparable prejudice in Article 41 of its Statute, nevertheless this prerequisite only indirectly derives from the overarching purpose enunciated therein regarding the preservation of rights. An eventual final judgment of the ICJ may not be executable absent interim protection, so in this way the Court protects chiefly the proper administration of justice and only subsidiarily the parties' rights.[141] Also, the exact meaning of irreparable prejudice is context specific. The Court will assess whether the alleged disregard of the rights deemed plausible by the Court is of such a character that could cause irreparable harm or entail irreparable consequences to those rights. As a rule of thumb, this will be the case when human rights are at stake, while sovereign rights are harder to support such a claim as they are generally capable of being

137 See eg ICJ, *Armed Activities on the Territory of the Congo* (*Democratic Republic of the Congo v. Burundi*), Order of 30 January 2001, ICJ Reports 2001 3. The DRC instituted new proceedings against Rwanda shortly afterwards by invoking new grounds for the establishment of the Court's jurisdiction, ICJ, *Armed Activities on the Territory of the Congo* (*New Application: 2002*) (*Democratic Republic of the Congo v. Rwanda*) (28 May 2002).

138 *Qatar v. UAE*, *Verbatim Record of the Oral Hearings 2018/15* (29 June 2018) 43[4].

139 Compare with the *Armed Activities* (*New Application: 2002*) DRC v. Rwanda, where the DRC had a much weaker jurisdiction case than Qatar, however the Court decided to retain the case in its List.

140 Miles, *supra* note 39, 225.

141 Kolb, *supra* note 53, 629.

remedied at the merits.[142] Further, urgency is strongly connected to the above, for according to the Court's case law it signifies 'a real and imminent risk that irreparable prejudice will be caused before the Court makes a final decision in the case'.[143] The latter condition is met when the acts susceptible of causing irreparable prejudice can occur at any moment before the Court renders its final decision.[144] Again, the assessment of the time-sensitive question of urgency depends on the factual background and is subject to an *ad hoc* examination. Overall, the case law does not show detailed or consistent examination of the prerequisite of irreparable prejudice and urgency. Rather, it reveals that interim protection is granted largely in two scenarios. First, when an ongoing obvious and flagrant violation of the rights claimed on the merits cannot be tolerated until the delivery of the final judgment.[145] Second, where the action causing a risk of irreparable prejudice has not yet occurred, so the *status quo ante* should be maintained.[146]

According to the Court, the former scenario was in play in *Qatar v. UAE*. The UAE emphasized during the oral round that the condition of urgency cannot be present when the application to the Court is made a whole year after the measures were instituted.[147] In return, Qatar complained about the 'continuous nature of the violations of the fundamental rights alleged', so that even a year on, the human rights situation of Qataris residing in the UAE remains stagnant. Qatar concluded that, since the damage is present and ongoing, the condition of imminence is fulfilled. The ICJ endorsed Qatar's viewpoint when dealing with this aspect. It declared the situation of Qataris residing in the UAE prior to 5 June 2017 to remain vulnerable with respect to their rights under Article 5 of CERD.[148] It is not relevant whether the situation complained of had already existed for a considerable time when the request was filed. Of importance is only the imminence of action prejudicial to the rights at stake. Therefore, it was the nature of the violation and of the rights sought to be guarded that determined the fulfillment of this criterion and not the temporal proxim-

142 Compare the Orders on *Pulp Mills* (2006), 131 [70] and 132 [74]–[76] and *1955 Treaty of Amity* (2018), 650 [91].

143 See e.g. *Application of CERD, Armenia v. Azerbaijan* (2023), 12 [57].

144 *Ibid.* 10 [46].

145 Oellers-Frahm and Zimermann, *supra* note 45, 1162.

146 ICJ, *Certain Documents and Data* (Timor-Leste v. Australia), Provisional Measures, Order of 3 March 2014, 157–8 [42]; ICJ, *Immunities and Criminal Proceedings* (Equatorial Guinea v. France), Provisional Measures, Order of 7 December 2016, 1169 [90].

147 *Qatar v. UAE, Verbatim Record CR 2018/13*, 62 [21].

148 *Qatar v UAE*, 430–1 [67] and 431 [69].

ity with the events under scrutiny. As with the link requirement, the ICJ seemingly gives priority to cases of human vulnerability,[149] and this may direct States to request interim protection in cases of human rights violations or to stress the humanitarian ramifications of their disputes.

Finally, the ICJ may take into consideration two pertinent contextual factors when assessing the urgency of the claim. Any relevant undertakings made by the defendant during the interim protection proceedings and the pursuit of other parallel dispute resolution mechanisms. Neither of the two was examined in *Qatar v. UAE*, nevertheless, they must be addressed since they shed light on the instrumentalization of ICJ interim protection. First, the commitments undertaken at this stage testify to the dispute resolution role of interim protection. When confronted with a legal determination of their inter-State relations, even a provisional one, States occasionally proffer unilateral commitments towards the other Party.[150] So, the Court will examine whether such undertakings sufficiently deprive the request of its urgent character. If this is the case, the Court may declare that the hypothesized prejudice is unlikely to arise. In *Questions relating to the Obligation to Prosecute or Extradite* for instance, Senegal 'gave a formal assurance [...] that it will not allow Mr. Habré to leave its territory before the Court has given its final decision'.[151] In view of this, the ICJ was convinced that the risk of irreparable prejudice to the right claimed by Belgium – that is, to bring criminal proceedings against Mr. Habré – was not apparent. In different circumstances however, unilateral commitments may not suffice. For example, the undertaking of the Attorney-General of Australia in *Certain Documents and Data* did not remove entirely the risk of an imminent irreparable prejudice to Timor-Leste's rights that would arise from Australia's seizure of confidential documents related to pending arbitral proceedings between the two States.[152] Or, Azerbaijan's public statement affirming its commitment 'to continue to take all steps within its power to guarantee the safety of movement [...] along the Lachin road',[153] did not remove entirely the imminent risk of irreparable prejudice created by the disruption in movement along this road.[154] All in all, by prompting States to modify their behavior and to commit to minimizing the prejudice on the

149 For a detailed analysis of the human dimension in ICJ jurisprudence *see* LA Sicilianos, *La dimension humaine du droit international*, 440 (2024) *RCADI*

150 Such statements are legally binding, as unilateral declarations, see Chr. Eckhart, *Promises of States Under International Law* (Hart, 2012) 172–3.

151 *Questions relating to the Obligation to Prosecute or Extradite, 2009 Order* 155 [71]–[72].

152 *Certain Documents and Data, 2014 Order* 159 [47]–[48].

153 *Armenia v. Azerbaijan, Verbatim Record* CR *2023/2*, 22 [30].

154 *Armenia v. Azerbaijan 2023 Order* 12 [56].

applicant's rights, ICJ interim protection proceedings may accelerate the resolution of the dispute[155] and fulfil a role beyond that of a provisional arrangement of inter-State relations.

Further, in order to assess the context in its entirety, and form an appreciation of urgency, the Court may examine the initiation of dispute resolution procedures running in parallel with the ICJ process. In theory, it is less likely to indicate interim protection when other parallel proceedings are already seized of the same subject-matter.[156] Such proceedings could take place before political institutions (e.g. the Security Council), judicial *fora* or bilaterally. Ongoing negotiations between the parties have been declared to affect the perception of urgency. In *Pakistani POW*, the Court was requested by the applicant to postpone deliberations on its interim protection application in order to facilitate bilateral negotiations. The Court held that since the parties had the luxury to suspend the ongoing judicial procedure the matter was no longer considered urgent.[157] To the contrary, the simultaneous seisin of a political body with respect to the same events, would not constitute an obstacle to the indication of provisional measures. According to the Court, the legal functions of the ICJ only complement and do not substitute any political determination by an organ with such a mandate.[158] The ICJ has confronted many scenarios where the Security Council has been seized concurrently of the matter, nevertheless to date the Court has never dismissed a request for interim protection for lack of urgency or for any other reason relating to the parallel pursuit of solution before political organs.[159] The million dollar question pertains to the parallel seizin of judicial *fora,* and in particular those that may issue binding provisional measures.

---

155 Arguably this happened in the *Passage through the Great Belt* where Denmark assured Finland that no physical hindrance for the passage through the Great Belt would occur before the end of 1994 (Finland v. Denmark), Provisional Measures, Verbatim Record CR 91/14, 17.

156 Kolb, *supra* note 53, 631.

157 ICJ, *Trial of Pakistani Prisoners of War* (Pakistan v. India) Order of 13 July 1973, ICJ Reports 1973, 331[14].

158 ICJ, *Armed Activities on the Territory of the Congo* (*DRC v. Uganda*), Provisional Measures, Order of 1 July 2000, ICJ Reports 2000, 126 [36].

159 Oellers-Frahm and Zimmermann, *supra* note 45, 1193. In *Lockerbie,* the Security Council determined legally (*sic*) the issue by acting under Chapter VII of the Charter while the Court was deliberating. Since Chapter VII obligations prevail over other international obligations of States, the Security Council precluded the rights claimed by Libya from 'be [ing] regarded as appropriate for protection by the indication of provisional measures', *Lockerbie* (Libya v. UK; Libya v. USA) Provisional Measures, Orders of 14 April 1992, 15 [40] and 126–7 [43] respectively.

The ICJ recently faced such a scenario in two cases, albeit its rulings do not provide sufficient guidance as to its position in this respect. The *Ukraine v. Russia* 26 March 2022 Order came in the aftermath of two binding ECtHR interim protection decisions on the 1st and 4th of March 2022 with both courts addressing the same factual matrix.[160] The ECtHR ordered Russia to refrain from military attacks against civilians and civilian objects, and to ensure unimpeded access of the civilian population to safe evacuation routes, healthcare, food and other essential supplies, rapid and unconstrained passage of humanitarian aid and movement of humanitarian workers respectively. Despite these measures, the Court did not contemplate the prospect of a lack of urgency regarding Ukraine's claim and indicated measures more comprehensive than those of the ECtHR. Namely, the general suspension of military operations commenced either by Russia or by forces it controls or directs. Without expressly referring to it, the Court considers the scope of its jurisdiction to be different from that of the ECtHR and therefore it deemed urgent to provisionally regulate the dispute from its own point of view.[161] Similarly, regarding the *Armenia v. Azerbaijan* 2023 Order, ECtHR measures – adopted in December 2022 – were not taken into consideration as a relevant factor by the Court. In this case, the difference in scope is not so straightforward since both courts requested that Azerbaijan guarantees the passage along the Lachin corridor as provided for in a 2020 agreement between the parties. The ECtHR decision referred to the safe passage 'of seriously ill persons in need of medical treatment in Armenia and others who were stranded on the Lachin road without shelter or means of subsistence'.[162] The ICJ held more generally that Azerbaijan shall 'ensure unimpeded movement of persons, vehicles and cargo along the Lachin Corridor in both directions'.[163] Once more, the Court reserves for itself the final say as to the interim regulation of the situation.

In both instances, ECtHR measures were not complied with before the delivery of the ICJ Orders, so practically it made sense for the Court to indicate without much ado measures different in scope but compatible with those of

160 Press release, 'The European Court Grants Urgent Interim Measures in Application Concerning Russian Military Operations on Ukrainian territory', 1 Mar 2022; Press release, 'Decision of the Court on requests for interim measures in individual applications concerning Russian military operations on Ukrainian territory', 4 March 2022.

161 This has been Ukraine's position during the Oral round regarding the relationship between parallel judicial proceedings, ICJ, *CR 2022/5* (7 March 2022), 61 [16].

162 European Court of Human Rights, *Armenia v. Azerbaijan*, App. No. 15389/22, Decision on Interim Measures, 21 Dec. 2022.

163 *Armenia v. Azerbaijan 2023 Order*, 14 [67].

the ECtHR. A pertinent legal question nevertheless persists: if the situation on the ground is already legally addressed by measures delivered by a different judicial *forum,* where is the urgency in reiterating the same substantive measures? From a normative viewpoint, the ICJ is entrusted with the preservation of different rights – than the ECtHR for example – so the Court may independently assess whether the rights at stake before it are faced with a real and imminent risk of irreparable prejudice. Hence, the adoption of and the compliance with previously indicated measures becomes a factual issue to be assessed by the Court when determining urgency. The absence of reference to the relevant ECtHR rulings and the Court's silence as to its relationship with these judicial proceedings, denotes that the ICJ does not make a systemic assessment of urgency and it is willing to exercise its interim jurisdiction irrespective of any relevant legal determinations by other *fora.* Unlike situations of parallel activity with a political organ where the ICJ has made clear the complementary nature of the relationship, the Court has yet to determine the nature of its interaction with organs that offer interim protection *in tandem* with it. But, if one must speculate, most probably the Court will be open to offer interim protection to applicants, if only to reiterate – or even to contradict – determinations already made by other *fora.* All in all, the Court's eagerness to ignore any parallel judicial proceedings when determining urgency is another factor that renders ICJ interim protection appealing to applicants and attests to the autonomous nature of this mechanism.

Finally, connected to their urgent character, another feature that renders provisional measures such an appealing choice is their highly disruptive nature. In the same way as they disrupt the judicial process and the ordinary 'flow' of the judicial determination of a dispute, they derange the power equilibrium between the parties. Since they may be requested at any time while the dispute is ongoing, and the Court will issue a decision in a short time-span, they may cause respondents to abruptly and unexpectedly enter into a defensive position. And also, to hastily construct a litigation and dispute settlement strategy. Following a joint application by Canada and the Netherlands in June 2023, Syria, for example, has to defend itself against allegations of violation of the Convention Against Torture that have occurred since 2011 and the beginning of the ongoing civil war.[164] While the Court for the first time in its modern history did not respond within the usual three-month

---

164 ICJ, *Application of the Convention Against Torture and Other Cruel, Inhuman or Degrading Treatment or Punishment* (Canada and the Netherlands vs. Syria), Request for the Indication of Provisional Measures, 8 June 2023, available at: https://www.icj-cij.org/sites/default/files/case-related/188/188-20230608-REQ-01-00-EN.pdf.

timeframe (testament to the increasing workload it has to negotiate),[165] still these proceedings are seen as the culmination of long-standing international efforts to hold Syria accountable for such crimes.[166] In the context of this swift process, Syria will have to address a wide array of allegations that spread across a wide time-span and eventually may be asked to revisit its civil war policy and suffer a severe blow to its international legitimacy.

The strategic use of ICJ interim protection in order to regulate a situation swiftly and with binding force, without, at the same time, going through a detailed examination of State consent, renders such measures a *prima facie* attractive judicial mechanism for interested States. As was the case with advisory opinions, the Court's willingness to intervene in inter-State disputes does not necessarily mean that the ICJ will effectively resolve bilateral disputes via the indication of provisional measures. The latter may play a critical role in this direction as *Qatar v. UAE* demonstrates, however the limits of the instrumentalization of this mechanism are defined by its quasi-autonomous standing and its capacity to offer strategic benefits to the State requesting such protection. Utilized by States as *means* and/or as *ends*, provisional measures are valuable for their self-standing value and/or their capacity to influence other procedures. The analysis of the *Qatar v. UAE* proceedings will highlight how States may get maximum benefits from such a mechanism in the context of a multi-*forum* strategy without at the same time abusing their right to request interim protection.

3 Instrumentalization of ICJ Interim Protection

On 5 January 2021, during a GCC Summit hosted by Saudi Arabia in the city of Al-'Ula all members of the regional organization and Egypt signed a declaration whereby the diplomatic rift was officially terminated. According to its terms, the States parties undertook to stand united in order to protect each other's sovereignty, security and people and further to strengthen their media coordination and their cooperation in combating terrorism (Article I). As a herald of the new era in their relations, the Quartet committed to the lifting of all sanctioning measures and Qatar to 'bringing an end to any claims, complaints, measures, protests, objections or disputes of any sort' (Article II). The declaration established a tight timeframe both for the implementation of Arti-

165 *Application of the CAT*, Order of 16 November 2023.

166 V Bellintanti and M Sharabati, 'State Responsibility for Acts of Torture: Netherlands/Canada v Syria at the International Court of Justice' *OpinioJuris* (17 July 2023).

cle II – one week to suspend or freeze all pending claims – and of Article I – two weeks to commence bilateral discussions on pending political and security issues between them.

To claim that the signing of the Al-'Ula declaration was effectuated solely due to Qatar's litigation strategy is a gross oversimplification. Other factors have certainly played a role – perhaps the most significant – in the resolution of the dispute; pressure by the US, especially towards Saudi Arabia,[167] and political linkages in the domestic sphere and the broader region, in particular the need for a GCC unified stance towards Iran and Turkey.[168] The role of domestic political coalitions in driving a State's decision to establish behavior that tends to comply with international law,[169] or the impact of reputational concerns that develop around regional standards of behavior in this respect,[170] have been examined elsewhere and need not be pushed further as they lie beyond the scope of the argument presented here. It is also oversimplifying to suggest that all Quartet members had a warm disposition towards ending the rift with Qatar and therefore all were equally pressured by the pending disputes. The UAE views Qatar as its most staunch opponent in the region, so unsurprisingly most Qatari judicial battles targeted the UAE. Saudi Arabia on the other hand, that has a coordinating role as the region's greatest power, had begun to signal as early as 2019 that reconciliation with Doha was on its agenda (e.g. by inviting Qatar's emir to the GCC 2019 meeting[171]). At the same time, the UAE had clearly a different perception on how the relationship with Qatar should unfold (e.g. the UAE's US ambassador stated in November 2020 that ending the dispute '[is] not on anyone's priority list'[172]). In fact, Saudi Arabia and its close ally Egypt led the way for reconciliation, slowly bringing the UAE and Bahrain aboard.[173]

This Section aims to assess whether a multi-*forum* litigation strategy that incorporates ICJ provisional measures may accommodate State policy objec-

167 A Cornwell and Gh. Ghantous, 'Saudis, Egypt embark on long road to ending Arab rift with Qatar' *Reuters* (19 March 2021).

168 A Occhiuto, 'Why are Saudi Arabia and the UAE moving apart on Qatar?' *Amwaj* (2 March 2021).

169 J Trachtman, 'International Law and Domestic Political Coalitions: The Grand Theory of Compliance with International Law' 11 (2010) *Chicago Journal of International Law* 127.

170 B Simmons, 'International Law and State Behavior: Commitment and Compliance in International Monetary Affairs' 94 (2000) *American Political Science Review* 819.

171 'Saudi king invites Qatar emir to Riyadh summit: Doha' *France 24* (3 December 2019).

172 I Levingston, 'UAE Envoy Says Ending Qatar Right 'Not on Anyone's Priority List'' *Bloomberg* (16 November 2020).

173 S Vakil, 'Qatar Crisis: A Beginning to the end?' *Chatham House* (8 January 2021).

tives. In this way, it aims to determine the limits of instrumentalization of provisional measures in this context. In order to do so, this Section will render intelligible the actual impact ICJ interim protection measures may have on disputing States when utilized in the course of a multi-*forum* litigation strategy. In particular, whether they possess the ability to promote State objectives either by ensuring compliance with their findings (provisional measures as *ends*) or by setting in motion other mechanisms (provisional measures as *means*). This correlation between the use of judicial mechanisms (the law) and the promotion of the requesting State's policy objectives (the facts) is the criterion determining the 'effectiveness' of the litigation strategy.[174] The main argument put forward here is that, as standalone actions, provisional measures exert limited influence on State behavior when used as *ends* and are, hence, not particularly impactful. In contrast, when used as *means* they may offer strategic benefits to the requesting State. But, when utilized either as *means* or as *ends* in the context of a multi-*forum* litigation strategy, their effects are maximized. And this realization, in turn, dictates the way in which this strategy may be utilized by States.

A caveat is in order before proceeding. This Section does not aim to measure the effectiveness of provisional measures *in abstracto* as a judicial mechanism, but instead to evaluate a strategy that incorporates provisional measures. Therefore, the intention is to examine whether provisional measures are impactful as a strategic choice. The analysis here adopts a biased viewpoint; namely, whether provisional measures as part of a multi-*forum* litigation strategy are effective in promoting in one way or another the policy objectives of the requesting State.[175] This is why, the methodology determining the effectiveness of a strategy must not be confused with the methodology determining the effectiveness of a judicial mechanism.

Scholars have put forward different ideas regarding the latter. For certain legal empiricists, one should evaluate a Court's effectiveness by comparing

---

174 Hernandez claims that the traditional understanding of effectiveness within international law is that of a 'bridge between normativity (law) and reality (facts), serving to sustain the relation between the two', Gl. Hernandez, 'Effectiveness' in J d'Aspremont and S Singh (eds) *Concepts for International Law* (Edward Elgar, 2019), 237, 239.

175 It is worth noting that provisional measures are seldom – if ever – resorted to for strategic purposes of a systemic nature, i.e. to contribute towards the development of international law. While in effect promoting such purposes may inform the role of the ICJ and consequently may not be 'just collateral side effect of adjudicatory practice', States will likely not initiate costly ICJ litigation with this as their main motivation, A von Bogdandy and I Venzke, 'Beyond Dispute: International Judicial Institutions as Lawmakers' 12 (2011) *German Law Journal* 979, 981.

whether its outputs correspond to its delineated goals,[176] or by assessing their exercise of their functions.[177] With respect to the ICJ, such benchmarks include conflict resolution, norm compliance, support for the operation of international regimes, legitimization of international governance,[178] or even law-making and the stabilization of normative expectations.[179] For others, it is connected to the *de facto* authority of this mechanism which they understand as the 'ability to influence practices in law, politics, and society'.[180] Measuring such authority entails two components, they suggest; whether interested actors recognize an obligation to comply with court rulings and, further, whether they engage in action to that effect.[181] *De facto* authority then relates to effectiveness if the latter is understood as 'the ability to move audiences in the direction indicated by the law'.[182] Hence, it can be examined solely by looking into the practices of the relevant actors. For proponents of the interpretative turn finally, measurement of this effect is near impossible because the inner subjective meanings and reasons of relevant actors are 'the key to unlock an explanatory account of social action'.[183] Authority of a court, they hold, is just one of the explanations why a State may comply with the findings of a court and the real reasons for compliance could be kept hidden from empirical observation.

The methodology adopted here to measure the effectiveness – and hence the limits – of multi-*forum* litigation strategy does not coincide with any of the

176 Y Shany, *Assessing the Effectiveness of International Courts* (OUP, 2014), 6ff.

177 Armin von Bogdandy and Ingo Venzke, *In Whose Name?: A Public Law Theory of International Adjudication* (OUP, 2014).

178 R Giladi and Y Shany, 'Assessing the Effectiveness of the International Court of Justice' in C Esposito and K Parlett, *The Cambridge Companion to the International Court of Justice* (CUP, 2023), 101, 105.

179 Bogdandy and Venzke, *supra* note 177, 8.

180 K Alter, L Helfer, and M Rask Madsen, 'International Court Authority in a Complex World' in K Alter, L Helfer and M Rask Madsen (eds) *International Court Authority* (CUP, 2018), 1, 13. That this analysis of '*de facto* authority' pertains to effectiveness is pointed out by Venzke, I Venzke 'International Courts De Facto Authority and Its Justification' in Ibid, 391, 393fn8. This empirical turn to explaining the authority of international courts has been analyzed in two issues of the Leiden Journal of International Law, *see* e.g. G Shaffer, 'The New Legal Realist Approach to International Law' 28 (2015) *Leiden Journal of International Law* 189.

181 K Alter, L Helfer, and M Rask Madsen, 'How Context Shapes the Authority of International Courts' in Alter et al. *supra* note 180, 24, 29.

182 Ibid 52. L Helfer, The Effectiveness of International Adjudicators, in K Alter. C Romano & Y Shany (eds) *The Oxford Handbook of International Adjudication* (OUP, 2014) 464.

183 P Capps and H P Olsen, 'Explaining power and authority in international courts' 34 (2021) *Leiden Journal of International Law* 1, 3, criticized as failing to distinguish authority from other relevant notions such as 'power' and 'consensus'.

said approaches, but it is closely connected to the purpose of the analysis. Thus, as noted above, the determination of the strategy's effectiveness depends on the correlation between the use of judicial mechanisms and the promotion of the requesting State's policy objectives. The analysis attempted here suggests that observable effects regarding the disposition of disputing parties may be attributed to a twofold strategic use of provisional measures; either as *ends* or as *means*. It is highly likely that the motivation behind changes in State disposition lies also in factors beyond empirical observation. This is why, in literature this attribution has occurred on the basis of anecdotal evidence.[184] Nevertheless, the present study is, deterministically, based on empiricism.

The argument proceeds as follows. First, the analysis will attempt to systematize and analyze the different ways in which a request for ICJ interim protection as a standalone action may in fact promote State objectives. While compliance with a concomitant Order is not expected (use of provisional measures as *ends*), the overall settlement of the dispute is indirectly promoted (use of provisional measures as *means*). Then, the attention will turn to how the impact of this judicial mechanism may differ when it forms part of a multi-*forum* litigation strategy. By following the unfolding of *Qatar v.* UAE, the next Section will appreciate the pressure exercised by the proceedings before international dispute settlement *fora* over the Quartet. To this end, it is important to understand the stage these proceedings were left at, at the date of the signing of the declaration. The ICJ interim protection measures occupied central place among these proceedings, for they were – and still are – the only judicial determination of the legality of the 2017 measures. With this in mind, this Section will finally expose the benefits a State is expected to achieve when incorporating this mechanism in a multi-*forum* litigation strategy. Of course, such benefits heavily rely on the context of every dispute, so any attempt to generalize the findings from *Qatar v.* UAE is made with caution.

3.1 *Provisional Measures as Standalone Actions*

3.1.1 Provisional Measures as *Ends*; Norm Compliance

The analysis attempted in this Section is informed by a speculative assumption; that, when using provisional measures as *ends*, compliance with the

184 R Giladi and Y Shany, *supra* note 178, 116; A Nollkaemper, 'The Role of Domestic Courts in the Case Law of the International Court of Justice', 5 (2006) *Chinese Journal of International Law*, 301; A Guzman, A Compliance-Based Theory of International Law, 90 (2002) *California Law Review*, 1823, 1838.

Court's Order is the main motive underpinning the request. In other words, that the main interest sought by the applicant State is that of safeguarding a right *pendente lite* or forestalling further aggravation of a dispute. In *Temple of Preah Vihear* (*Interpretation*) for instance, Cambodia filed an application requesting interpretation of the 1962 judgment almost 50 years after the delivery of the initial judgment and asked simultaneously for the indication of provisional measures. It is highly likely that interim protection was Cambodia's primary focus since compliance with the Court's Order would terminate the border skirmishes between the parties.[185] Nevertheless, it cannot be excluded that (also) other expectations beyond compliance may inform a decision to pursue ICJ interim protection even when no interest in other procedures is evident.[186] For example, the prospect of tangential diplomatic gains could have animated Yugoslavia's request in *Use of Force*. In an attempt to move the Court, Yugoslavia brough to the Court's attention a substantial volume of photographic material as evidence of the NATO bombing campaign in Kosovo. And this strategy paid off since the ICJ did not limit itself to declaring its incompetence to rule upon the case. It held *obiter* that it 'is deeply concerned with the human tragedy, the loss of life, and the enormous suffering in Kosovo which form the background of the present dispute, and with the continuing loss of life and human suffering in all parts of Yugoslavia' and further instructed the parties to comply with the Charter and not to aggravate the dispute.[187] In view of the evident lack of ICJ jurisdiction in this case, these *dicta* were probably all Yugoslavia was after with its request. This underscores that requests for interim protection may be backed by different motives and in this respect a degree of speculation is inevitable.

As a rule of thumb, it can be said that immediate compliance with the Court's interim protection Orders depends heavily on consent.[188] Compliance is understood here as the voluntary observance of a judicial decision.[189] It will

---

185 M Ghantous, 'Les mesures conservatoires indiquées par la Cour internationale de Justice dans le cadre de conflits territoriaux et frontaliers. Développements récents', (2012) *The Canadian Yearbook of International Law*, 78.

186 Treves, *supra* note 41, 466.

187 *Legality of Use of Force* (*Yugoslavia v. Spain*), 1999 Order, 768 [15] and 773 [37]–[39].

188 For political scientists, the 'design of delegation [to the authority of an international court] is politically consequential' K Alter, E Hafner-Burton and L Helfer, 'Theorizing the Judicialization of International Relations' 63 (2019) *International Studies Quarterly* 449, 450.

189 Voluntary in the sense that no enforcement power equivalent to that of the executive in a domestic legal system is discernible in the international system, JS Warioba, 'Monitoring Compliance with and Enforcement of Binding Decisions of International Courts' 5

occur when States are being one way or another pressured to align their behavior with the determinations of the Court.[190] In cases of genuine consent to the Court's jurisdiction, compliance is expected because States are in principle willing to have their dispute resolved by the ICJ. Therefore, compliance with provisional measures in such cases is a non-issue as the disposition of litigant States towards resolution of the dispute is not affected by the indication of provisional measures. The million-dollar question then pertains to cases of defective consent. Can the Court ensure compliance with an interim protection Order when the respondent objects to the exercise of the Court's jurisdiction? This is the case if provisional measures may influence disputing parties and have the power to alter their disposition towards the resolution of the dispute. Until recently, the Court lacked the necessary legal enforcement tools (that is, a legitimation strategy that creates pressure on governments to comply) and the political determination to render provisional measures attractive or effective as *ends*.[191] Put differently, when examined independently from its connection to other proceedings, this judicial mechanism utilized as an *end in itself* does not adequately promote the resolution of a dispute.

This is so, because ICJ provisional measures have shown a notably low level of compliance despite their functioning as a separate yet premature mechanism for settling disputes.[192] And such a poor record should be

---

(2001) *Max Planck Yearbook of United Nations Law* 41, 42. In international law compliance can be understood as the 'conformity between behavior and international law', I Wuerth, 'Compliance' in J d'Aspremont and S Singh (eds) *Concepts for International Law* (Edward Elgar, 2019),117. More generally, compliance may be defined as 'the interaction between rules and behavior', B van Rooij and D Sokol, 'Introduction: Compliance as the Interaction between Rules and Behavior, in *Cambridge Handbook of Compliance* (CUP, 2021), 1, 4.

190 Orthodox international legal scholarship suggests that States comply with international law because of negative incentives, that is external pressure (e.g. sanctions) or internal pressure (e.g. concern for reputation). For an overview *see* M Bothe, 'Compliance' (2010) *Max Planck Encyclopedia of Public International Law* R Wolfrum (ed.). Others suggest that positive incentives may also promote compliance, *see* A van Aakcen and B Simsek, 'Rewarding in International Law' 115 (2021) *AJIL* 195; O Ben Shahar and A Bradford, 'Efficient Enforcement in International Law', 12 (2012) *Chinese Journal of International Law*, 375. It would exceed the remit of the analysis to delve deep into whether States react to negative incentives based on the rational actor model, constructivist or process-based theories. For an overview, *see* Wuerth, *supra* note 189, 119ff.

191 See *infra* this Section notes 199–209 and accompanying text.

192 Leonhardsen, *supra* note 35, 309. In a recent empirical account of the level of compliance with ICJ provisional measures Orders, Alexianu observed that in seven out of the 15 post-*LaGrand* disputes States took no action to comply, in three such disputes States com-

expected, as the pressure deriving from the legal standing of provisional measures is minimal for two reasons; first, due to the weak enforcement means available to the Court and second because of its limited formal or *de jure* authority when adjudicating provisional measures. The reputational cost a State may face in case of non-compliance notwithstanding. The new legal obligations created by an Order of the Court place the losing party in front of a dilemma; either adjust its behavior to match the judicial Order or damage its reputation. The reputational cost dilemma is one of the main consequences deriving from a failure to implement a decision of an international court and a factor upon which international tribunals rest in order to induce compliance with legal rules.[193] The effectiveness of the reputational cost ensuing from non-compliance is relative, i.e. it depends heavily on the circumstances of the case, the nature of the dispute and the subjects at hand.[194] In view of the compliance record with interim protection Orders however, reputational costs do not adequately promote immediate compliance with the Court's determinations.[195]

At first blush, the normative status of interim protection Orders would militate in favor of a high compliance record. It is now settled that Article 41 of the Statute, despite its unclear wording, empowers the Court to indicate legally

plied partially and only in five instances he records full compliance, Alexianu, *supra* note 43.

193 Guzman has been the most fervent proponent of this idea, A Guzman, 'International Tribunals: A Rational Choice Analysis' 157 (2008) *University of Pennsylvania Law Review* 171, 181. This is based on a 'rational' account of how international law may influence State action. Others openly challenge it, J Goldsmith and E Posner, *The Limits of International Law* (OUP, 2007) and others find limitations, R Brewster, 'The Limits of Reputation on Compliance', 1 (2009) *International Theory*, 323.

194 Eg Gr. Shaffer, M Elsig and S Puig attribute the effectiveness of WTO Appellate Body reports mainly to 'reciprocity and reputational effects', in 'The World Trade Organization's Dispute Settlement Body: Its Extensive but Fragile Authority', *International Court Authority, supra* note 180, 300, 328–9.

195 Theoretically, *eo ipso* the request for interim protection may generate reputational costs, and thus pressure the respondent to change behavior, when an unfavorable ruling is expected. It is debatable whether this was the case with respect to Germany's 2022 request in the – still pending – *Jurisdictional Immunities* case. The day after Germany's request, Italy published in its Official Gazette a decree whereby it addressed the central concern informing the request for provisional measures, causing Germany to withdraw, ICJ, *Questions of Jurisdictional Immunities of the State and Measures of Constraint Against State-Owned Property* (Germany v. Italy) Order, 10 May 2022, General List no. 183. Due to the short timespan between request and compliance, it is unclear whether the publication of the decree can be attributed to the interim protection request.

binding provisional measures. Clearly stipulated for the first time in the *LaGrand* judgment,[196] such measures impose on disputing States an obligation of compliance.[197] Therefore, non-compliance with provisional measures is a breach of an international obligation entailing all the consequences stemming therefrom, including international responsibility.[198] Nevertheless, the ineffective implementation mechanisms ensuring such compliance keep the pressure deriving from the binding nature of the indicated measures very low. Countermeasures are possible according to most commentators,[199] but, such measures have not been adopted by an injured State up to date since they adhere to strict requirements, and they are likely to aggravate the dispute. And intervention by the Security Council under Articles 94(2) or 41(2) UN Charter is not legally possible.[200] What is more, determination of a breach was – until recently – reserved for the merits.[201] This *ex posto facto* determination, ran counter to their anticipatory rationale and meant that a substantial amount of time would elapse until a determination of breach was made

196 ICJ, *LaGrand* (Germany v. United States) (Judgment) [2001] ICJ Rep 466, 502–3 [101]–[103]. Until then, it was debated whether the provision reflected a legal or a moral obligation of compliance. For a summary *see* Miles, *supra* note 39, 276ff.

197 ICJ, *Armed Activities on the Territory of the Congo* (DRC v Uganda) (Judgment) [2005] ICJ Rep 168, 258 [263].

198 ICJ, *Construction of a Road* (Nicaragua v. Costa Rica) (Judgment) (Separate Opinion Judge Cançado Trindade) 39–40 [26]; M Mendelson, 'State Responsibility for Breach of Interim Protection Orders of the International Court of Justice' in D Sarooshi and M Fitzmaurice (eds), *Issues of State Responsibility before International Judicial Institutions* (Hart, 2003) 35; Rieter, *supra* note 87, 63.

199 In favor of the legality of countermeasures as a response to a breach of provisional measures M Lando, 'Compliance with Provisional Measures Indicated by the International Court of Justice' 8 (2017) *Journal of International Dispute Settlement* 22, 27–8, and Miles, *supra* note 39, 324–5; against K Oellers-Frahm, 'Article 41', in A Zimmermann, K Oellers-Frahm, Chr. Tomuschat and Chr. Tams (eds), *The Statute of the International Court of Justice: A Commentary* (OUP, 2012), 1026, 1068–9. M Alexianu holds that countermeasures may be taken also by third-parties to the dispute, especially when compliance with *erga omnes* obligations is sought, 'Third-Party "Provisional Countermeasures": A Proposal to Give Teeth to Provisional Measures' *Ejil:talk!* (20 March 2024).

200 Lando, *supra* note 199, 26ff.

201 See e.g. ICJ, *Alleged Violations of the 1955 Treaty of Amity, Economic Relations, and Consular Rights* (*Iran v. USA*), Preliminary Objections, Judgment, ICJ Reports 2021, 16 [13]. For a critique on how the ICJ may exercise its jurisdiction to assess compliance with provisional measures, *see* N Panagis, 'Jurisdictional Entanglement: the Relationship between the Jurisdiction over a Dispute and the Jurisdiction to Assess Compliance with Provisional Measures' 23 (2024) *The Law and Practice of International Courts and Tribunals* 7.

rendering compliance with them counter intuitive.[202] And when the Court was to make a relevant finding the usual remedy ordered was that of a declaration of a breach in the main judgment.[203] Only in extreme circumstances of non-compliance, equivalent to Nicaragua's stance in *Border Area,* the ICJ would go so far as to order compensation.[204] More intrusive compliance mechanisms, such as levying costs against the non-complying party according to Article 64 of the ICJ Statute,[205] awarding damages, withholding the judgment,[206] or implementing a 'public shame' system when referring to the UN General Assembly[207] have never been utilized by the Court.

Nevertheless, this is subject to change. In order to better the compliance record with provisional measures and to push further the autonomous nature of interim protection, the ICJ instituted a novel implementation mechanism. According to Article 11 of its Internal Judicial Practice, the Court will respond institutionally and swiftly to any issues of compliance with interim protection Orders through the formation of a three-member *ad hoc* Committee. Its mandate is to 'assist the Court in monitoring the implementation of provisional measures' and also to 'recommend [...] potential options for the Court' which will adopt any relevant decision. While not provided expressly, it stands to reason that such Court decisions may be different from the final judgment on the merits. With this provision, the Court hits two birds with one stone. It determines by its own initiative –

202 Institut de Droit International, 'Provisional Measures' (78)2017 *Annuaire de l'Institut de Droit international* 107 (Cançado Trindade).

203 ICJ, *Application of the International Convention for the Suppression of the Financing of Terrorism and of the International Convention on the Elimination of All Forms of Racial Discrimination* (*Ukraine vs Russia*) Judgment of 31 January 2024, 111 [401]; Miles, *supra* note 39, 329. It has been argued that the reputational cost accompanying a declaration of breach renders this reparation tool an effective sanction, P Palchetti, 'Making and enforcing procedural law at the International Court of Justice', 61 (2019) *QIL Zoom-out,* 5, 18; *contra* G Zyberi, 'Provisional Measures of the International Court of Justice in Armed Conflict Situations' 23 (2010) *Leiden Journal of International Law* 581.

204 ICJ, *Certain Activities Carried Out by Nicaragua in the Border Area* (*Costa Rica v. Nicaragua*) *and Construction of a Road in Costa Rica along the San Juan River* (*Nicaragua v. Costa Rica*), Judgment, ICJ Reports 2015, 665, 712–4 [51]–[53].

205 Ibid. Joint Declaration of Judges Tomka, Greenwood and Sebutinde and Judge ad hoc Dugard, 757 [8]. Proposed for the first time by G Barile, 'Osservazioni sulla indicazione di misure cautelari nei procedimenti davanti alla Corte internazionale di giustizia' 4 (1952) *Comunicazioni e Studi* 154.

206 Both have been proposed by Schachter but do not seem to have a basis in the Statute, O Schachter, 'International Law in Theory and Practice: General Course in Public International Law' (1982) 178 *Recueil des Cours* 223

207 Lando, *supra* note 199, 50.

irrespective of any claim by the parties – whether provisional measures have been complied with, possibly also in the absence of jurisdiction on the merits of the dispute. More interestingly for present purposes, irrespective of the invocation of responsibility by the injured party, the Court will impose sanctions on the non-complying party *sua sponte*. In this way, the ICJ attests that the regime of responsibility for non-compliance with provisional measures functions autonomously from the respective regime of responsibility for the breaches alleged in the main claim. Whether this change will promote a new attitude towards compliance with provisional measures and enhance the effectiveness of this mechanism remains to be seen. But, given the Court's reluctance to use it in *Gambia v. Myanmar* where Myanmar is allegedly not complying with its reporting obligation as per the 2020 Order,[208] casts some early doubts as to the willingness of the ICJ to make use of this mechanism to pressure non-compliant States. All in all, bindingness is not a guarantee of compliance,[209] rather it is only one of the possible sources of pressure towards non-compliant States.

Further, another factor testifying to the low pressure exercised on States to comply with an interim protection Order is the Court's limited *de jure* or legitimate authority when adjudicating provisional measures. That is, the extent to which a court is justified in exercising its authority over the parties.[210] Legitimate authority derives in international judicial dispute settlement from an act of delegation, and essentially justifies the court's granted competence to resolve a dispute in a binding fashion.[211] Given the consensual form of international adjudication, this delegation suggests that States willingly concede part of their sovereignty to judicial determination,[212] and at the same time 'no State is obliged to [...] give an account of itself to any

208 While little public information on the reports submitted by Myanmar is available, there is little doubt that there is a lack of compliance, Pr. Pillai, 'The Gambia v. Myanmar and Ukraine v. Russian Federation: A Tale of Two Cases at the International Court of Justice' *OpinioJuris* (14 July 2022).

209 J d'Aspremont, 'Bindingness' in J d'Aspremont and S Singh (eds) *Concepts for International Law* (Edward Elgar, 2019), 67, 78.

210 K Gorobets, (2022) *Contemplating an Uneven Landscape: The Authority of International Law* (PhD Thesis, University of Groningen), 78.

211 A Bradley and J Kelley, 'The Concept of Delegation' 71 (2008) *Law and Contemporary Problems* 1; Y Shany, 'Chapter 2: Jurisdiction as Delegated Authority' in *Questions of Jurisdiction and Admissibility before International Courts and Tribunals* (CUP, 2015), 22ff; I Hurd, 'Authority and International Courts: A Comment on "Content-Independent" Social Science', in International Court Authority, *supra* note 180, 422, 426.

212 J Crawford, *Brownlie's Principles of Public International Law* (OUP, 2019), 697.

international tribunal'.[213] Of course, in cases of genuine expression of consent this may naturally amount to recognition of an obligation to comply and eventually lead to compliance.[214] However, provisional measures are indicated after only a *prima facie* examination of the consent requirement and hence any pronouncement may be questioned by the losing side as lacking such authority. This is more so in the context of a multi-*forum* litigation strategy, where the establishment of consent is *ab initio* defective and defendants are already negatively inclined towards affirming the *de jure* authority of the Court.[215] *Qatar v. UAE* is a case in point. The Court's reluctance to interpret Articles 1(1) and 22 CERD in its 2018 Order gave the UAE a strong foothold to question the ICJ's competence to rule on the case and refuse compliance with the Court's ruling.[216]

Overall, the answer to the question posed above is a negative one. When defective consent is present, compliance is not expected, and provisional measures are not impactful when utilized as *ends*. It is now pertinent to turn the focus to the use of provisional measures as *means* and examine whether in such instances interim protection may promote resolution of the dispute. When States request interim protection but in essence they squint towards other dispute settlement methods, clearly the main motivation underpinning the request is not immediate compliance with the ICJ's Order. The next Section claims that motivation must be sought in the ability to exert political influence and thus promote the resolution of the dispute through alternative mechanisms.

3.1.2 Provisional Measures as Means; Pursuing Strategic Benefits

By pursuing interim protection, the applicant State may not promote compliance effectively, nevertheless it may efficiently raise the cost of non-compliance via the exercise of political pressure. And, in this way, promote

213 M Shaw, *Rosenne's Law and Practice of the International Court: 1920–2015*, vol.ii (Brill, 2016), 571.

214 For more on the *de jure* authority of international courts and its relationship with compliance and with *de facto* authority, see *infra* Chapter 2.

215 P Kovacs, 'Interim Measures in the Practice of the International Court of Justice and the International Criminal Court' in *Provisional Measures 2021*, *supra* note 59, 147, 166.

216 According to Qatar, the UAE had no intention to negotiate a way-out nor to modify its policy to comply with the ICJ's ruling, *Qatar v. UAE*, Memorial of the State of Qatar (25 April 2019), 350 [6.15]. According to the UAE, Qatar is hampering the UAE's attempts to assist Qatari citizens, so any compliance failure is attributable to the applicant, *Qatar v. UAE*, Request for Provisional Measures submitted by the UAE (22 March 2019) 21–4 [49]–[54].

State objectives indirectly, through alternative dispute resolution mechanisms.[217] As noted earlier with respect to *Qatar v. UAE*, political pressure will likely derive from non-legal mechanisms too, but, at the same time, it would be unjust to downplay the role performed by international judicial bodies in this respect.[218] It may be that such institutions have *ab initio* a limited role to play in the resolution of an inter-State dispute where no consent is provided by the respondent. This is more so in disputes involving Islamic law States[219] that have a preference toward non-confrontational dispute settlement and are less willing to accept the authority of international judicial bodies.[220] Nevertheless, due to their peculiar characteristics, provisional measures may prove to be an efficient mechanism for the promotion of State objectives when utilized as *means*. First, they may readjust the balance of bargaining power in favor of the requesting State, second, they may quickly generate reputational costs for the respondent, and finally, they may open up unwelcome possibilities for both parties.[221] This is not a closed list though. On top of those enumerated *infra*, provisional measures offer certain benefits that pertain to international dispute resolution in general, such as the generation of domestic audience costs and the increase in the resolve of the winning side.[222] Nevertheless, the latter are not presented in further detail here, because they very rarely constitute the main reason for incorporating interim protection in a litigation strategy. For present purposes, it is

217 Similar argument with respect to UNCLOS, S McLaughlin Mitchell and A Owsiak, 'Judicialization of the Sea: Bargaining in the Shadow of UNCLOS' 115 (2021) *AJIL* 579.

218 For an overview of the courts' potential effects on interstate bargaining, see K Alter, 'Delegation to International Courts and the Limits of Recontracting Political Power' in Hawkins et al. (eds) *Delegation and Agency in International Organizations* (CUP, 2009), 312; K Alter, E Hafner-Burton and L Helfer, 'Theorizing the Judicialization of International Relations' 63 (2019) *International Studies Quarterly* 449.

219 I borrow Powell's definition of the term as: a State, a substantial part of whose official legal system is directly based on the Koran, EJ Powell, 'Islamic Law States and the International Court of Justice', 50 (2013) *Journal of Peace Research* 203.

220 EJ Powell, Islamic Law States and the Authority of the International Court of Justice: Territorial Sovereignty and Diplomatic Immunity, 79 (2016) *Law and Contemporary Problems*, 209, 217, 234. It is telling that the ICJ is the only international judicial institution to hear cases involving Islamic states, EJ Powell, *Islamic Law and International Law: Peaceful Resolution of Disputes* (Oxford University Press, 2020).

221 Leonhardsen, *supra* note 35.

222 Sh. Scott, 'Litigation versus dispute resolution through political processes', in N Klein (ed), *Litigating International Disputes: Weighing the Options* (CUP, 2014), 24. The relevant literature with respect to courts in general is vast. For a succinct, although somewhat outdated, overview see M Pollack, 'Political Science and International Adjudication' in *Oxford Handbook of International Adjudication*, *supra* note 132, 357.

important to relate costs and benefits to their legal characteristics as analyzed in the previous Section. And further assess whether utilizing provisional measures to promote strategic benefits in an indirect fashion may be considered abusive. Finally, it is equally important to examine to what extent such instrumentalization may have a spill-over effect to similarly situated third parties.

3.1.2.1 *Creating the Shadow of the Law*

First, a successful interim protection application functions as a temporary resolution of the dispute and as such it confers bargaining power to the requesting State. This happens as the normative force of provisional measures inevitably affects any future attempt to resolve the dispute. The so-called 'shadow of the law', advanced by Mnookin and Kornhauser, suggests that the outcome of any dispute settlement process will be influenced by the result or even the pendency of any relevant litigation and the presence and behavior of a third-party adjudicator.[223] In *Diallo* for example, the applicant requested the Court to delay the assessment of compensation in order to give the parties time to negotiate on the 'shadow' of the 2010 merits judgment.[224] While they operate in the background, provisional measures color any future attempt to settle and in this way they 'reverse the settlement games from domestic law by allowing for a unilateral request by the parties, which sees the legal dispute come first, the real negotiations subsequently'.[225] The introduction of institutional structures to a bargaining process and the concomitant change to the rules that govern this process constitutes perhaps the most significant strategic gain a State can expect to acquire from a successful interim protection request.

Second, ICJ provisional measures operate as an expedited dispute settlement mechanism. If the application is successful, within three months from the request, the parties interact on the basis of new legal relations. This swift reaction places the losing party in front of the reputational cost dilemma explained above, perhaps sooner than expected.[226] Further, the form of obligations created through the process of adjudication, public and highly visible commitments, exposes non-compliant States significantly. So, it has been

223 *Supra* note 35.

224 ICJ, *Ahmadou Sadio Diallo (Republic of Guinea v. Democratic Republic of the Congo)*, Merits, Judgment, ICJ Reports 2010, 639, 691[162]–[163].

225 Leonhardsen, *supra* note 35, 332.

226 Miles, *supra* note 39, 455.

forcefully argued that the inflicted reputational cost might cause States to seek a negotiated settlement.[227] An exemplary case in this respect is *Certain Documents and Data* where Australia sought an amicable settlement of the dispute after the ICJ provisionally held that it had interfered in the communication between Timor-Leste and its legal advisors. In this sense, a successful application for interim protection may generate pressure for settlement through the creation of a 'reputational trap'. As was the case with their use as *ends,* the effectiveness of this trap is, when used as *means*, context-dependent and the respondent's reaction to the indication of provisional measures may vary. They have taken their toll on Australia, they had no apparent effect on the Azerbaijani stance towards Armenia,[228] and caused the opposite effect from the intended on the US in its rift with Iran.[229] Also, the rare overturn of pronouncements in provisional measures regarding jurisdiction and plausibility at a later stage, allows the applicant to portray them as *faits accomplis* and hence generate extra pressure. All in all, by pressuring respondent States to adopt a position that may tarnish their public image, provisional measures function as an accelerator of settlement procedures.

Finally, the ICJ does not resolve a dispute in a vacuum, and it is attentive to any attempts at dispute resolution being pursued as the proceedings evolve. In principle, the Court has recognized the possibility of States pursuing alternative dispute settlement mechanisms even in parallel with the exercise of its functions.[230] In the same vein, it may secure acceleration of settlement also by inviting the parties to rethink their position with respect to the dispute while the Court's final judgment is pending. This is essentially

227 Leonhardsen, *supra* note 35, 330ff.

228 Despite signs in negotiations following the ICJ Order that Azerbaijan is willing to unblock transport (European Council, 'Press remarks by President Charles Michel following the trilateral meeting with President Aliyev of Azerbaijan and Prime Minister Pashinyan of Armenia' 14 May 2023, available at: https://shorturl.at/bppYO), the blockade of the Lachin road continues to this date (European Parliament, 'Question Time: Relations between Armenia and Azerbaijan, and the situation in Nagorno-Karabakh and at the Lachin corridor' 9 June 2023, available at: https://www.europarl.europa.eu/RegData/etudes/ATAG/2023/749774/EPRS_ATA(2023)749774_EN.pdf).

229 The ICJ 2018 Order, relying on the 1955 Treaty of Amity with Iran, ordered unanimously the US to cancel its recent sanctions against Iran, *Alleged Violation of the 1955 Treaty 2018 Order,* 33 [102]. The Trump administration withdrew from this treaty right after the ICJ Order and likely because of it, M Sahimi, 'A Century of Economic Blackmail, Sanctions and War against Iran' in S Davis and I Ness (eds) *Sanctions as War: Anti-Imperialist Perspectives on American Geo-Economic Strategy* (Brill, 2021), 165, 182.

230 ICJ, *Frontier Dispute* (*Burkina Faso v. Mali*), Provisional Measures, Order of 10 January 1986, ICJ Reports 1986, 3, 10 [24].

an extortion mechanism, achieved through a warning from the Court that dire consequences may ensue should a party continue unaltered its course of action. Miles considers this an enunciation of the 'proceed at own risk' principle,[231] while for Rosenne mere advice from the Court.[232] Either way, it is up to discussion whether this way to promote out-of-court settlement falls within the ICJ's dispute settlement role.[233] Especially, when such promotion of alternative resolution of the dispute occurs in an overt fashion via *obiter dicta*. This stratagem precipitated settlement in *Great Belt* where the Court indicated with respect to Denmark's construction of a bridge over an international channel, that 'the possibility cannot and should not be excluded a priori of a judicial finding that such works must not be continued or must be modified or dismantled'.[234] Similar comments were made in *Pulp Mills*[235] and in *Construction of a Road*[236] but they did not affect the parties' disposition towards dispute resolution as both States took the risk of ignoring the Court's pronouncement. They may not have been effective in fact, however, the Court's *dicta* put Argentina and Costa Rica respectively in the position of calculating afresh the costs of continuing their course of action and rethinking the possibility of early settlement.

3.1.2.2 *An Abusive Litigation Strategy?*

Pursuing such goals that extend beyond the protective scope of Article 41, begs the question whether it is abusive to do so in extreme cases. The invocation of an abuse of process objection may form part of the litigation strategy itself.[237] Before the ICJ, abuse of process has been alleged mainly in relation to the use

231 Miles *supra* note 39, 448–9.

232 Sh. Rosenne, *Provisional Measures in International Law: The International Court of Justice and the International Tribunal for the Law of the Sea* (OUP, 2014), 213.

233 Ibid 213–4; ICJ, *Passage through the Great Belt* (*Finland v. Denmark*), Provisional Measures, 29 July 1991, ICJ Reports 1991, 12 Separate Opinion of Vice-President Oda, 25.

234 *Passage through the Great Belt 1991 Order*, 19 [31].

235 ICJ, Pulp Mills on the River Uruguay (Argentina v. Uruguay), Provisional Measures, Order of 13 July 2006, ICJ Reports 2006, 113, 133 [78]: Uruguay necessarily bears all risks relating to any finding on the merits that the Court might later make [...] the Court points out that their construction at the current site cannot be deemed to create a fait accompli.

236 *Construction of a Road 2013 Order*, 404 [23]: should Costa Rica's construction activities continue, in particular on the 41-km stretch of road running along the San Juan River upstream from its intersection with the San Carlos River, there is a possibility that Nicaragua's right to be free from transboundary harm, which it seeks to protect by the second provisional measure requested, may be further affected.

237 R Kolb, *Good Faith in International Law* (2017), 221. See also: Fr. Baetens, 'Abuse of Process and Abuse of Rights Before the ICJ: Ever More Popular, Ever Less Successful?', *EJIL: Talk!* (15 October 2019).

of incidental proceedings due to their 'highly disruptive nature in the judicial process'.[238] However, the alleged conduct has never been recognized as abusive. The ICJ has not provided any definition of what ought to be considered an abuse of process, but it has been defined elsewhere as

> the use of procedural instruments or rights by one or more parties for purposes that are alien to those for which the procedural rights are established, especially for a fraudulent, procrastinatory or frivolous purpose, for the purpose of causing harm or obtaining an illegitimate advantage, for the purpose of reducing or removing the effectiveness of some other available process or for purposes of pure propaganda.[239]

From this all-encompassing definition it is evident that the list is indicative and some bad faith element must be evident for the foundation of a concomitant claim. Thus, the motive of influencing a different dispute settlement procedure, even if proven, is not as such sufficient to sustain abuse of process and additional evidence is necessary.

What this evidence may be remains unclear nevertheless, as ICJ jurisprudence is nebulous on this issue and the Court dispatches such objections without blinking an eye.[240] In fact, the only claim regarding an abusive use of provisional measures was made in *Certain Activities* by Costa Rica, since Nicaragua had – allegedly – requested the same measures five times in the context of the same judicial process.[241] It is worth noting that the ICJ did not even mention the allegation in its Order (*sic*). Most such claims have been made in the context of requests for preliminary objections and recently the Court indicated that any finding made in that context is applicable with respect to concomitant claims made in intervention requests.[242] There is no reason why this analogy should not extend to provisional measures also. According to well-settled caselaw, the ICJ will accept such a claim only in 'exceptional circumstances' for it is not inclined to enquire into the motivation behind the

238 Lemey, *supra* note 40, 9. She suggests that this allegation has become somewhat of a trend in ICJ proceedings and provides an exhaustive account of relevant practice until 2021, Ibid 8–10.

239 R Kolb, 'General Principles of Procedural Law', in *The Statute of the International Court of Justice: A Commentary* (OUP, 2019), 998.

240 This uncertainty was pointed out by Judge Koroma, ICJ, *Certain Activities Carried Out by Nicaragua in the Border Area (Costa Rica v. Nicaragua)*, Provisional Measures, Order of 8 March 2011, ICJ Reports 2011, Separate opinion of Judge Koroma, 32–3 [13].

241 *Construction of a Road*, Oral proceedings, Verbatim record CR 2013/29, 42–5.

242 *Allegations of Genocide*, Order of 5 June 2023, 12 [56]–[57].

request[243] nor to weigh the possible consequences deriving from the requesting State's conduct.[244] The only clarification as to the relevant threshold comes from *Bosnian Genocide*. In that case, the ICJ was ready to accept abuse of process when the sole motivation behind the claim was to delay the normal course of proceedings.[245] This logic will probably not work in provisional measures, because the proceedings before the Court run for a limited time and the ICJ will reply in a timely manner, notwithstanding recent complaints about the availability of resources to effectively do so.[246] Nevertheless, their disruptive nature as to the Court's overall workflow is evident, but this in itself is not good enough reason to consider their pursuit as abusive. Because the disruption is not caused on the delivery of justice in the particular case. So, whatever the principal motivation underpinning the provisional measures application, for the Court to reject it as abusive 'anything short of a brazen admission of guilt' will not do the trick.[247]

The overly high threshold in establishing abuse of process is strategically important and will likely induce respondent States to utilize this mechanism to go in the offensive. Either during the same proceedings or by instituting a new application for main proceedings. In recent history this has occurred three times; first, in the joined *Construction of a Road* and *Certain Activities* cases, second, in *Qatar v. UAE* and third, in *Application of CERD (Armenia v. Azerbaijan)* and *Application of CERD (Azerbaijan v. Armenia)*. In all three instances the ICJ did not grant the measures requested by the initial respondent while it did offer interim protection to the initial applicant. The conflict over Nagorno Karabakh is the most characteristic example in this respect. Despite the appearance in the Court's docket of two separate cases, these proceedings have been moving *in tandem*.[248] In this context, Azerbaijan

243 *Supra* note 36.

244 ICJ, *Certain Phosphate Lands in Nauru (Nauru v. Australia)*, Preliminary Objections, Judgment, ICJ Reports 1992, 240, 255 [38].

245 *Bosnian Genocide*, Preliminary Objections, ICJ Reports 1996, 622 [46]: 'solely designed to delay the normal course of the proceedings, without clarifying the legal situation in question.'

246 Donoghue, *supra* note 49, 10. Of note is the withdrawal of the interim protection request by Equatorial Guinea in its dispute with France in *Return of Property* 'so that the Court may settle the dispute at the earliest opportunity', ICJ, *Request Relating to the Return of Property Confiscated in Criminal Proceedings (Equatorial Guinea v. France)*, Order, 21 October 2022, General List no. 184, 2.

247 Miles, *supra* note 39, 469–70.

248 While they are based on distinct facts, it has been argued that their disconnection is mainly formal. For a short description of how the two applications interrelate see F Fontanelli, 'The Disputes Between Armenia and Azerbaijan: The CERD Compromissory Clause as a One-way Ticket to Hague' *Ejil:talk!* (11 November 2021).

filed two interim protection requests, reactionary to Armenia's respective requests and both Azerbaijani claims were evidently a strategic move to influence the proceedings initiated by Armenia. Reactionary because the requests by Azerbaijan were made a week after Armenia submitted its requests and both times they concerned allegations that were legally and – to some extent – factually unconnected to those of Armenia. It is safe to assume then, that Azerbaijan was not interested in its own applications for interim protection, but rather it intended with this move to score points in the other proceedings that were running in parallel. Put differently by Armenia's counsel: 'Azerbaijan plainly hopes that by bringing its own request for provisional measures, the Court will be tempted to treat the two requests as somehow equivalent and accord both sides similar treatment'.[249] Hence, the use of provisional measures as *means* is not a privilege reserved for the applicant. Respondents may also put forward their claims and in pursuance of a strategy of 'whataboutism', they hope to convey the image of the victim State and hence move the Court to rule in their favor in the proceedings that really matter, that is the main proceedings.

3.1.2.3 *The Spill-Over Effect of Strategic Benefits*

Article 59 of the ICJ Statute specifies that '[t]he decision of the Court has no binding force except between the parties and in respect of that particular case'. This rule limits the legal effect of ICJ rulings and provides an escape hatch for States, non-parties to the judicial dispute, to avoid Court-created international legal obligations. Nevertheless, this provision does not foreclose the impact of an ICJ ruling on the practice of third parties, especially similarly situated actors. What has been elsewhere been termed *erga omnes* effectiveness,[250] intermediate legal authority,[251] or 'ultra-compliance'.[252] According to Alter several factors suggest that, in general, the ICJ does not possess the ability to affect the behaviour and decisions of potential future litigants and government officials charged with implementing rules as interpreted by the Court.[253] But, isolated examples may prove otherwise. With respect to the case examined here it is pertinent to ask whether the indication of ICJ provi-

249 *Azerbaijan v. Armenia* Verbatim Record CR2021/27 (19 October 2021), 26.

250 L Helfer, 'The Effectiveness of International Adjudicators' in Alter et al., *supra* note 222, 464, 470–3.

251 Alter, Helfer and Madsen, *supra* note 180, 31.

252 R Howse and R Teitel, 'Beyond Compliance: Rethinking Why International Law Matters' 1 (2010) *Global Policy* 127.

253 K Alter, 'The International Court of Justice in Comparison: Understanding the Court's Limited Influence' 21 (2021) *Melbourne Journal of International Law* 1, 18.

sional measures was capable of inducing a settlement between Qatar and the UAE or, more broadly, affect the disposition of the other members of the Quartet in settling the dispute?

The question is important for a comprehensive understanding of the impact of provisional measures and hence of their usefulness when incorporated in a litigation strategy. But the answer can only be politically consequential, based on anecdotal evidence and thus speculative to such an extent that it is rendered unscientific. To the best of the writer's knowledge, no quantitative empirical studies have analyzed the effect of provisional measures on the behavior of States non-parties to a dispute.[254] It has been claimed that theoretically they have the capacity to generate political pressure and force third States to strategic readjustments,[255] albeit such claims possess questionable probative value. Characteristically, a handful of States decided to suspend arms trade with Israel after the beginning of the Gaza war,[256] but, reportedly, the relevant ICJ Order in *South Africa v. Israel* only influenced the respective decisions regarding weapons arriving from Belgium[257] and Japan.[258]

---

254 Ie. such studies have targeted the ECtHR, L Helfer and E Voeten, 'International Courts as Agents of Legal Change: Evidence from LGBT Rights in Europe' 68 (2014) *International Organization* 77, and the WTO, M Busch and E Reinhardt, 'Bargaining in the Shadow of the Law: Early Settlement in GATT/WTO Disputes' 24 (2000) *Fordham International Law Journal* 158.

255 Leonhardsen, *supra* note 35, 335.

256 UN Human Rights Office of the High Commissioner, 'Arms Exports to Israel Must Stop Immediately: UN Experts' *Press Release, Special Procedures* (23 February 2024) available at: https://www.ohchr.org/en/press-releases/2024/02/arms-exports-israel-must-stop-immediately-un-experts. In the Netherlands, such a governmental decision ensued after the ruling of a domestic court, L Castellanos-Jankiewicz, 'Dutch Court Halts F-35 Aircraft Deliveries for Israel' *Verfassungsblog*, 14 February 2024. Other States held individual assessments, see Press Release, *UK suspends around 30 arms export licences to Israel for use in Gaza over International Humanitarian Law concerns* (2 September 2024), available at: www.gov.uk/government/news/uk-suspends-around-30-arms-export-licences-to-israel-for-use-in-gaza-over-internationalhumanitarian-law-concerns.

257 Business and Human Rights Resource Centre, 'Belgium: Regional govt suspends arms export licenses to Israel, citing ICJ ruling ordering Israel to prevent genocidal acts' (6 February 2024), available at: https://www.business-humanrights.org/en/latest-news/belgium-regional-govt-suspends-arms-export-licenses-to-israel-citing-icj-ruling-ordering-israel-to-prevent-genocidal-acts/.

258 It was the private Japanese company Itochu, and not the State of Japan, that decided to cut ties with Israel, but this decision ensued after "[t]aking into consideration the International Court of Justice's order on 26 January, and that the Japanese government supports the role of the Court, [...]", "Japan's Itotchu to End Cooperation with Israel's Elbit amid Gaza War" *Reuters* (5 February 2024).

An array of factors may be relevant in this respect, some of them are contextual and only pertinent *ad hoc*, as *Qatar v UAE* demonstrates. First, whether third States are in the same legal position as the respondent. The issue of arms trade with Israel mentioned above, is particularly on point. Even if all States do not feel the pressure after the *South Africa v. Israel* Order that does not explicitly refer to this issue, third States will definitely feel compelled to halt arms exports after a concomitant Order in *Nicaragua v. Germany* where this issue lies at the heart of the matter. In the case at hand, this holds true only partially. To the extent that the sanctions adopted by all Quartet members were identical and all four adopted a common defense narrative it does. It does not, to the extent that Saudi Arabia, Egypt or Bahrain are not potential respondents in a similar procedure before this same court due to the lack of a jurisdictional basis. Second, whether Islamic law and international law are aligned with respect to the matters regulated by the Court, such as access to courts and education. The proposition that a potential disjuncture between international law and Islamic law is a factor limiting the effect of ICJ judgments on Islamic law States has been made forcefully elsewhere,[259] and it would exceed the remit of this study to assess the level of accordance with Islamic law in the present case. Finally, whether judicial proceedings that could be affected by the indication of provisional measures were looming against third States. As the next Section will demonstrate, the existence of such procedures may weigh in in the decision of third States to settle the case. In view of the above, it is likely that the 2018 ICJ Order caused some concern to Saudi Arabia, Egypt and Bahrain. To what extent though, if at all, it has pressured these States to seek settlement of their dispute is impossible to evaluate precisely.

What can be stated with certainty though – and this is the claim of the next, and final, Section – is that, overall, it was important that this Order formed part of a multi-*forum* litigation strategy. Because with the pending lawsuits before CERD, the PCA, the WTO and investment tribunals, the Quartet was subject to judicial scrutiny for the implementation of their sanctions against Qatar, and, as the Al-'Ula Declaration shows, all four States were not indifferent to the outcome of such procedures. The impact of provisional measures lies, as explained *supra* in their capacity to generate pressure, and this has been the case in *Qatar v UAE* also because of the interaction of ICJ provisional measures with other judicial proceedings. Thus, it is only logical for States to incorporate interim protection in a litigation strategy that would capitalize on

259 EJ Powell, 'The International Court of Justice and Islamic Law States: Territory and Diplomatic Immunity' in *International Court Authority*, *supra* note 180, 277, 288.

this and hence maximize the potential benefits deriving therefrom. The attention turns to this right away.

3.2 *Provisional Measures as Part of a Multi-*forum *Litigation Strategy*

Article II of the Al-'Ula Declaration suggests that Qatar's multi-*forum* litigation strategy eventually bore fruit and was used *per se* in the bargaining game as a bargaining chip and as a mechanism applying pressure on all sanctioning States. According to this provision, all signatory States were 'committed to bringing an end to any claims, complaints, measures, protests, objections or disputes of any sort against any other State party to the Declaration, including by dropping, withdrawing or rescinding them, and to stopping implementation of the measures'. But the four sanctioning States were not equally affected by Qatar's litigation strategy. In this respect, the Quartet can be in split into three different categories: the UAE was the sole respondent in the ICJ case and co-respondent with Bahrain and Saudi Arabia in most proceedings, consequently the most heavily influenced. Bahrain and Saudi Arabia were respondents in several non-ICJ judicial proceedings, none of which came to a close. Finally, Egypt was affected the least since it was involved only in the PCA proceedings, which did not last long and probably were of small economic interest when compared to the WTO cases or the investment arbitrations. Egypt went along with the whims of the other GCC States to settle the case, mostly with Saudi Arabia who it sees as a strong ally, and in an attempt to benefit commercially from Qatari investments it spearheaded the resumption of diplomatic relations with Qatar.[260] Against this background, this Section will examine how Qatar's decision to engage a plurality of judicial and quasi-judicial fora has promoted the signing of the Al-'Ula declaration.

3.2.1 *Qatar v. UAE*: Provisional Measures at Centre-Stage

The only institution that had made a legal determination of the measures before the Al-'Ula declaration was the ICJ with its interim protection 2018 Order. The Court held that the measures interfered with basic rights of Qataris as they are protected under Article 5 CERD.[261] And it ordered the reunification of mixed (Qatari-Emirati) families, the continuation of studies for Qatari students studying at the UAE, and the uninhibited access to UAE courts for Qataris.[262] The next salvo in this dispute, the Court's 2019 Order on provisional measures requested by the UAE was also favorable to Qatar. The UAE sought

260 Cornwell and Ghantous, *supra* note 167.

261 *Qatar v. UAE 2018 Order*, 427 [54].

262 Ibid, 433–4 [79].

a withdrawal of Qatar's CERD communication, and a halt of Qatar's efforts to aggravate the dispute and to compromise the implementation of the 2018 Order.[263] The Court considered UAE's claims unrelated to plausible rights and saw no reason to alter the 2018 Order which, according to the Court, adequately regulated the relations between the parties.[264] In both occasions, the ICJ had deferred for the merits the question whether discrimination on the basis of nationality was *rationae materiae* within the scope of the CERD. But, as noted earlier, given the low expectation that the Court would reverse its decision on jurisdiction at a subsequent stage, the UAE probably considered the battle on jurisdiction to be lost. This was exacerbated by the CERD committee's 2019 twin decisions in the communications against the UAE and Saudi Arabia whereby it labeled the nationality issue as an admissibility issue[265] and held that differences on treatment based on nationality fall within the scope of the Convention.[266] And, because the ICJ complaint was based on the same legal instrument as the one before the CERD, if the ICJ were to follow the CERD committee's logic, the prospect of two – ICJ and CERD – unfavorable rulings on the merits was more than likely and loomed large for the Quartet.

By that time, no other institution had rendered a final decision on the dispute. Proceedings before the PCA and investment tribunals are confidential, so no valuable information is extractable from either of them. But drama ensued before the WTO dispute settlement mechanism. In summer 2017, Qatar lodged complaints against three sanctioning States (the UAE, Bahrain and Saudi Arabia) related to the direct effects of the 2017 sanctions in trade in goods (claiming violations of the GATT), services (violations of the GATS), and in trade-related intellectual property rights (violations of the TRIPS).[267] The cases against Bahrain and Saudi Arabia ended in 2017 at the consultations stage. However, the case against the UAE was about to come to a close at the

---

263 *Qatar v. UAE 2019 Order*, 366 [12].

264 Ibid. 371–2 [32].

265 CERD, *Decision on the jurisdiction of the Committee in respect of the inter-State communication submitted by Qatar against Saudi Arabia* (27 August 2019), UN Doc C/99/5, 8 [52]; CERD, *Decision on the jurisdiction of the Committee in respect of the inter-State communication submitted by Qatar against the UAE* (27 August 2019), UN Doc C/99/3, 11–2 [56].

266 CERD, *Decision on the admissibility of the Committee in respect of the inter-State communication submitted by Qatar against Saudi Arabia* (27 August 2019), UN Doc C/99/6, 3 [19]; CERD, *Decision on the admissibility of the Committee in respect of the inter-State communication submitted by Qatar against the UAE* (27 August 2019), UN Doc C/99/4, 13 [63].

267 WTO case nos: *DS526* (v. UAE), *DS527* (v. Bahrain) and *DS528* (v. Saudi Arabia).

panel stage – the panel report was expected in the first quarter of 2021 – before it was dropped by virtue of the Al-'Ula declaration. There are grounds to believe that the UAE dodged another unfavorable ruling by reaching a mutually agreed solution at the GCC Summit.

This is so because in the meantime, two procedures pertaining to the diplomatic rift were brought before WTO organs and the findings therein hinted at the non-conformity of the Quartet's measures with WTO law. The first procedure, terminated by virtue of the Al-'Ula declaration, between Qatar and Saudi Arabia concerned Saudi Arabia's alleged failure to provide effective judicial protection to intellectual property rights held by the Qatari company *beIN*.[268] By virtue of the 2017 sanctions, Saudi Arabia prevented *beIN* from obtaining Saudi legal counsel to enforce its intellectual property rights through civil enforcement procedures before Saudi courts. And this was deemed by a WTO panel in 2020 to be in violation of the TRIPS agreement,[269] although this finding was never verified by the appellate body due to the suspension of the proceedings. Two things stand out from this. First, Saudi Arabia's refusal throughout the proceedings to interact or engage in any way with Qatar, the Panel shifting to an exclusively written format and modifying accordingly its Working Procedure. And second, the alignment between the WTO Panel's report and the ICJ's interim protection Order concerning the illegal nature of the restricted access to domestic tribunals under WTO law and CERD respectively.

The second procedure was short-lived, but of heightened significance. In January 2019, the UAE claimed that the Qatari government had imposed a ban on the import, sale and distribution of Emirati products.[270] The complaint relates to Qatari retaliatory measures that prohibited retailers and pharmacies there from selling certain goods originating in or exported from the UAE. Adopted in May and June 2018 as countermeasures to the 2017 sanctions,[271] the measures at hand had an effect analogous to that of their 2017 counterparts. Unsurprisingly, soon thereafter they were withdrawn and on 8 August 2019, the UAE discontinued the case.[272] The swift revocation of the 2018 Qatari measures once the UAE complaint at the WTO was filed, is impor-

268 WTO case no: *DS567* (v. Saudi Arabia).

269 WTO Panel Report, *Saudi Arabia – Measures Concerning the Protection of Intellectual Property Rights*, WTO Doc no. WT/DS567/R (16 July 2020), 124 [8.1].

270 WTO case no: DS576 (v. Qatar).

271 *Qatar – Certain Measures Concerning Goods from the UAE*, 'Request for the Establishment of a Panel by the UAE', WTO Doc. no. WT/DS576/2, 16 April 2019, 1 [8].

272 *Qatar – Certain Measures Concerning Goods from the UAE*, 'Communication from the UAE', WTO Doc no. WT/DS576/3, 9 August 2019.

tant for many reasons. First, it suggests that these measures were considered by Qatar to be incompatible with WTO law. If this was not the case, Qatar would not have rescinded them and would have been willing to engage in a legal battle that it might have won. Further, to the extent that the Qatari measures had a similar market effect to the concomitant Quartet measures, the latter would have had the same fate when examined by a WTO panel. Finally, the revocation is testament to the political pressure exercised upon States by judicial dispute settlement bodies. The exchange of complaints before the trade body was a first-class opportunity for both parties to the dispute to give their respective grievances a public airing. Keeping in effect measures that are not WTO-compliant though, and thus being exposed to an open condemnation by a WTO panel, lay in sharp contrast with Qatar's attempt to construct the image of the boycotted victim. Characteristically, Qatar's Ministry of Foreign Affairs presented the UAE's withdrawal from the case as a win for Qatar since the latter 'continues to, uphold and comply with its obligations under the WTO' and concluded that 'the allegations made against Qatar were false and baseless.'[273] So, the end of the WTO saga found Qatar with two pending complaints with good chances of success, and strategically, it exposed the image-making strategy pursued by Qatar.

Timing was of the essence for the fruition of Qatar's litigation strategy. Less than one month after the signing of the declaration, the ICJ held not to have jurisdiction on the inter-State dispute. Qatar would have lost all benefits from the resort to the ICJ since lack of jurisdiction would automatically mean the termination of the provisional measures indicated. As all other procedures were pending at the time, pressure from ongoing litigation was at its peak in January 2021. It is pertinent to examine then the different ways in which Qatar benefited from its litigation strategy to arrive at the signing of the Al-'Ula declaration.

3.2.2 Maximizing Strategic Benefits

Judicial proceedings are objectively a nuisance for any litigant, especially for respondents. Even more so for States that are involved in this capacity in high-stakes international disputes.[274] Respondents are dragged before a third-party and must bear all the costs that accompany a judicial procedure of interna-

273 Qatar Ministry of Foreign Affairs, *Qatar Prevails over the UAE in trade dispute at the WTO*, Statement of 9 August 2019, available at: https://www.mofa.gov.qa/en/statements/qatar-prevails-over-the-uae-in-trade-dispute-at-the-wto.

274 The type of disputes likely to end up in multi-*forum* litigation are those labelled as 'high politics' or these related to national-interest and security of concern to governments,

tional nature: hiring and paying lawyers, getting involved in the construction of a litigation strategy (e.g. the appointment of arbitrators), communicating with the judicial body etc. The level of nuisance will be context-dependent, although two factors are certainly taken into consideration. How many resources does the State estimate to spend in the course of these proceedings? What will be the reputational and material cost any ensuing court proncouncements? Evidently, when judicial procedures are multiplied this nuisance is exacerbated. This policy consideration may not be the main justification underlying the principles of *lis pendens* and *abuse of process* according to which the pursuit of parallel proceedings may be considered illegal. It is, nevertheless, a tangential inconvenience, so it is not surprising that the UAE argued before the ICJ and CERD that it should not be 'required to simultaneously defend itself against the same allegation in two overlapping and parallel procedures'.[275] First of all then, in and of itself multi-*forum* litigation is unpleasant for respondents and such a prospect may affect the respondent's willingness to settle, all the more when the applicant has chances of success.

Qatar v. UAE testifies that, when examined in the context of a multi-*forum* litigation strategy, an ICJ interim protection application is transformed into a more impactful mechanism than when examined as a standalone action. This is so for two main reasons analyzed in the previous Chapter. First, if such an application is successful it puts on the table the threat of a domino effect of like-minded rulings. And in turn, this threat may be used as a bargaining chip. Since the adjudication of ICJ interim protection requests is a fast-track procedure, it will likely precede other rulings. Through its connection with the latter and its capacity to influence them, it maximizes the pressure exercised by judicial mechanisms towards non-complaint States. As alluded to by the counsel for Ukraine during the provisional measures oral round in *Ukraine v. Russia,* the Court holds such an important role in the international system, that its Order may be the "essential spark that will inspire other competent international organs and agencies to take the further steps necessary".[276] In this sense, provisional measures are utilized as *means*. Second, due to its image-making effect, any interim protection request promotes a particular

---

political leaders, and militaries, K Alter and M Rask Madsen 'The International Adjudication of Mega-Politics' 84 (2022) *Law and Contemporary Problems* 1.

275 *Supplemental response of the United Arab Emirates to the Request made by the State of Qatar pursuant to article 11 of the CERD, dated 29 November 2018*, as quoted in: *Jurisdiction of the Inter-State Communication submitted by Qatar against the UAE*, UN Doc. CERD/C/99/3 (30 August 2019), fn 27; *Qatar v UAE, Request for Provisional Measures by the UAE,* 18 [41].

276 *Ukraine v. Russia, Genocide, Verbatim Record 2022/5*, 61 [16] (Koh).

strategic narrative.[277] So that opposing States are pressured to abandon any counternarrative. In this way, provisional measures are utilized – as *ends* – for the pressure they generate, and not for their connection with other proceedings. By pursuing a multi-*forum* litigation strategy, thus by increasing the judicial mechanisms that are used as platforms of communication or as agents of pressure, this image-making potential is maximized. *In casu*, it is debatable whether Qatar's litigation strategy in fact promoted settlement in one of the aforementioned ways. Beyond dispute is however the following: even if this was not the case, Qatar still had in hand a negotiatory tool. Because a settlement whereby the Quartet decides to repel the 2017 sanctions without at the same time asking for anything in return would have been one-sided and one that the Quartet would not likely endorse, or project to third parties. Then, the usefulness of multiple proceedings is not exhausted in promoting settlement via exercising pressure, but it extends to providing bargaining chips that may facilitate the settlement process.

In *Qatar v. UAE* the relationship between the ICJ and CERD procedures was such that the two UN bodies were seemingly engaged in a mutual feedback loop. Besides, both complaints hinged on the same factual and legal basis. The ICJ 2018 and 2019 Orders influenced the CERD decisions on jurisdiction and admissibility against the UAE and Saudi Arabia, and, in turn, the latter were expected to influence the ICJ final judgment on the merits. The CERD decisions on admissibility interpreted Article 22 of the Convention in accordance with relevant ICJ caselaw, and then concluded that discrimination based on 'nationality' – an issue the ICJ had deferred for the merits – is protected by Article 1(1) of the Convention. In view of CERD's position as a specialized body and the ICJ's previous position in *Diallo* 'that it should ascribe great weight to the interpretation adopted by this independent body [nb the Human Rights Committee] that was established specifically to supervise the application of that treaty', a judgment upholding ICJ jurisdiction along the lines of CERD's decisions was likely.[278] So, some were perplexed when the ICJ *ex posto facto* arrived at a different interpretation of Article 1(1),[279] and consequently this

277 A Miskimmon, B O'Loughlin and L Roselle define a strategic narrative as: 'a means to construct a shared meaning of the past, present and future of international politics to shape the behavior of international and national actors' A Miskimmon, B O'Loughlin, and L Roselle, 'Introduction' in A Miskimmon, B O Loughlin, and L Roselle (eds), *Forging the World: Strategic Narratives and International Relations* (University of Michigan Press, 2017) 1, 2.

278 *Diallo*, 664[66].

279 K Pan, 'Difference Between the ICJ and the CERD Committee: A Comment on the Application of the International Convention on the Elimination of All Forms of Racial

stance generated a debate on which institution should be the lead agency for the interpretation of the CERD Convention.[280] In view also of the Report by the UN Special Rapporteur on Unilateral Sanctions which held the Quartet's sanctions incompatible with international law, it was possible that UN organs would hold a unified stance with respect to the merits of the issue and not contradict each other.[281] The strong possibility of this domino of unfavorable rulings by UN organs, all based upon a common stance, is important because it bears the risk of elevating such position to *the* UN position on the matter. And this is ultimately a more serious stain than that imposed by a single adverse ICJ Order or Judgment. Overall, the Court performs its functions within the general framework of the political organization of the international society, and when understood as part of the UN machinery its outputs acquire a different political *gravitas*.

Further, the other parallel procedures were lesser attached to the ICJ case legally. Though factually all circled around the consequences of the imposed sanctions. At this point, not much can be said about the PCA proceedings since they are confidential and no relevant caselaw is available in order to speculate how the ICJ Orders may influence these proceedings. With respect to the WTO and investment proceedings though, the ICJ's authority might have contributed to influencing them to align with any relevant interim ICJ determinations. The only available WTO ruling, the panel report in the *beIN* case, confirms this. Ditto, the investment tribunals will likely take into consideration any relevant ICJ determination if not for legal reasons,[282] for reasons of legitimacy. And both the investment and WTO claims exercise considerable pressure on respondents, because the financial repercussions from either one are substantial even for the wealthy Gulf States.[283] The importance of the WTO

Discrimination (Qatar v. United Arab Emirates) Case' 21 (2022) *Chinese Journal of International Law* 195.

280 G Ulfstein, 'Who is the Final Interpreter in Human Rights: the ICJ v CERD?', *EJIL:Talk!* (22 February 2021).

281 As the 2020 Order in *Gambia v. Myanmar* demonstrates, the ICJ takes seriously under consideration relevant findings by UN organs, 23–4 [55]–[56].

282 Arguably, this can be the case if the *Qatar Airways* tribunals follow the decision in *HICEE v. Slovakia* regarding the derivative nature of investor rights (UNCITRAL, PCA Case No. 2009–11). This tribunal has claimed that inter-State obligations (e.g. ICJ pronouncements) will have 'effect on an investor claiming derivatively through the rights procured for it by one of those States', Ibid [139].

283 The claim on the investment arbitration is allegedly 5 billion dollars, *supra* note 33. And the financial repercussions of non-compliance with a WTO ruling is the imposition of trade sanctions or countermeasures that disrupt trade, according to Article 3.7 of the WTO's Dispute Settlement Understanding, WTO, *Dispute Settlement System Training*

cases for international trade was evident from the number of participating third parties in these processes.[284] Third party governments may pressure the respondent to comply by increasing the publicity of the dispute, monitoring implementation, and making enforcement more likely.[285] The investment system also offers many reasons why States may be pressured to comply with awards for damages, notwithstanding voices that recognize a gap between the investment regime's authority and effectiveness:[286] attraction of investment, reputational considerations, pressure or fear of retribution from the investor's home State or from other international actors, avoidance of penalties in the sovereign bond arena, appease of domestic political constituencies.[287] In this way, Qatar was able to benefit from the extra pressure exercised upon the Quartet via the ensuing possibility of a domino effect of unfavorable judgments within the UN and by other dispute settlement mechanisms.

In parallel, provisional measures may be utilized in a communication strategy as an effective means to mount a public relations campaign. In an attempt to increase their international legitimacy and influence international affairs, States are strategically communicating their position as a means of persuasion.[288] In disputes that develop *in tandem* with the judicial proceedings, States will instrumentalize the possibility offered by the oral round in ICJ provisional measures to publicly elaborate judicial claims while the tensions are still high. ICJ provisional measures have arguably been used – and possibly abused[289] – as a means of giving a public airing to a State's claims in *Legality of Use of Force* as noted above,[290] the *2002 Armed Activities on the Territory of the*

Module: Chapter 6, available at: https://www.wto.org/english/tratop_e/dispu_e/disp_settlement_cbt_e/c6s1p1_e.htm.

284 L Peritz, 'When are International Institutions Effective? The Impact of Domestic Veto Players on Compliance with WTO Rulings' 64 (2020) *International Studies Quarterly* 220, 221. In the Qatar-UAE case that was about to come to a close at the panel stage 18 third parties intervened, and in the Qatar-Saudi Arabia *beIn* case 19.

285 L Johns, and Kr. Pelc, 'Who Gets to Be in the Room? Manipulating Participation in WTO Disputes' 68 (2014) *International Organization* 663.

286 E Gaillard and I Mitrev Penushliski, 'State Compliance with Investment Awards' 35 (2020) *ICSID Review* 540.

287 M Hirsch, 'Explaining Compliance and Non-Compliance with ICSID Awards: The Argentine Case Study and a Multiple Theoretical Approach' 19 (2016) *Journal of International Economic Law* 681.

288 Miskimmon *et al.*, *supra* note 277, 2. See *infra* Chapter 2, Section 4(C).

289 Chr. Gray, 'The Use and Abuse of the International Court of Justice: Cases concerning the Use of Force after *Nicaragua*' 14 (2003) *EJIL* 867, 888ff.

290 *Supra* note 187.

Congo[291] and the *1995 Nuclear Tests* applications.[292] In such cases, applicant States were not interested in how the ICJ ruling may affect other proceedings, rather they intended to capitalize on the open and public procedure before the Court to utilize provisional measures as *ends*. Without pushing the argument further, the UAE complained about this in the oral proceedings,[293] for it was worried that Qatar may maximize its soft power, or its 'ability to obtain preferred outcomes by attraction rather than coercion or payment'.[294]

By communicating the dispute to many audiences and by capitalizing on the capacity of provisional measures to provide bargaining chips, States instrumentalize this mechanism in an attempt to delegitimize the opponent's position. With this in mind, Qatar utilized international judicial *fora* as part of an official communication strategy so as to convey an image of transparency and legality, and further to create a narrative whereby it respects international commitments and takes seriously the international institutions it belongs to.[295] Indisputably, such objectives are more easily attained, and the strategy is rendered more effective the more platforms are involved. When a claim reaches different audiences it may mobilize them, maximize its image-making potential and thus promote a certain strategic narrative. The added value of engaging judicial mechanisms as agents of communication, is that the essence of the narrative acquires a moral dimension: the State has been wronged to such an extent that it is committed to using the law in order to vindicate its rightful claim. Given the resources spent for the projection of claims via parallel recourse to international judicial mechanisms, it may be a costly means of communication. Albeit, because judicial platforms are independent third parties with the authority to dictate and apply the law, they constitute an appealing choice for a State's public diplomacy strategy.

291 ICJ, *Armed Activities on the Territory of the Congo* (*New Application: 2002*) (*Democratic Republic of the Congo v. Rwanda*) Provisionai Measures, Order, 10 July 2002, ICJ Reports 2002, 219.

292 France was forced to justify afresh its nuclear tests despite the Court not having jurisdiction to adjudicate, ICJ, *Request for an Examination of the Situation in Accordance with Paragraph 63 of the Court's Judgment of 20 December 1974 in the Nuclear Tests case* (*New Zealand v. France*), ICJ Reports 1995, 288.

293 *Supra* note 138.

294 J Nye, 'Soft power: the origins and political progress of a concept' 28 (2022) *The Journal of International Communication* 1.

295 AIG Santamaría, 'Qatar's communication strategy and the resolution of the diplomatic conflict in the Gulf' (2021) *Thematic dossier International Relations and Social Networks* 131, 140.

4 The Court as a Crisis-Manager

Back in early 2021, the continuation of Qatar's isolation was not seen in a positive light by either side. Qatar confronted unprecedented economic challenges after the blockade,[296] and the Quartet (especially Saudi Arabia) saw no benefit in prolonging division in the Gulf ahead of significant geopolitical changes for the region that demanded a united front.[297] At the time though, proceedings were ongoing before many judicial fora. The pendency of such proceedings gave Qatar bargaining leverage and gave the Quartet something to trade for in exchange for lifting the sanctions. If only for this, Qatar's multi-*forum* litigation strategy was instrumental in providing an escape hatch for both sides to the conflict.

ICJ provisional measures played a key role in this strategy. Their unique features render them a suitable option for addressing developing situations. But, the same factors that render ICJ provisional measures a fitting option for the applicant, are the ones chipping away the ICJ's *de jure* authority and expose their limited capacity to address developing situations.

First, the strategic use of ICJ interim protection in order to regulate a situation swiftly and with binding force, without, at the same time, going through a detailed examination of State consent, renders provisional measures a *prima facie* attractive judicial mechanism for applicant States. In particular, the possibility of awarding provisional measures in cases where the respondent would object to the exercise of the Court's jurisdiction ('defective consent') renders this mechanism particularly pertinent in the context of a multi-*forum* litigation strategy. On the other hand, the epidermic examination of a situation (*prima facie* examination of jurisdiction and weak elaboration of the factual background) limits the *de jure* authority of an ICJ Order and makes it easier for States to resist any consideration of the Court's pronouncements.

Further, the expansion of the purposes fulfilled by provisional measures, and hence of the measures indicated, is another sign that States will resort to the Court in order to capitalize on the integrated resolution of the dispute.

---

296 Arguably, the ensuing transformation of Qatar's economy renders this rift a 'blessing in disguise' for the small peninsular State, albeit at the time it was seen as a nuisance, S Umar and S Ghurab, 'The 2017 Gulf Crisis and Changes in Qatar's Economic Landscape' in M Rahman and A Al-Azm, *Social Change in the Gulf Region* (Springer, 2023), 457.

297 These changes were mainly Joe Biden's arrival in the White House and the changing stance of Iran towards Gulf States, A Jacobs, 'Gulf Arab Reconciliation Hides Simmering Tensions' *InternationalCrisisGroup* (12 July 2023).

Provisional measures are increasingly being utilized as a fast-track way of managing a dispute. States have picked up on this potential of the mechanism and are tactically using it to advance arguments on the merits in an attempt to create *faits accomplis*. But again, the ICJ's choice to adjudicate measures beyond what could be justified according to the stated purpose of this mechanism, does not favor the Court's legitimate authority and the future compliance with such Orders. So, the already poor compliance record with provisional measures Orders is only expected to become poorer.

Finally, a third feature that renders provisional measures such an appealing choice is their highly disruptive nature. They derange the power equilibrium between the parties as they may cause respondents to abruptly and unexpectedly enter into a defensive position. However, they also disrupt the Court's workflow and the sheer number of such requests has strained the Court's resources.[298]

Not surprisingly then, State interest in resorting to this mechanism has lately peaked. In developing situations the expectation that the Court will assess the legality of State behavior while the crisis is ongoing ranks high in the priorities of applicant States. In his latest address to the UNGA, the incumbent President of the Court himself disapproved the attempt of applicant States to put forward arguments on the merits via provisional measures.[299] It comes as no surprise that, when instrumentalizing interim protection States expect from the ICJ to act as a crisis-manager. The barrage of requests with respect to the Gaza conflict and the Nagorno Karabakh war testify to this. The engagement of the Court in the ongoing persecution of the Rohingua people, in the large-scale torturing of detainees in Syria and possibly in the position of women in Afghanistan point to the same direction. The phenomenon of instrumentalization of provisional measures impacts the Court's docket: it accounts for the increase in applications, but also for the nature of cases that make their way to the Court as most of them are now presented as ongoing crises.

There are signs that the Court is aware of the trend to utilize provisional measures. The ICJ hinted lately that there are limits to this tactic. The summary rejection of South Africa's second request (12 February 2024) via a deci-

298 *Donoghue, supra* note 50, 8.

299 *Speech of HE Judge Nawaf Salam, President of the International Court of Justice, On the Occasion of the Seventy-Eighth Session of the United Nations General Assembly*, 24 October 2024, available at: https://www.icj-cij.org/sites/default/files/press-releases/0/000-20241024-sta-01-00-en.pdf, 6.

sion,[300] and without the holding of an oral round, suggests that the Court views the request as clearly unmeritorious, if not abusive. In this way, the Court puts the brakes on States that wish to strategically engage ICJ provisional measures as a reactionary mechanism to any development on the ground, and it also sends a message that in this way States 'may be entering into a world of diminishing returns'.[301] Further, the latest Order in *Nicaragua v. Germany* where the Court departed from its established approach and refused to indicate measures after an examination of the factual background – a scrutiny unbecoming for this stage of the proceedings[302] – is another indication that the Court is willing to get away from the 'straitjacket' of provisional measures so as to put the brakes on States that wish to capitalize on ICJ interim protection.

The ICJ is experiencing an unprecedented level of provisional measures requests. And this phenomenon must somehow be managed. In order to disincentivize their instrumentalization and thus uphold its legitimate authority, the Court is willing to sacrifice doctrinal consistency. Time will whether this approach will pay dividends, but in the present author's opinion the Court is likely caught in a catch-22 situation where in order to save face the ICJ may be opening new doors for criticism.

---

300 The Court's decision was published one day after Israel's reply to the request and consisted of three brief paragraphs, ICJ, *Application of the Convention on the Prevention and Punishment of the Crime of Genocide in the Gaza Strip* (*South Africa v. Israel*) 'Decision of the Court on South Africa's request for additional provisional measures', Decision No. 2024/16 (16 February 2024).

301 Becker, *supra* note 123. Albeit, South Africa's pressure eventually bore fruit as the Court modified its previous Order after the third request ICJ, *Application of the Convention on the Prevention and Punishment of the Crime of Genocide in the Gaza Strip* (*South Africa v. Israel*) Order on the Request for the Modification of the Order of 26 January 2024 Indicating Provisional Measures, General List no. 192 (28 March 2024).

302 M Becker, 'Nicaragua Comes Up Empty: Provisional Measures in Nicaragua v Germany at the ICJ' 1 May 2024, *Verfassungsblog*.

CHAPTER 4

Advisory Opinions: Bilateral Disputes in a Multilateral Setting

The One Where Postal Stamps Herald Justice

1 Introduction

On 28 September 2004, the Minister for Foreign Affairs of Mauritius, while addressing the United Nations General Assembly (UNGA), affirmed that "Mauritius has always favoured a bilateral approach in our resolve to restore our exercise of sovereignty over the Chagos Archipelago" and stated further that "we shall use all avenues open to us in order to exercise our full sovereign rights over the Chagos Archipelago".[1] The bilateral dispute between the UK and Mauritius regarding sovereignty over the Chagos Archipelago has given rise to a judicial saga before domestic and international tribunals that began in 1998 and has almost come to a close.[2] The events summarized below demonstrate that Mauritius has repeatedly sought adjudication or arbitration of that dispute and the UK has consistently refused its consent thereto.[3] Recurring, and perhaps central, issue in all proceedings before international courts has been the competence of these bodies to adjudicate on issues that – directly or indirectly – concern the question of sovereignty. Given the UK's stance, Mauritius has been playing a 'cat and mouse' game with international courts, whereby it has endeavored to cloth its sovereignty claim in an alternative legal garment without at the same time denying that a sovereignty dispute

1 United Nations General Assembly, Official Records of the General Assembly, Fifty-Ninth Session, 14th Plenary Meeting, Tuesday, 28 September 2004, 3 p.m. (Verbatim record A/59/PV.14) [extract], dossier No. 300.

2 On 3 October 2024, UK and Mauritius have reached a political agreement on the exercise of sovereignty over the Chagos archipelago. The agreement itself is not public and a concomitant legal agreement is still expected, Press Release, *UK and Mauritius joint statement* (3 October 2024) available at: https://www.gov.uk/government/news/joint-statement-between-uk-and-mauritius-3-october-2024.

3 For a detailed explanation of the background to the dispute see Arbitral Tribunal Constituted Under Annex VII of the United Nations Convention on the Law of the Sea, *Chagos Marine Protected Area Arbitration* (*Mauritius vs. UK*), PCA, Award, 18 March 2015, Chapter III; ICJ, *Legal Consequences of the Separation of the Chagos Archipelago from Mauritius in 1965,* Advisory Opinion, 25 February 2019, [92]–[131]. The summary provided here relies on these sources.

 | DOI:10.1163/9789004704565_005

exists between itself and the UK.[4] Since the UK has sturdily opposed any such determination, the turning point to promoting a settlement of the dispute has been the *Chagos* advisory opinion rendered by the ICJ on 25 February 2019. Thus, this Chapter will use the sovereignty dispute over the Chagos archipelago as a vehicle in order to demonstrate how ICJ advisory opinions can be incorporated in a multi-*forum* litigation strategy and constitute an effective dispute resolution mechanism.

It is pertinent to provide from the outset an account of the background to the dispute and the attempts made by Mauritius to bring it to a closure. The Republic of Mauritius consists of a group of islands in the Indian Ocean. The main island of Mauritius is located about 2,200 km south-west of the Chagos Archipelago. The largest island in the archipelago is Diego Garcia, which accounts for more than half of the archipelago's total land area. Between 1814 and 1965, the Chagos Archipelago was administered by the UK as a dependency of the colony of Mauritius and in accordance with GA resolution 66(I), the UK as the administering Power regularly transmitted information to the UNGA concerning Mauritius as a non-self-governing territory. In 1964, the US expressed an interest in establishing a military facility in Diego Garcia. So, the UK commenced talks with Mauritius regarding the detachment of the Chagos Archipelago from Mauritius. Despite the concerns voiced by the Secretary of State for the Colonies,[5] the bargain essentially was: independence for Mauritius in turn for the detachment of Chagos.[6] These talks led to the conclusion on 23 September 1965 of an agreement (Lancaster House agreement) on the detachment of the entire Chagos archipelago from Mauritius. Shortly afterwards, the UK established a new colony known as the British Indian Ocean Territory (BIOT) consisting of the Chagos Archipelago, detached from Mauritius, and the Aldabra, Farquhar and Desroches Islands, detached from

4 Mauritius' oral statement before the ICJ: "Existe-t-il un différend entre Maurice et la puissance administrante? Oui, évidemment; personne ne le nie, je crois, et certainement pas Maurice elle-même", *Chagos Opinion,* Public Sitting held on 3 September 2018, *CR 2018/20*, 35.

5 According to the Secretary of State, the United Kingdom would be accused of "creating a … colony in a period of decolonization and of establishing new military bases when we should be getting out of the old ones", Colonial Office, Note for the Prime Minister's Meeting with Sir Seewoosagur Ramgoolam, Premier of Mauritius, 22 September 1965, PREM 13/3320.

6 Record of a Conversation between the Prime Minister and the Premier of Mauritius, Sir Seewoosagur Ramgoolam, at No. 10, Downing Street, at 10 a.m. on Thursday, 23 September 1965, FO 371/184528: Prime Minister Wilson told Ramgoolam that "in theory, there were a number of possibilities. The Premier and his colleagues could return to Mauritius either with Independence or without it."

Seychelles.[7] And finally, on 30 December 1966 the US and the UK agreed to a 50-year lease of Diego Garcia and to the resettlement of any inhabitants (called Chagossians). The main forcible removal of Diego Garcia's population took place in July and September 1971. On the basis of two inter-State agreements, in 1972 and 1982 respectively, Mauritius accepted payments from the UK to meet the cost of resettlement of persons displaced from the Chagos Archipelago and to fully and finally settle all claims arising therefrom.[8] As a condition for collecting the funds, the islanders were required, by virtue of the 1982 agreement, to renounce the right to return to the Chagos Archipelago. On 30 December 2016, when the 50-year period covered by the 1966 Agreement came to an end, it was extended for a further period of twenty years, in accordance with its terms.

These events gave rise to both an inter-State sovereignty dispute and to another dispute, intertwined with the first, between the Chagossians and the British government over the legality of their removal and whether they have a right to return and resettlement. The attempts of the Chagossians before UK courts to claim back their fatherland did not bear fruit. In 1998, the claimants challenged the validity of UK legislation denying them the right to reside in the Chagos Archipelago (*Bancoult* case). The Divisional Court ruled in their favour and quashed the ordinance that prohibited Chagossians from returning to the Chagos Archipelago.[9] Immediately, the Government replaced it with another immigration ordinance that lifted for Chagossians all entry and residence restrictions to the Chagos Archipelago, with the exception of Diego Garcia. Another claim, brought in 2002, demanding compensation and restoration of property rights was dismissed by the High Court on the grounds that no tort was committed by the removal of the Chagossians and that compensation for property loss was precluded by the 1980 Limitation Act and the 1982 agreement.[10] However, the restrictions were reinstituted in 2004. And when the former inhabitants challenged afresh the validity of the restricting orders

7 British Indian Ocean Territory Order 1965 (S.I. 1965/1920).

8 The 1982 agreement was the outcome of negotiations initiated due to the *Vencatessen v Attorney General* litigation. The latter was introduced in 1975 before UK courts and was hence discontinued, see *Chagos Islanders v Attorney General and the BIOT Commissioner* [2003] EWHC 2222, [54]–[84].

9 *Regina (Bancoult) v. Secretary of State for Foreign and Commonwealth Affairs and Another (No. 1)* [2001] QB 1067 (LJ Laws and J Gribbs).

10 *Chagos Islanders v. Attorney General* [2003] EWHC 2222 (9 October 2003) (Ouseley J). The Court of appeal denied leave of appeal on 22 July 2004, *Chagos Islanders v. Attorney General* [2004] EWCA Civ 997 (Sedley LJ).

(*Bancoult no.2* case), the House of Lords held in the Government's favor.[11] The case made its way to the European Court of Human Rights (*Chagos Islanders v. UK*). On 11 December 2012, the ECtHR declared inadmissible the application made by a group of 1,786 Chagossians against the UK for breach of their rights under the European Convention on Human Rights. The main ground for the decision was that the claims of the applicants had been settled through implementation of the 1982 agreement between Mauritius and the UK.[12] In a third, and final up to date, set of proceedings (*Bancoult no.3* case) the Chagossians challenged the 2010 declaration of a marine protected area (MPA) by the UK around the Chagos Archipelago. On 8 February 2018, the Supreme Court dismissed the contention that the declaration of the world's largest MPA had been made for the improper purpose of rendering impracticable the resettlement of the Chagos islanders on the archipelago.[13]

In the meanwhile, on 12 March 1968 Mauritius becomes an independent State, and on 26 April 1968 it is admitted to membership in the UN. Since at least 1980, Mauritius consistently asserts its sovereignty over Chagos. Initially, its claim was put forward in various political fora, including in bilateral communications with the UK and in statements to the United Nations. Mauritius challenged the circumstances under which the Lancaster House agreement was negotiated, questioned the validity of the Mauritius Council of Ministers' approval of this agreement and asserted the incompatibility of the agreement with applicable international law on decolonization. Further, unilaterally Mauritius enshrined a claim to sovereignty over the Archipelago in its Constitution and legislation, and declared its own exclusive economic zone in the surrounding waters. But, the effort to bring the matter before an international court begins in 2001 when Mauritius proposed that the two States take their dispute to the International Court of Justice.[14] The UK did not agree because its 1 January 1969 optional clause declaration excluded disputes with Commonwealth States, so that declaration could not serve as the basis for the Court's jurisdiction in a contentious case.[15] And in 2004, after Mauritius indicated that it would withdraw from the Commonwealth in order to provide a basis for the Court's jurisdiction, the UK amended its optional clause declara-

11 *Regina (Bancoult) v. Secretary of State for Foreign and Commonwealth Affairs (No. 2)* [2008] UKHL 61

12 *Chagos Islanders v. the United Kingdom*, no. 35622/04, 12 December 2012 [81].

13 *Regina (Bancoult) v. Secretary of State for Foreign and Commonwealth Affairs (No. 3)* [2018] UKSC 3.

14 ICJ, *Chagos Opinion*, Written Statement of the United Kingdom, Annex 62.

15 Ibid., [5.12].

tion to exclude disputes with States that are or have been members of the Commonwealth.[16] Despite Mauritius' efforts, the dispute was not brought under the resolution mechanism of the International Convention on the Elimination of All Forms of Racial Discrimination (CERD) either. On 20 October 2011, Mauritius proposed to the UK negotiations withe meaning of Article 22 of the CERD treaty on the basis that Mauritius "has sovereignty over the Chagos Archipelago", and that Mauritius "does not recognize the so-called 'BIOT' which the United Kingdom purported to create by illegally excising the Chagos Archipelago from Mauritius prior to its independence".[17] The UK denied the existence of a dispute within the meaning of Article 22 of the CERD and hence declined to negotiate.[18]

It was the creation of the MPA by the UK that gave Mauritius a strong foothold to bring an inter-State claim before an international court. On 20 December 2010, Mauritius instituted proceedings pursuant to Article 287 of the United Nations Convention on the Law of the Sea (UNCLOS or the Convention) before an Arbitral Tribunal constituted under Annex VII of the Convention. In those proceedings, it made two types of submissions.[19] The first ones were related to the sovereignty dispute. Specifically, Mauritius asked the Court to pronounce on whether the UK or Mauritius was a coastal State entitled to declare the MPA. The second type related to violations of UNCLOS without prejudice to the question of sovereignty. On 18 March 2015, the tribunal rendered its award where it found by a marginal majority (3–2) that it lacked jurisdiction on Mauritius' first type submissions, and unanimously that it had jurisdiction to consider the second. With respect to the former, the Tribunal noted that the sovereignty dispute was the "real issue in the case" and the "object of the claim".[20] It was hence impossible to detach the meaning of the words "coastal State" from the issue of sovereignty. And since "[t]he parties' dispute regarding sovereignty over the Chagos Archipelago d [id] not concern interpretation or application" of UNCLOS, ruling upon these submissions extended beyond the Tribunal's jurisdiction.[21] With respect to

16 Ibid., [5.19(b)].

17 *Chagos Opinion*, Written Statement of the United Kingdom, Annex 70.

18 *Chagos Opinion*, Written Statement of the United Kingdom, Annex 71.

19 PCA, Annex VII Arbitral Tribunal, *In the Matter of the Chagos Marine Protected Area* (*Mauritius v United Kingdom*) (Final Award) [18 March 2015] PCA 2011–03, 69[158].

20 Chagos MPA, 89[220]. Clear reference to [30] of the ICJ's *Nuclear Test* (*New Zealand v. France*) case, where the ICJ held that: 'it is the Court's duty to isolate the real issue in the case and to identify the object of the claim'.

21 Chagos MPA, 85–90[203]–[221] and 92–3[228]–[230]. *Contra* Judges Kateka and Wölfrum who thought that the disassociation of these submissions from the sovereignty

the second type of submissions however, the tribunal found, that, in establishing the MPA the UK had breached its obligations under Articles 2(3), 56(2) and 194(4) of UNCLOS. In particular, the undertaking in the Lancaster House agreement – which the tribunal found to be binding on the UK – to return the archipelago to Mauritius when no longer needed for defense purposes, gave "Mauritius an interest in significant decisions that bear upon its possible future use".[22] By ignoring Mauritius' repeated calls for bilateral consultations before the creation of the MPA, the UK extinguished Mauritius' rights in the territorial sea, failed to pay due regard to Mauritius' rights in the EEZ and finally failed to endeavor to harmonize policies on marine pollution.[23]

Overall, the award must be understood as a balancing exercise. On the one hand, it gave due consideration to the UK's main legal argumentation. The sovereignty claim, according to the tribunal, was not ancillary or incidental to a claim that can be brought under UNCLOS, rather it lied at the heart of the matter. But at the same time, the tribunal struggled to give some recognition to Mauritius' interests without contravening its previous *dictum* regarding sovereignty. By virtue of the Lancaster House agreement's binding nature, Mauritius has a saying as to what happens in the Chagos archipelago. And while the tribunal found that the manner in which the MPA was established contravened UNCLOS, it called the parties to negotiate in order to achieve a mutually satisfactory arrangement.[24] Mauritius then failed to directly challenge UK's sovereignty over the archipelago, but its strategic interests were, for the first time, judicially recognized. Subsequent bilateral discussions came to nothing and the matter was left *in limbo*.

So, Mauritius took the matter to the UNGA. Undaunted, it successfully lobbied the UNGA to seek an advisory opinion from the ICJ on whether the separation of the Chagos Archipelago during the process of decolonization was unlawful. The drafting of the questions posed to the Court, as matters that concern the international community as a whole, unlocked the ICJ's door for Mauritius. The vote – 94 to 15 with 65 abstentions – was a 'humiliating defeat'

---

dispute was possible and the exercise of jurisdiction over them: "We differ in respect of the qualification of the dispute, which is for us a dispute about the interpretation of Article 56 of the Convention, and we consider it permissible to decide incidentally about sovereignty issues", Dissenting and Concurring Opinion, 12 [45].

22 Chagos MPA, 203 [521].

23 As noted by Waibel, the UK "simply assumed that the MPA was in the interest of Mauritius – without ever asking Mauritius", 'Mauritius v. UK: Chagos Marine Protected Area Unlawful', Ejil:talk!, (17 April 2015).

24 MPA Award, 212 [544].

for the UK.[25] Two factors were crucial in this respect.[26] First, the presentation of the dispute as a matter of decolonization and not one of sovereignty.[27] Second, the alleged use by the US of Diego Garcia as a 'black site' in the CIA's post-9/11 rendition program.[28] In this way, a bilateral dispute made its way to the UN court, with Mauritius holding the moral upper hand as the ICJ was seized of the matter.

Against this background, this Chapter will follow the unfolding of the Chagos archipelago saga to examine the utilization of ICJ advisory opinions in a multi-*forum* litigation strategy. In order to be incorporated in such a strategy, the function and nature of such opinions will be scrutinized and particularly whether they constitute a dispute settlement mechanism.

Section 2 analyses the terms under which the ICJ exercises its advisory jurisdiction in inter-State disputes. The main argument is that the Court is prepared to advise on any dispute, by circumventing the (lack of) consent of interested States to have their dispute determined by the Court. In order to do so, it invokes two justifications, one pertaining to jurisdiction and the other to admissibility. First, the Court can in principle exercise its jurisdiction since the non-binding nature of the proceedings renders any consent requirement *ab initio* irrelevant. Second, when the dispute is of acute interest to the UN, it is appropriate for the Court as the principal judicial organ of the organization to

25 O Bowcott, 'EU members abstain as Britain defeated in UN vote on Chagos Islands', *The Guardian*, (22 June 2017).

26 Brexit may have also been a third contributing factor as noted by Br. Kuźniak and D Kabat-Rudnicka, 'Advisory Opinion or Judgment? The Case of the Chagos Archipelago' 13 (2021) *Adam Mickiewicz University Law Review*, 45, 64–6.

27 M Milanovic, 'ICJ Advisory Opinion Request on the Chagos Islands', *Ejil:talk!* (24 June 2017). During parliamentary debates, a UK official held that the GA's resolution secured such an overwhelming support as it was framed 'around the emotive theme of decolonisation', House of Commons Debates 3 July 2019, vol 662, cols 584–6.

28 A high-ranked US official admitted this in 2015 (Vice News, 'Exclusive: CIA Interrogations Took Place on British Territory of Diego Garcia, Senior Bush Administration Official Says', 30 January 2015, available at: https://www.vice.com/en/article/pa8njm/exclusive-cia-interrogations-took-place-on-british-territory-of-diego-garcia-senior-bush-administration-official-says), while since 2007 the UK parliament has stated that: '[t]here have been repeated, credible and concurrent claims that Diego Garcia has played a major role in the US system of renditions and secret detention', House of Commons Foreign Affairs Committee, 'Enforced Disappearance, Illegal Interstate Transfer, and other Human Rights Abuses involving The UK Overseas Territories', 18 October 2007, available at: https://publications.parliament.uk/pa/cm200708/cmselect/cmfaff/memo/147/uc7302.htm.

render an opinion despite contrary State will. With respect to the latter, relevant jurisprudence suggests that the UNGA is prepared to place any dispute in this category irrespective of its specific features. This renders an advisory opinion a *prima facie* attractive judicial mechanism for interested States.

Section 3, in turn, focuses on the policy objectives that may be pursued by instrumentalizing advisory opinions. In view of their legal and political ramifications, such proceedings are appealing for States as they are viewed as a *de facto* dispute resolution mechanism. While the ICJ is using the non-binding nature of advisory opinions as the key consideration in order to entertain disputes, recent practice shows that its opinions are not perceived as such. Rather, they are understood to carry a normative weight akin to a dispute settlement mechanism. Arguably, this carrot and stick situation, exemplified in the UK-Mauritius dispute, may provoke a backlash from States. Especially, in view of the strong moral and political effects that ICJ advisory opinions may produce. Testament to that is Israel's reaction to the successful attempt by Palestine to bring their long-standing dispute before the Court for an advisory opinion.

The penultimate Section juxtaposes the concomitant effects of advisory opinions rendered by the Inter-American Court of Human Rights which have recently been used in the context of multi-*forum* proceedings but have not yielded similar results. Contrary to the ICJ, the regional court due to its limited authority has been more attentive to State interests and has declined to render opinions when to do so could provoke extreme State backlash.

The main contention in the final Section is that both the nature and the function of ICJ advisory opinions have been redefined after *Chagos*. This will likely give new life to ICJ advisory opinions for it develops their potential to accelerate the resolution of international disputes and hence their capacity to be used in the context of a multi-*forum* strategy. Nonetheless, in view of the severe political ramifications of its opinions, the ICJ may need to be more prudent when delivering them in order to anticipate unintended consequences.

2 The ICJ's 'Compulsory' Advisory Jurisdiction on Inter-state Disputes

2.1 *PCIJ Advisory Opinions as a Dispute Settlement Instrument*

In order to fully understand how the Court perceives its advisory function when this is somehow related to the resolution of bilateral disputes, it is important to put this in a historical perspective. The ICJ's precursor, the Permanent Court of International Justice (PCIJ), was frequently resorted to in order to deliver advisory opinions. Seventeen out of the twenty-seven opinions requested in total, concerned the settlement of inter-State disputes.[29] Advisory opinions were considered a dispute settlement procedure, provided for in the League of Nations' Covenant and applicable in the disputes arising between the member States of the international organization. Through their participation in the Covenant, State-members were considered to have given *a priori* their consent to such a dispute settlement procedure. And both States and League of Nations organs complied with PCIJ advisory opinions. Understandably then, advisory opinions at the time were not incorporated in a multi-*forum* litigation strategy, but were rather used as the sole *forum* for the settlement of disputes.

Basis of the PCIJ's competence was Article 14 of the Covenant of the League of Nations that held as follows: "The Council shall formulate and submit to the Members of the League for adoption plans for the establishment of a Permanent Court of International Justice. The Court shall be competent to hear and determine any dispute of an international character which the parties thereto submit to it. The Court may also give an advisory opinion upon *any dispute or question* referred to it by the Council or by the Assembly" (emphasis added).[30] Even when the initiative was taken by the States parties to a dispute, all requests for advisory opinions were made by a unanimous Council since it was the organ responsible to "endeavour to effect a settlement of [a] dispute".[31] Article 14 was incorporated within the cluster of provisions (Articles 12–16) that established a dispute settlement procedure applicable on disputes

29 For an account of the relevant practice see ZCr Reghizzi, 'The Internaitonal Court of Justice's Advisory Jurisdiction, Dispute Settlement and State Consent: An Historical Perspective', (2021) *Rivista di Diritto Internazionale* 139, 145.

30 The Statute of the Permanent Court approved in December 1919 did not contain any provision on advisory jurisdiction. An amendment adopted in 1929 and entered into force on 1st February 1936 introduced a new chapter IV of the Statute devoted to advisory opinions (Articles 65 to 68): see PCIJ Publications, Series D, No. 14, 13ff, 27ff.

31 Article 15 of the Covenant. E.g. with respect to Advisory Opinion no.14, the parties agreed in writing to request the Council to submit three questions to the Court for advisory opinion, which agreement was then sent to the Council via the League's Secretary General, League of Nations Official Journal (1927) 151 and 233. The unanimity rules was not provided for in the Covenant, but was developed by the Council's practice, M Aljaghoub, *The Advisory Function of the International Court of Justice 1946–2005*, (Springer, 2006), 25.

arising between member States of the League.[32] Also, with a modification of the Rules of the Court in 1927, Article 31 of the PCIJ's Statute – regulating the composition of the Bench in contentious cases – was declared applicable to advisory proceedings that pertained to "a question relating to an existing *dispute* between two or more States" (emphasis added).[33] This pronouncement coupled with the broad formulation of Article 14 noted above, suggest that the rationale behind the introduction of advisory opinions as part of the PCIJ's competence was the creation of a new means of judicial dispute settlement, equivalent and alternative to, contentious jurisdiction. And the PCIJ's practice is testament to that.[34] Though formally not binding, the PCIJ advisory opinions were considered as *de facto* binding given the record of compliance with them.[35] Hence, the *Institut de Droit International* held in 1937: "la procedure consultative, facilitant le règlement judiciaire des conflits internationaux là où l'arbitrage obligatoire fait défaut, rend les plus grands services à la solution pacifique des différends".[36] Thus, a *sui generis* procedure was created whereby a political organ of the League of Nations – the Council – would seek the legal advice of a judicial organ of the same organisation – the PCIJ – in order to resolve a dispute or a question that was pending before it.

---

32 Article 17 of the Covenant established a respective procedure regarding disputes between a member and a non-member.

33 The PCIJ appointed *ad hoc* judges in five advisory proceedings (*Jurisdiction of the Courts of Danzig*; *Greco-Bulgarian "Communities"*; *Railway Traffic between Lithuania and Poland*; *Polish War Vessels in the Port of Danzig*; *Treatment of Polish Nationals in Danzig*) and in one case (*Greco-Turkish-Agreement (Final Protocol*), the two States waived their right to appoint judges *ad hoc*). For an analysis of the relevant pactice *see* E Jiménez de Aréchaga, "Judges ad hoc in Advisory Proceedings", 31 (1971) *ZaöRV* 697.

34 Ch. De Visscher, Les avis consultatifs de la Cour permanente de justice internationale, 26 (1929) *Recueil des cours*, 41; D Négulesco, L'évolution de la procédure des avis consultatifs de la Cour permanente de justice internationale, 57 (1936) *Recueil des cours* 64.

35 Judges Loder, Moore and Anzilotti in a report they prepared for the Court in 1927 concluded that "the difference between contentious cases and advisory cases is only nominal [...]. So the view that advisory opinions are not binding is more theoretical than real", P.C.I.J., Publications, Series E, No. 4, 76.

36 "The advisory procedure, facilitating the judicial regulation of international disputes where compulsory settlement is defective, serves to the maximum the pacific settlement of disputes" author's translation Institut de droit international, Session de Luxembourg, résolution sur La nature juridique des avis consultatifs de la Cour permanente de Justice internationale, leur valeur et leur portée en droit international, 3 September 1937, available at www.idi-iil.org.

In two instances, the PCIJ was called upon to advise on disputes between a member and a non-member of the League. The first, was the *Status of Eastern Carelia* opinion that concerned a dispute between Finland and Russia, a non-member of the League at the time.[37] Russia had been recalcitrant regarding the League's intervention in the dispute because it considered the question of the status of Eastern Carelia to be a domestic issue. So, Russia denied both the examination of the dispute by the Council in political formation and also did not consent to the Council's request for the rendering of an advisory opinion by the PCIJ. The latter rejected the request and the reason animating this decision was, according to the PCIJ, "the lack of competence of the League to deal with a dispute involving non-member States which refused its intervention".[38] Russia's lack of consent to the judicial procedure was not relevant in and of itself as a prerequisite for the rendering of the advisory opinion.[39] On this point, the PCIJ clarified that "there has been some discussion as to whether questions for an advisory opinion, if they relate to matters which form the subject of a pending dispute between nations, should be put to the Court without the consent of the parties. It is unnecessary in the present case to deal with this topic".[40] Rather, what was relevant was Russia's consent to bring the dispute under the Council's – not the PCIJ's – competence, a *conditio sine qua non* underpinning the Council's engagement with the dispute.[41] It is clear therefore, that the institutional

37 PCIJ, Publications, Series B, No. 5, 7 ff.

38 *Advisory Opinion of 16 October 1975 on Western Sahara*, ICJ Reports, 1975, 23[30]. Similar *dictum* in *Advisory Opinion of 21 June 1971 on Namibia*, ICJ Reports, 1971, 23[31].

39 DW Greig, "The Advisory Jurisdiction of the International Court and the Settlement of Disputes between States" 15 (1966) *International and Comparative Law Quarterly* 325, 334: "where the competence of the Council was directly involved, the Court regarded the 'consent' of the parties to the proceedings as irrelevant". *Contra see* Individual and Dissenting Opinions of Judges Azevedo, Winiarski, Zoričić and Krylov appended to the advisory opinion of 30 March 1950 in the *Case Concerning the Interpretation of Peace Treaties with Bulgaria, Hungary and Romania*, ICJ Reports, 1950, 79 ff., 89 ff., 98 ff. and 105 ff.; Sh. Oda, "The International Court of Justice Viewed from the Bench (1976–1993)", 244 (1993) *Recueil des cours* 92; M Pomerance, "The ICJ's Advisory Jurisdiction and the Crumbling Wall between the Political and the Judicial 99 (2005) *The American Journal of International Law* 26, 35.

40 *Eastern Carelia* 27.

41 *Eastern Carelia* 27–28, "The submission, therefore, of a dispute between them [nb non-member States] and a Member of the League for solution according to the methods provided for in the Covenant, could take place only by virtue of their consent"; Reghizzi, *supra* note 29, 152; G Abi-Saab, *Les exceptions préliminaires dans la procédure de la Cour internationale*, (Pédonne, 1967) 79; K Keith, *The Extent of the Advisory Jurisdiction of the International Court of Justice*, (Seitjoff, 1971), 494 ff.

aspect was predominant, and this accords with the nature of an advisory opinion as a dialogue between the Council and the PCIJ.

The other advisory opinion of the PCIJ that involved a non-member State was the one on *Article 3, paragraph 2 of Treaty of Lausanne*.[42] This provision referred the determination of the boundary line between Turkey and Iraq – which was under UK mandate – to the Council of the League of Nations "[i]n the event of no agreement being reached between the two Governments within nine months".[43] Turkey was not a member of the League but after the failure of negotiations with the British, it agreed to the involvement of the Council and took part in proceedings before the latter. When the PCIJ was asked by the Council whether the latter's function was to render a binding arbitral award or to offer its good offices, it did not decline to deliver an opinion despite Turkey's refusal to participate in the judicial proceedings.[44] In its reasoning, the PCIJ did not clarify why it had competence to render the opinion, however the record of a private sitting between PCIJ members shed some light as to the difference with the *Eastern Carelia* case "the circumstances in the present case were distinctly different, since the questions before the Court referred not to the merits of the affair but to the competence of the Council, which had been duly seized of the affair and could undoubtedly ask for the Court's opinion on points of law".[45] The institutional dimension is once more critical for the PCIJ to assert its competence;[46] once the Council is seized of the dispute, the latter comes under the Covenant's dispute resolution spectrum and hence the PCIJ has the competence to deal with it. All in all, advisory proceedings in the League of Nations era were a) considered a dispute-settlement instrument equivalent to contentious jurisdiction, and b) resorted to even against the consent of the disputing parties when the organization had the competence to intervene in the dispute.

42 PCIJ, Publications, Series B, No. 12, 6 ff.

43 PCIJ, Publications, Series B, No. 12, 19.

44 Turkey contended that it would be improper for the Court to render the opinion since the questions posed were of an "extremely political" and not of a legal nature, Speech of Tevfik Rouschdy Bey at the 35th Session of the Council, PCIJ, Ser. C, No. 10,127. See also the telegram sent by the Turkish Foreign Minister to the Registrar of the Court on October 8, 1925: "Turkish Government [..] is convinced that the questions [...] are of a distinctly political character and, in the Turkish Government's opinion, cannot form the subject of a legal interpretation" (Ser. B, No. 12, 8).

45 P.C.I.J., Publications, Series E, No. 2, 164.

46 M Pomerance, *The Advisory Function of the International Court in the League and UN Eras*, (Johns Hopkins University *Press, 1973*), 75–78, 289–90; Keith, *supra* note 41, 101: 'this case and Eastern Carelia can be read consistently only on the basis that they turned on the competence of the Council'; Reghizzi, *supra* note 29, 155.

2.2 *ICJ Advisory Opinions as Advice against or despite State Consent*

2.2.1 The Normative Framework: a New Role For Advisory Opinions

In the UN era, a new approach towards the advisory jurisdiction of the ICJ has been put forward. An approach that is based upon a clear separation between advisory and contentious proceedings. And this is reflected both in the normative framework outlining the Court's jurisdiction and the relevant institutional practice. Thus, opinions are no longer considered a dispute-settlement instrument and consent to advisory proceedings has acquired a novel significance. It is telling that the ICJ has been resorted to for the delivery of an opinion in its 78-year history, as many times as the PCIJ had in its 24-year history. And from the twenty-seven opinions rendered by the ICJ, only a handful were closely related to inter-State disputes. This new approach brings with it a new role for advisory proceedings, one that is compatible with their incorporation in a multi-*forum* litigation strategy for the resolution of international disputes.

The relevant normative framework under the Charter is an indicator of this change in perception on the Court's advisory function. While it is comparable to that under the Covenant, some notable differences stand out. Article 96 [1] of the Charter leaves out "any dispute" as a possible subject matter of a request for advisory opinion, and provides instead that "any legal question" can be entertained. This is also reflected in Article 65 of the ICJ's Statute. This change echoed the concerns of the drafters to prevent the Court from giving opinions on non-legal, ie political matters,[47] and it is debatable whether it has affected the competence of the ICJ to render an opinion on inter-State disputes.[48] Article 102 [3] of the Rules of the Court however, would suggest a permissive interpretation since it recognises the Court's competence with respect to "a legal question actually pending between two or more States" and extends the application of Article 31 of the Statute in such proceedings, notwithstanding the appointment of *ad hoc* judges. Further, Article 96 [2] of the Charter opens up the spectrum of bodies that may request the delivery of an opinion when compared to the League era. Apart from the UNGA (equivalent to the Assembly in the League of Nations) and the Security Council (equivalent to the

---

47 Sh. Rosenne, *The Law and Practice of the International Court, 1920–2005*, vol. I (OUP, 2006), 285–6.

48 Most publicists believe that no substantial difference exists, *see* M Shaw, *Rosenne's Law and Practice of the International Court: 1920–2015*, (Brill, 2017) 294 and R Kolb, *The International Court of Justice* (Hart, 2013) 1062; *contra* Dissenting Opinion Judge Azevedo, *Interpretation of Peace Treaties with Bulgaria, Hungary and Romania*, ICJ Reports, 1950, 86.

Council), also "other organs of the UN and specialised agencies [...] may also request advisory opinions". This novel provision heralds a new 'organisational' perception of the Court's role. The latter is henceforth self-identified as the principal judicial organ of the UN, and, as the analysis of the jurisprudence will demonstrate *infra*, this will heavily influence the interpretation of the Court's advisory competence.[49]

Further, the procedure leading up to the request for an opinion under the Charter is substantially different from the respective one under the Covenant. The unanimity rule prevalent in the League of Nations has been replaced in the UN by a majority voting system.[50] Thus, while the League of Nations Council showed reluctance in adopting a request by a majority vote, the UN organs show no such reticence.[51] This means that requests for advisory opinions regarding politically sensitive matters may be referred to the Court by a political majority despite significant opposition.[52] The *Interpretation of the Agreement of 25 March 1951 Between WHO and Egypt* has been the closest call so far with the World Health Assembly upholding the request by 53 votes to 43.[53] So, opinions have been used as a form of political pressure for propaganda purposes against the minority.[54] This has allegedly been the case with the *Expenses* opinion. According to the Soviet representative to the UNGA, "the proposal to ask the International Court of Justice to issue an advisory opinion is merely an attempt in this case to find the means for exerting pres-

49 M Pomerance, 'The Advisory Role of the International Court of Justice and its "Judicial" Character: Past and Future Prisms', in A Muller et al. *The International Court of Justice: Its Future Role After Fifty Years* (1997) 271, 290; Reghizzi, *supra* note 29, 157. For more see *infra*.

50 Since no relevant provisions exist in the UN Charter, in the ICJ's Statute or in the Rules of the Court, the voting procedure for the adoption of a referring resolution must be determined in accordance with the general rules governing voting by the concerned organ; M Amr, *The Role of the International Court of Justice as a Principal Judicial Organ of the United Nations* (Kluwer, 2003) 75–78. According to Article 18 of the Charter, the General Assembly, that has referred to the ICJ 16 opinions, decides with a two thirds majority of those present and voting on "important questions" and with simple majority on "other questions". In the *Wall, Kosovo* and *Mauritius* opinions, the requesting resolutions were adopted by a shorter than two thirds majority, nevertheless they were assumed to be duly adopted.

51 S Rosenne and Y Ronen, *The Law and Practice of the International Court of Justice, vol. I* (Brill, 2006), 286.

52 For an evaluation of the voting records see Shaw, *supra* note 48, Chapter 5, 292ff[60].

53 WHO Resolution No. WHA 33.16 of 1980. Relatedly, ten times a request has been put to a vote and has not acquired the necessary votes in order to reach the ICJ, M Aljaghoub, *supra* note 31, 246.

54 Greig, *supra* note 39, 340.

sure on those States which on very good grounds – on political and juridical grounds – do not feel that it is possible for them to participate in the financing of [...] the Emergency Force in the Middle East or the United Congo Operation".[55]

Undoubtedly, voting patterns affect both the reception of the opinion by States and UN organs,[56] and also the attitude of States during the procedure before the ICJ. For example, objections to the Court's competence in delivering the opinion have become standard practice. It is no wonder then that the record of implementation of advisory opinions, which was automatic with respect to the PCIJ, has become an issue for the ICJ.[57] Characteristic in this respect has been the stance of nuclear powers after the delivery of the *Legality of the Threat or Use of Nuclear Weapons* advisory opinion; given the political sensitivity of the matter, the Court's timidity to clearly pronounce on the main issue and the weak majority by which the resolution requesting the opinion was adopted (78 to 43 with 38 abstentions), it is no surprise that these States regarded the opinion as importing no legal, political or moral obligation.[58] The institutional environment, then, has dictated the new direction advisory jurisdiction has taken in the UN era.

2.2.2 Jurisprudential Practice: the Non-binding and Intra-organizational Character of Advisory Opinions

This direction crystallised mainly through the Court's jurisprudence. The ICJ had to rediscover the proper function and nature of advisory proceedings in the UN era and to assert its own stance *vis-à-vis* these proceedings. Many times, the ICJ has recognized that underlying a request for an advisory opinion is a controversy which has led to making the request: "Differences of view amongst States on legal issues have existed in practically every advisory pro-

55 G.A.O.R., 16th Session, Plenary 57.

56 Pomerance, *supra* note 46, Chapter 4.

57 Implementation in this context does not denote adherence to legal obligations since advisory opinions cannot produce legal rules. It rather pertains to the attitude of UN or League of Nations organs towards the opinion and the willingness of States to align with the opinion's outcome which is usually a resolution by the requesting organ. Goodrich claims that PCIJ opinions were generally accepted by the Council with no discussion and States themselves almost uniformly accepted the solution indicated in the Court's advisory opinions, 'The Nature of the Advisory Opinions of the Permanent Court of International Justice, 32 (1938) *American Journal of International Law* 738, 747. On the other hand, the 'very acceptance and implementation [of ICJ opinion's] has frequently arisen heated discussions', Pomerance, *supra* note 46, 355.

58 John Burroughs, *The Legality of Threat or Use of Nuclear Weapons* (LIT Verlag, 1997), 153–155.

ceeding; if all were agreed, the need to resort to the Court for advice would not arise".[59] But, this "existence, in the background, of a dispute the parties to which may be affected as a consequence of the Court's opinion, does not change the advisory nature of the Court's task, which is to answer the question put to it".[60] In principle then, advising upon a dispute is not incompatible with the ICJ's advisory function. But to what extent is it akin to the dispute settlement role undertaken by the PCIJ? And how does the Court's new 'organisational' self-perception, noted above, determine the limits of its engagement with disputes in advisory proceedings? The ICJ faced these questions early on in its life, in the 1950 *Peace Treaties* opinion.

In *Peace Treaties* the distinction between advisory and contentious jurisdiction was unearthed by the Court so as to justify its engagement with inter-State disputes. The case concerned the interpretation of the peace treaties of 1947 between Bulgaria, Hungary and Romania and certain Allied and Associated Powers and whether the former States were under an obligation to carry out the provisions of those treaties relating to the settlement of disputes. The three affected States – not UN members at the time – objected to the Court's jurisdiction; the delivery of an opinion on the pending dispute would essentially constitute, they claimed, a violation of the overarching principle of consent to adjudication. The ICJ dismissed the applicability of that principle in advisory proceedings on a twofold basis. First, since the Court's reply has no binding force it does not constitute a means of dispute settlement substantially equivalent to contentious jurisdiction.[61] This was further refined in *Nuclear Weapons* where the Court held that the "purpose of the advisory function is not to settle – *at least directly* – disputes between States, but to offer legal advice to the organs and institutions requesting the opinion" (emphasis added).[62] An opinion which is not legally binding either upon the State thus indirectly interested or upon the organ receiving the opinion, does not interfere with State sovereignty and no need for protection of that State's consent

59 *Namibia*, Advisory Opinion, ICJ Reports (1971), 24 [34]; *Wall*, Advisory Opinion, ICJ Reports (2004), 158[48].

60 *Judgement no. 158 (Review)*, Advisory Opinion, ICJ Reports (1973), 171–2[14].

61 *Peace Treaties*, 71. They may not produce *res judicata*, however, advisory opinions have been invoked in subsequent cases where the same point has arisen for decision, eg in the preliminary objections phase of the *South West Africa* cases the ICJ had to consider the effect of the advisory opinion concerning the *International Status of South West Africa*, ICJ, *South West Africa Cases (Ethiopia and Liberia v South Africa)*, Preliminary Objections, 21 December 1962, ICJ Reports 1962, 334.

62 *Nuclear Weapons*, 236[15].

arises.[63] For three judges, however, the absence of consent constitutes a *non possumus* for the Court, since an advisory opinion is essentially a dispute settlement mechanism capable of encroaching on State sovereignty.[64] Second, the opinion is not addressed to States but to the UN organ that requested it. Hence, the Court's reply represents its participation in the activities of the Organization and "no State, whether a Member of the United Nations or not, can prevent the giving of an Advisory Opinion which the United Nations considers to be desirable in order to obtain enlightenment as to the course of action it should take".[65] It is the nature of advisory proceedings, as non-binding and intra-organizational, that gives the ICJ the power to detach the determination of its jurisdiction from the consent of the interested parties when a dispute constitutes the subject-matter of advisory proceedings.

In this way, the ICJ puts to the side any argument relating to the objective for which the opinion was sought. This was introduced in *Nuclear Weapons* and further clarified in the *Kosovo* opinion. When discussing the referring resolution with respect to the latter opinion, Serbia stated that:

> Supporting this draft resolution would also serve to reaffirm a fundamental principle: the right of any Member State of the United Nations to pose a simple, basic question on a matter it considers vitally important to the Court. To vote against it would be in effect a vote to deny the

63 H Lauterpacht, *The Development of International Law by the International Court*, (CUP, 1958) 355. Lauterpacht analyses how the Court attempted unconvincingly to distinguish *Peace Treaties* from *Eastern Carelia*. The ICJ introduced a distinction between a question that relates directly to the main point of the dispute (*Eastern Carelia*) and one that touches upon procedural matters for the purpose of enlightening the General Assembly (*Peace Treaties*). Arguably, the more convincing explanation of the distinguishing element between the two lies in that the Treaty of Dorpat conferred no functions at all upon the League of Nations while the Treaties of Peace of 1947 did so by express reference to the Secretary-General of the United Nations, Ibid. 356–8.

64 Separate opinion of Judge Azevedo (p. 79), dissenting opinions of Judges Winiarski (p. 89) and Zoričič (p. 98). Insightfully, Gross notes that in *Peace Treaties* "[t]he Court wrote a prologue for the future, the minority wrote an epilogue for the past", 'The International Court of Justice and the United Nations' 120 (1967) *Recueil des cours*, 313, 416.

65 *Peace Treaties*, 71. Reproduced in subsequent cases; e.g. *Western Sahara*, Advisory Opinion, ICJ Reports (19715), 24–5[32]; *Wall*, 157–8 [47]. The ICJ held in the *Mazilu* opinion that this reasoning is equally valid in a legal question pending between the UN and a member State, *Mazilu*, Advisory Opinion, ICJ Reports (1989), 188–91[31].

> right of any country to seek – now or in the future – judicial recourse through the United Nations system.[66]

It was obvious then that the advisory opinion was meant to serve as a sort of judicial recourse by Serbia against the unilateral declaration of independence by Kosovo and the recognition of Kosovo by several UN member States.[67] Many participants argued that the ICJ should not respond to the request because its opinion is used to serve the interests of one State and not to assist the UNGA in the exercise of its functions. The Court appealed once again to the nature of advisory jurisdiction in order to reply to this contention: advisory jurisdiction "is not a form of judicial recourse for States [...] and it is for the organ which requests the opinion, and not for the Court, to determine whether it needs the opinion for the proper performance of its functions".[68] And it was not within the Court's competence to assess the usefulness of the opinion for the requesting organ nor to speculate on the motives of States supporting the requesting resolution. Then, advisory opinions may not typically constitute a dispute settlement mechanism, but the ICJ cannot control whether they are in fact used as such when a dispute underlies the request made to the Court.

2.2.3 Jurisprudential Practice: Placing the Dispute in a 'Broader Frame of Reference'

Nevertheless, the Court in *Peace Treaties* qualified its capacity to deliver advisory opinions when the latter are closely related to international disputes. According to the ICJ, starting point for the examination of every request for advisory opinion is that it should not be refused, at least in principle.[69] Subsequently, it noted that Article 65 of the Statute, given its permissive wording, "gives the Court the power to examine whether the circumstances of the case are of such a character as should lead it to decline to answer the Request".[70] Subsequent case-law has further elaborated on this *dictum*.[71] The examination of such circumstances, applies once the Court is satisfied it has jurisdiction to entertain the opinion, and therefore it should be understood as an admissibil-

66 UN Doc. A/63/PV.22, 1.

67 *Kosovo*, [32]–[33].

68 Ibid [33]–[34].

69 *Peace Treaties*, 71.

70 Ibid 72. *ILO Administrative Tribunal Judgment No. 2867*, Advisory Opinion, ICJ Reports (2012), 24[33], *Wall*, 156[44]; *Kosovo*, 415–6[29]. It must be noted that the Court has never declined to respond to a request for an advisory opinion.

71 *Wall*, 156 [44]; *Kosovo*, 415–6[29].

ity issue.[72] The criteria for this determination are not provided for in Article 65, so only compelling reasons should lead the Court to refuse its opinion.[73] These reasons are attached to the notion of judicial propriety which restricts the ICJ's discretion vested upon it by virtue of Article 65.[74] In exercising such discretion, the Court has to have regard to its character, both as a principal organ of the United Nations and as a judicial body.[75]

It is pertinent to examine at this point the criterion set by the ICJ that would render inappropriate the delivery of an advisory opinion when the latter is closely connected to a bilateral dispute. This was articulated by the Court in the *Western Sahara* opinion. The question of consent, rejected by the Court as irrelevant for the determination of its jurisdiction in advisory opinions, becomes a relevant factor in the admissibility issue of judicial propriety.[76] State consent should be protected when, according to the circumstances, to give a reply would have the effect of circumventing the principle that a State is not obliged to allow its disputes to be submitted to judicial settlement without its consent.[77] Nonetheless, fulfilment of this criterion as a result of the rendering of the opinion itself seems unlikely; it would run counter to the ICJ's *dictum* in *Peace Treaties* whereby advisory opinions do not have a binding effect and hence do not constitute a means of judicial settlement. Circumvention could arise however, when the advisory opinion is used by a UN organ "in order that it may later, on the basis of the Court's opinion, exercise its powers and functions for the peaceful settlement of that dispute".[78] So, while the opinion itself may not effectively amount to circumvention of the consent

72 *Wall*, 156[44]; Kolb, *The Elgar Companion to the International Court of Justice* (Elgar, 2016), 274. Through an analysis of the ICJ's jurisprudence, Thirlway explains how 'all State parties to the Statute hav[e] thus given unconditional consent to the exercise of advisory jurisdiction' and only the limits set by the texts of the Statute and the Charter themselves could give rise to a jurisdictional issue in such proceedings, *The Law and Procedure of the International Court of Justice, vol. I* (OUP, 2013), 824–8.

73 *Namibia*, 27[41]

74 *Kosovo* 416[30]; *Cumaraswamy*, Advisory Opinion, ICJ Reports (1999), 78–9[29]. On the relationship between discretion and judicial propriety *see* Judge Cançado Trindade Dissenting Opinion, *Kosovo*, [26]–[27] who holds that discretion is a term attached to political organs not to judicial bodies. Similar argumentation by Kolb who argues that the ICJ has no 'true' discretion to refuse an opinion on the basis of Article 65, but according to a legal norm, it must refuse to deliver an opinion if, in doing so, it would be forced to undermine its judicial integrity, Kolb, *supra* note 72, 274.

75 *ILO Administrative Tribunal Judgment No. 2867*, Advisory Opinion, ICJ Reports (2012), 24–5[33].

76 *Western Sahara* 24–5[32].

77 Ibid 25[33].

78 Ibid 26–7[39].

principle, this could be the case indirectly via the procedure before the UN organ that requested the advisory opinion. The context in which the opinion was requested automatically acquires great significance.

The *Western Sahara* opinion is a case in point that demonstrates the difficulty of applying this criterion. It pertained to the claims over the territory of Western Sahara by Spain, the former colonial power and administering power of Western Sahara at the time of advisory proceedings one the one hand, and Morocco and Mauritania on the other. Spain endeavored to convince the Court that its lack of consent to the advisory proceedings was reason enough for the Court to deny to exercise its jurisdiction. Based on the origin and scope of the dispute, the Court rejected Spain's contention on a twofold basis.

The first one was to place the dispute in a broader frame of reference than that of a bilateral dispute between Spain and Morocco or Spain and Mauritania. This was evinced by two considerations. First, the legal controversy in this case had arisen during the UNGA debates, not in bilateral relations, and was always attached to the UN decolonization proceedings. And second, the UNGA did not bring the dispute before the Court with the purpose of exercising its dispute-settlement function, but rather its function relating to the decolonization of the territory. This was evident from the terms of resolution 3292 requesting the opinion and in particular the application of resolution 1514 *On the Granting of Independence to Colonial Countries and Peoples* in the case at hand.[79] By showing deference to the referring resolution, the ICJ attempted to give precedence to the institutional dimension of the request. This approach was followed in subsequent case-law, such as the *Wall* and the *Chagos* opinions, as a means to go around the circumvention argument.[80]

While the ICJ never explained how these two aforementioned considerations interrelate,[81] it did not recognize that the guidance offered to the General Assembly for decolonization purposes can be premised or conditioned upon the resolution of a bilateral dispute. While the object of the request is not formally the resolution of a dispute, this may in fact be inferred through the back door. And Spain invoked an argument to this effect before the Court. In particular, it argued:

79 Ibid 25–7[34]–[39].

80 Albeit it was evident that in *Wall* and *Chagos* the advice was not sought for the purpose of resolving a concrete question pending for the requesting institution, D Akande, 'Selection of the International Court of Justice as a Forum for Contentious and Advisory Proceedings (Including Jurisdiction)' 7 (2016) *Journal of International Dispute Settlement* 320, 339.

81 Thirlway, *supra* note 72, 845.

> that the subject of the dispute which Morocco invited it [Spain] to submit jointly to the Court for decision in contentious proceedings, and the subject of the questions on which the advisory opinion is requested, are substantially identical; thus, the advisory procedure is said to have been used as an alternative after the failure of an attempt to make use of the contentious jurisdiction with regard to the same question.[82]

The ICJ did not find the scope of the two requests by Morocco to be identical, but this argument highlights the belief that advisory opinions can in fact be equivalent to any other dispute resolution mechanism. In *Western Sahara* the relationship between the two competences of the General Assembly – dispute settlement and decolonization – was never clarified by the ICJ and it stands to reason that these two may very well overlap. The overarching question then is whether placing the dispute in a broader frame of reference, i.e. labelling a dispute as pertaining to the functions (not dispute-settlement) of a UN organ, justifies the delivery of an opinion by the Court in any case.[83] This will acquire new significance in view of the *Wall* and the *Chagos* opinions, as it will be argued *infra*.

Nevertheless, the Court did not stop there and invoked another argument as to why Spain's lack of consent was irrelevant for the determination of the ICJ's discretion to entertain the case. The Court held that Spain's legal position will not be compromised from the rendering of the advisory opinion, because the latter pertains to Morocco's rights over Western Sahara at the time of decolonization and not at the time of the advisory proceedings.[84] To present this as a consideration pertinent to the scope of the request is perplexing. Irrespective of the context in which they are requested, advisory opinions are generally not capable of altering the legal position of States *tout court*. The ICJ could not have compromised Spain's *legal* rights by answering the General Assembly's request, only its *political* claim to have the dispute settled

---

82 *Western Sahara*, 22[14].

83 A similar issue was at stake at the *Namibia* opinion. By reference to the referring Security Council resolution, the ICJ found that the request did not relate to a pending dispute and, *obiter*, that the objective of the Security Council was to seek legal advice on the consequences and implications of its own decisions, *Namibia*, 24 [32].

84 *Western Sahara*, 27[42]: 'The issue between Morocco and Spain regarding Western Sahara is not one as to the legal status of the territory today, but one as to the rights of Morocco over it at the time of colonization. The settlement of this issue will not affect the rights of Spain today as the administering Power, but will assist the General Assembly in deciding on the policy to be followed in order to accelerate the decolonization process in the territory.'

in its favor.[85] So, it is not evident why the ICJ invoked this argument, unless the ICJ believes that the effect of its advisory opinions is such that can potentially alter the legal position of States. It is important though because the Court evokes the non-binding nature of advisory opinions, to justify 'the real (*sic*) significance in this case of the lack of Spain's consent'.[86] Ostensibly, the Court suggests that compromising the legal position of an interested State can constitute another way of circumventing the principle that a State is not obliged to allow its disputes to be submitted to judicial settlement without its consent. To accept this, however, would effectively amount to distorting the nature and function of advisory opinions. This second argument of the Court is instructive nevertheless, for it pinpoints the ICJ's difficulty to contextualise and specify the criterion that renders inappropriate the delivery of an advisory opinion.

The fact that the ICJ has not declined to answer any request for advisory opinion up to date, shows that it is trying hard to put the dispute in context in order to reject the circumvention argument. This was even more striking in the *Wall* opinion. The UNGA convened an emergency session and asked for urgent advice on the question of: "the legal consequences arising from the construction of the wall being built by Israel, the occupying Power, in the Occupied Palestinian Territory, including in and around East Jerusalem'.[87] Israel invoked a line of defence similar to that of Spain in *Western Sahara*, More specifically, it held that the question underlying the request is an integral part of the wider Israeli-Palestinian dispute concerning questions of terrorism, security, borders, settlements, Jerusalem and other related matters.[88] This dispute did not arise in the context of decolonisation however, and the Court arguably stretched even further its discretion to advise on disputes despite the consent of interested States. In order to demonstrate that the dispute was located in a frame of reference that was broader than a bilateral dispute, the ICJ referred to the powers and responsibilities of the United Nations in general, when issues relating to international peace and security are in play. The responsibility of the organisation, held the Court, extends to the resolution of "the question of Palestine [...] in all its aspects".[89] Therefore, the wall's construction is of particularly acute concern to the United Nations

---

85 Thirlway, *supra* note 72, 846. On the political ramifications of advisory opinions see *infra* Section 3.2.2, 201ff.

86 *Western Sahara*, 27[42].

87 UNGA Res ES-10/14 (8 December 2003).

88 *Wall*, 157[46].

89 Ibid. 158–9[49].

and this renders appropriate the delivery of the advisory opinion in this particular case. Key takeaway from the *Wall* opinion is that the consent of an interested State loses its relevance for the propriety of giving an advisory opinion if the question before the Court is also a matter 'of particularly acute concern' to the United Nations.

This reasoning is very generic, revisionary of previous case-law and unconvincing. Generic because the Court did not invoke specific functions of the General Assembly for which the UN organ needed guidance from the ICJ, as it did in *Western Sahara*. Rather, it needed the advisory opinion for the proper exercise of its functions.[90] Arguably then, the UNGA requested the opinion in order to exercise powers upon the dispute. It is revisionary because, as Higgins suggests, by leaving in essence this point unaddressed "this Opinion by its very silence essentially revises, rather than applies, the existing case law".[91] Finally, this part of the judgment is unconvincing, since the ICJ minimized the 'dispute' nature of the question before it and correspondingly emphasized its 'organizational' aspects.[92] In paragraphs 49 and 50 of the opinion, the ICJ rules that in some circumstances the interests of the international community in obtaining an advisory opinion on a point of law which is also the subject of a specific dispute between two states may override the right of each of those States not to have the dispute judicially determined without their consent. This is a defensible position and could have been stated as a ground for rejecting Israel's objection. But, as Thirlway observes, it is idle to pretend that because the dispute issue was located in a much broader frame of reference the dispute between Israel and Palestine disappeared, or that if there was such a dispute, the Court's opinion would not have the effect of ruling upon it, even if only indirectly.[93] Once more, the ICJ does not address the overarching question posed above and repeated now with emphasis: when placing the dispute in a broader frame of reference, the delivery of an opinion by the Court is always justified? The Court leaves the matter open for speculation and all in all, it remains unclear under what circumstances the circumvention argument could prevail. What is clear though, is that the ICJ is prepared to subsume any

90 Ibid 159[50].

91 Higgins, Dissenting Opinion, *Wall* 210[12]–[13]: Higgins concludes by saying that 'the Opinion by its very silence essentially revises, rather than applies, the existing case law.'

92 Pomerance, *supra* note 39, 33.

93 Thirlway, *supra* note 72, 1724. P d'Argent, 'Article 65' in A Zimmermann, Chr. Tams, K Oellers – Frahm, et al. (eds), *The Statute of the International Court of Justice. A Commentary* (OUP, 2019), 1783, 1807.

bilateral dispute within UN competence and hence offer its opinion on the merits of any dispute.

2.3 *Compelled to Advice: the* Chagos *Opinion*

This eagerness of the Court to advise on any dispute irrespective of the particular circumstances surrounding the request for the opinion, is further accentuated by the particularities surrounding the *Chagos* opinion.[94] The questions posed to the Court in UNGA resolution 71/292 are as follows:

> (a) Was the process of decolonization of Mauritius lawfully completed when Mauritius was granted independence in 1968, following the separation of the Chagos Archipelago from Mauritius and having regard to international law, including obligations reflected in General Assembly resolutions 1514 (XV) of 14 December 1960, 2066 (XX) of 16 December 1965, 2232 (XXI) of 20 December 1966 and 2357 (XXII) of 19 December 1967?;
> (b) What are the consequences under international law, including obligations reflected in the above-mentioned resolutions, arising from the continued administration by the United Kingdom of Great Britain and Northern Ireland of the Chagos Archipelago, including with respect to the inability of Mauritius to implement a programme for the resettlement on the Chagos Archipelago of its nationals, in particular those of Chagossian origin?

As expected, the UK resisted the delivery of the advisory opinion on two fronts.[95] First, on the basis that the *MPA* arbitral award has already determined the substantive issues at stake and second, by putting forward the familiar circumvention contention; namely, that determination of sovereignty is the real object of the request and a pronouncement on this cannot be made without UK's consent.[96] The UK strongly opposed what it perceived to be the judicial settlement of a bilateral sovereignty dispute, yet its

94 ICJ, *Legal Consequences of the Separation of the Chagos Archipelago from Mauritius in 1965*, Advisory Opinion 25 February 2019, I.C.J. Reports 2019, 95. The events leading up to the request for the opinion were summarized in the introduction to this Chapter.

95 Ph. Webb, 'The United Kingdom and the Chagos Archipelago Advisory Opinion: Engagement and Resistance' 22 (2021) *Melbourne Journal of International Law* 726–748.

96 ICJ, *Legal Consequences of the Separation of the Chagos Archipelago from Mauritius in 1965*, Written Statement of the United Kingdom, 15 February 2018, 154[9.21] and Chapter VII respectively.

resistance was notably tinged with regret for its treatment of the Chagossians.[97]

The ICJ classified both considerations as potential 'compelling reasons' that could lead the Court to decline to give the advisory opinion. Arguably, the first concerned the preclusive *res judicata* effect of the *MPA* award in relation to the ICJ advisory proceedings.[98] According to this effect, it is impossible to reopen a settled case between the same parties.[99] Many States – not only the UK – during the UNGA debates,[100] and in their written statements before the Court,[101] noted Mauritius' attempt to bring the sovereignty dispute for a second time under judicial scrutiny. So, for the first time in its jurisprudence, the ICJ commented on the value of relevant previous judicial findings for the delivery of its opinion. The Court clarified that, while it 'will consider any relevant judicial or arbitral decision', *res judicata* cannot affect its capacity to undertake a request for an advisory opinion.[102] This is so, because the purpose of rendering such an opinion is to assist the organ that requested it and not to help States settle a dispute (which is the purpose of a binding award). Hence, an advisory opinion can in principle always re-examine previous legal findings. The importance of this *dictum* has gone largely unnoticed in literature perhaps because the Court found *obiter,* that even if *res judicata* was a relevant consideration, its prerequisites would not have been fulfilled.[103] In particular, the issues determined by the *MPA* award were different from those before the ICJ, so there was no subject-matter identity between the two proceedings.[104]

---

97 Ibid 2[1.5].

98 JH Fahner, 'Two Takes on Chagos: Reconciling the Advisory Opinion with the *Res Judicata* Effect of the UNCLOS Arbitral Award' in T Burri and J Trinidad (eds) *The International Court of Justice and Decolonisation: New Directions from the Chagos Advisory Opinion* (CUP, 2021) 71.

99 Gr. Walters, 'Fitting a Square Peg into a Round Hole: Do Res Judicata Challenges in International Arbitration Constitute Jurisdictional or Admissibility Problems?' 29 (2012) *Journal of International Arbitration* 651.

100 General Assembly, verbatim record, 71st Session, 88th Plenary Meeting, Thursday, 22 June 2017, 10 a.m. (A/71/PV.88), 16–21 (Australia, Canada, Croatia, France, Germany, Israel, Mexico, Myanmar, New Zealand, Sweden, UK, USA).

101 Eg Written Statement of Germany, 13 [35]; Written Statement of Israel 7–8[3.8].

102 *Chagos Opinion* 116[81].

103 But *see* G Puma, 'Preliminary Questions in the ICJ Advisory Opinion on the Legal Consequences of the Separation of the Chagos Archipelago from Mauritius in 1965' 79 (2019) *Zeitschrift für ausländisches öffentliches Recht und Völkerrecht* 841, 864; Fahner, *supra* note 98, 84 .

104 Ibid. '*In any event*, the Court further notes that the issues that were determined by the Arbitral Tribunal in the Arbitration regarding the Chagos Marine Protected Area [..] are not the same as those that are before the Court in these proceedings." (emphasis added)

The reasoning of the ICJ merits close attention. The critical issue here concerns the binding effect of judicial awards rendered in the course of contentious proceedings.[105] In order to justify that the scope of *res judicata* of such awards does not cover subsequent advisory proceedings, the Court appeals solely to the purpose of rendering an advisory opinion. The examination of the *ad hoc* relationship between the two sets of proceedings, identity of *personae, petitum* and *causa petenti,* becomes irrelevant.[106] It is only logical nevertheless, that the Court will adopt the same approach with respect to the application of *lis pendens,*[107] that is when contentious proceedings run in parallel with advisory proceedings. For *lis pendens* and *res judicata* address similar concerns, are comparable and can be invoked when the same prerequisites are in play.[108] Therefore, the ICJ in *Chagos* rules that advisory proceedings, even if they pertain to a bilateral dispute, can always be resorted to irrespective of any relevant judicial pronouncements either preceding the opinion or running in parallel with it. Such a view on the relationship between advisory opinions and related bilateral litigation limits even further the set of circumstances under which the ICJ will decline to render an advisory opinion. Also, in view of the legal effects of ICJ advisory opinions, explained in detail in the next Section, this view is unduly formalistic and some nuance in this *dictum* would have been welcome. In effect, the ICJ in *Chagos* may be circumspect on the question of the interaction of its advisory opinion with other relevant past litigation, but with its stance the Court is demonstrating an eagerness to intervene in, and perhaps settle, bilateral disputes.

The second objection to the rendering of the opinion concerned the circumvention of UK's consent. This was premised on the contention that at the heart of the matter lied the bilateral sovereignty dispute and not decolonization as a matter of international concern.[109] The recognition of the bilateral

105 This consideration should not be confused with the incapacity of advisory opinions to qualify as *res judicata*. As noted above, this was clarified by the ICJ in *Peace Treaties, see supra* note 61.

106 *Contra* Fahner who holds that the ICJ implicitly refers to the prerequisite of the identity of parties, *supra* note 98, 84. Be that as it may, the crucial consideration at this point is that the different nature of proceedings renders the principle of *res judicata* inapplicable in such scenarios.

107 Kolb argues that this will be the case with respect to *lis pendens* because advisory and contentious proceedings are not 'of equivalent value' and also the *causa petendi* will probably be different, *supra* note 48.

108 C McLachlan, *Lis Pendens in International Litigation* (Brill, 2009) 356–357; S Schaffstein, *The Doctrine of Res Judicata before International Commercial Arbitral Tribunals* (OUP, 2016) 235[6.55].

109 *Chagos opinion*, 112[60] and 116–7[83].

nature underlying Mauritius' previous claim before the PCA, was testament to the bilateral nature of the present request also, some participants argued. The ICJ nevertheless, was undeterred. By following a reasoning *alla Western Sahara,* the Court dismissed the argument without blinking an eye. Initially, it repeated the *dictum* from that opinion that "the lack of consent of an interested State may render the giving of an advisory opinion incompatible with the Court's judicial character".[110] To hold subsequently that the circumstances of the case justify a disaggregation between the questions of decolonisation and sovereignty. Neither the purpose of the GA's request, nor the longstanding divergent views between the two States were pointing towards an opinion on a bilateral territorial dispute.[111] The Court's pronouncement in paragraph 89 is indicative of the disposition with which the Court examines this objection: "the fact that the Court may have to pronounce on legal issues on which divergent views have been expressed by Mauritius and the United Kingdom does not mean that, by replying to the request, the Court is dealing with a bilateral dispute". Given the ink spilled and the hours of pleadings spent on this issue before the Court, to treat it in one fell swoop was disappointing, to say the least. With relative ease then, the ICJ placed the dispute in the broader frame of reference of decolonisation and this finding, in and of itself, functioned as a 'get out of jail free card'.

Once again, the ICJ missed an opportunity to acknowledge and pronounce on the relationship between decolonization – a UNGA function of acute concern for the UN – and resolution of a bilateral dispute which is undoubtedly underlying the request for an advisory opinion.[112] That a bilateral dispute existed between the two States was not denied even by Mauritius.[113] The ICJ ignores the underlying dispute and one would expect a more elaborate justification as to why decolonization can be separated from the claim on sovereignty. By glossing over the consequences arising from the existence of such

110 Ibid 117[85].

111 Ibid 117–8[86]–[89].

112 Same criticism with respect to the *Wall* opinion, *supra* note … and accompanying text. The bilateral character of the underlying dispute was more pronounced in *Chagos* than in *Wall* for two reasons. First, because Mauritius is – contrary to Palestine – an established State and hence able to settle disputes in a position of formal equality with the UK (FL Bordin, 'State Responsibility in Advisory Proceedings: Thoughts on Judicial Propriety and Multilateralism in the Chagos Opinion', in *The ICJ and Decolonization, supra* note 98, 95, 103) and second, due to the nature of the dispute as 'it is difficult to imagine any dispute that is more quintessentially bilateral than a dispute over territorial sovereignty', *Chagos*, Dissenting Opinion Judge Donoghue 266[21].

113 Oral Submissions of Mauritius 35 [6].

a dispute for the decolonization issue, the ICJ examines the circumvention argument in a superficial way. In her dissenting opinion, Judge Donoghue, criticizes the outcome of the opinion in dealing with the circumvention argument and the respective methodology used by the majority. "It is necessary", she urges, "to compare the subject-matter of this bilateral dispute with the issues presented by the request".[114] Donoghue compared the two in detail and arrived at the opposite outcome from the majority, namely that the question of decolonization and that of sovereignty are inseparable.[115] The crucial aspect here is not the difference in evaluation, but rather the appropriate reasoning and methodology via which Donoghue arrived at this outcome. A counterpoint to Donoghue's opinion was offered by Vice-President Xue who acknowledged the existence of an underlying bilateral dispute and concluded that it does not change the nature of the issue as a matter of decolonization.[116] It is exactly this lack of argumentation in the majority's reasoning that renders the *Western Sahara* incantation -repeated with approval in *Chagos*, hollow. The ICJ continues to chip away from the circumvention principle, until what is left after *Chagos* is but a name.

One wonders then, under what circumstances will the ICJ decline to render an advisory opinion for 'compelling reasons'. To turn once more to the overarching question running through this Section, the Court's stance is steadfast: irrespective of the nature of the bilateral dispute underlying the request for an advisory opinion, its relationship with the request for an advisory opinion, the judicial organs that may have been seized of the dispute and the position of the interested parties, lack of consent cannot affect the delivery of an ICJ advisory opinion. In an imaginary scenario, even if both interested parties were unwilling to have the dispute brought before the ICJ, the Court would have been entitled to deliver its opinion, assuming of course that the referring organ had adopted legally the referring act. While this is a defensible position in view of the normative framework regulating the functioning of the Court, nevertheless, the ICJ's jurisprudence seemingly points to a different direction. By pretending that *Western Sahara* is still alive, the Court wants to have the cake and eat it too. In name, to preserve the integrity of its two functions (settling legal disputes in contentious cases and responding to requests in advisory opinions) and in practice to undertake any request for advisory opinion hereby undermining this very integrity. Overall, the UK argument that "[i] f the principle of non-circumvention is not to be upheld in this case, [...] then

114 *Chagos*, Dissenting Opinion Judge Donoghue, 263[10].
115 Ibid. 264–6[16]–[22].
116 *Chagos*, Declaration of Vice-President Xue, 146–7[19].

it appears that the principle may be taken as abandoned altogether" reflects the state of affairs.[117]

The *tour d' horizon* of the relevant ICJ jurisprudence, suggests that advisory opinions may be used as a fallback option in any bilateral dispute. As Judge Tomka noted in *Chagos*, "advisory proceedings have now become a way of bringing before the Court contentious matters".[118] Provided of course that the subject-matter of the request falls within the functions of the requesting organ.[119] This explains why the UNGA has been the requesting organ in the latest opinions (*Wall*, *Kosovo* and *Chagos*) where arguably the advice is not sought for the purpose of resolving a concrete question pending for the requesting institution.[120] Due to the wide spectrum of functions the UNGA undertakes, it is easy to camouflage the request as a matter of multilateral concern and thus hide the real intentions of the interested party. And the ICJ's jurisprudence to extract the purpose of the request solely by its framing and to ignore the overriding circumstances, demonstrates its willingness to put under the rug any underlying dispute. In this way, the Court detaches its capacity to deliver an opinion from the positions of the interested parties. This strategic use of advisory opinions in order to override State consent renders such opinions a *prima facie* attractive judicial mechanism for interested States, especially since they are delivered by the principal judicial organ of the UN. This 'open-door' policy however, does not necessarily mean that the ICJ will effectively resolve bilateral disputes via the delivery of non-binding opinions. This will be determined by the way ICJ opinions are perceived by both States-parties to a dispute and other actors involved in the dispute settlement process that may be called to pronounce on the issues determined by the advisory opinion. The judicial adventure of the Chagos Archipelago provides illuminating insights in this respect too.

---

117 UK Written Statement, (15 February 2018) [7.21]. *Contra* Z Cr. Reghizzi, 'The Chagos Advisory Opinion and the Principle of Consent to Adjudication', in *The ICJ and Decolonization, supra* note 98, 51, 67: 'circumvention of consent has not become purely theoretical with Chagos'.

118 *Chagos,* Declaration of Judge Tomka 148[2].

119 Note the refusal of the ICJ to deliver an opinion on the request by the WHO regarding the legality of the use of nuclear weapons for reasons relating to the competences of the requesting organization, ICJ, *Advisory Opinion on the Legality of the Use of Nuclear Weapons* (1994).

120 D Akande, 'Selection of the International Court of Justice as a Forum for Contentious and Advisory Proceedings (Including Jurisdiction)' 7 (2016) *Journal of International Dispute Settlement* 320, 339.

3 Instrumentalization of ICJ Advisory Opinions in the UN Era

3.1 *The Curious Legal Effect of ICJ Advisory Opinions*

The *Chagos* opinion was a win for Mauritius. With respect to question (a), the Court held that the process of decolonization of Mauritius was not lawfully completed when that country acceded to independence in 1968. The circumstances under which the Lancaster House agreement was negotiated were such, that it did not reflect the free and genuine expression of the will of the people concerned.[121] Therefore, both the detachment and the subsequent creation of the BIOT were unlawful actions, violating the UK's international obligation to respect the territorial integrity of Mauritius.[122] It is worth noting that the ICJ did not pronounce explicitly on the issue of sovereignty, and it could not have done so since it rejected the UK's submission that it was essentially dealing with a bilateral dispute concerning sovereignty.[123] Whether it did so implicitly, is a matter of interpretation.[124] One way or the other, the Court's answer to question (a) clearly undermines the UK's position as to sovereignty.[125] As does the answer to the second question put to the Court. With respect to the legal consequences of the continuing administration of Chagos by the UK, the Court was equally critical towards the colonial power. It declared that the UK's stance constitutes nothing less than a wrongful act entailing the international responsibility of that State, and that the UK consequently has an obligation to bring its administration of the Chagos Archipelago to an end "as rapidly as possible".[126] Acting prudently, the ICJ left the modalities for the completion of Mauritius' decolonization to the UNGA.[127] It is telling that the latter's reaction to the opinion was to set a six-month deadline to the UK in order to "withdraw its colonial administration … unconditionally".[128] Finally, according to the Court, the decolonization pro-

121 *Chagos* 137[172].

122 Ibid 137[173]–[174].

123 *Chagos* 117–8[86]–[88].

124 Donoghue asserts that the determination of sovereignty over the Archipelago is the only possible reading of the Court's opinion, *Chagos*, Donoghue Dissenting, 265[19].

125 Chris Monaghan, 'Reflections on the UK's Assertion of Sovereignty over the Chagos Archipelago in the Wake of the *Chagos* Advisory Opinion' in *The ICJ and Decolonization, supra* note 98, 144, 158.

126 *Chagos* 138–9[177], 139–40[182].

127 Ibid [178]–[179].

128 *Advisory Opinion of the International Court of Justice on the Legal Consequences of the Separation of the Chagos Archipelago from Mauritius in 1965* GA Res 73/295, 73rd session, 83rd plenary meeting, Agenda Item 88, Supp No 49, UN Doc A/RES/73/295 (24 May 2019) [3] (voting record: 116–6–56).

cess will be completed with the co-operation of all UN members and the UNGA that will address the issue of resettlement of the Chagossians. After these pronouncements of the ICJ, the development of the dispute has taken a different turn.

The intervention of the Court has been perceived to have a dispute resolution effect and this is evinced by the ITLOS preliminary judgment of 28 January 2021 where the next act of the Chagos judicial drama took place.[129] The UK played no direct role in this judicial procedure as the disputing parties were Mauritius and Maldives. Since 2001, Mauritius reached out to the Maldives asking to begin negotiations regarding the delimitation of their continental shelves around the Chagos Archipelago.[130] These broke down in 2011 and the undertaking provided for in the joint communiqué of 12 March 2011 "to make bilateral arrangements on the overlapping area of extended continental shelf of the two States around the Chagos Archipelago" was not upheld. And on 18 June 2019, Mauritius instituted arbitral proceedings against the Maldives under Annex VII of the UNCLOS. After consulting with the President of the tribunal, a special agreement was concluded between the two States and the case was transferred to a Special Chamber formed under Article 15(2) of the ITLOS Statute. Mauritius asked the Special Chamber to delimit its exclusive economic zone, inner and outer continental shelf from that of the Maldives and to find that the Maldives had violated its procedural obligations under articles 74(3) and 83(3) of the UNCLOS to enter into provisional arrangements pending an agreement on delimitation and not to jeopardise the reaching of a final agreement.

Unsurprisingly, before the Special Chamber Maldives reiterated the main UK contention before the ICJ. The case before the Special Chamber, as well as the one before the ICJ, argued the Maldives, primarily concerns a long-standing and unresolved bilateral dispute between Mauritius and the United Kingdom about territorial sovereignty.[131] Both the first and second preliminary objections of the Maldives to the Special Chamber's jurisdiction were linked to the determination of the UK's legal position in relation to the parties; the first, pertained to the application of the indispensable third party (*Mone-*

129 ITLOS, *Delimitation of the Maritime Boundary between Mauritius and Maldives in the Indian Ocean* (*Mauritius/Maldives*) (*Preliminary Objections*), Judgment, International Tribunal for the Law of the Sea, Case No 28, 28 January 2021.

130 For an account of the factual background to the dispute, see Ibid 19–23[56]–[68].

131 *Delimitation in the Indian Ocean* 33[104].

tary Gold) principle.[132] The second, to the necessary examination of a preliminary issue – territorial sovereignty – that lies beyond UNCLOS and hence outside the competence of the Special Chamber.[133] Deciding on both objections, said the tribunal, depended on the validity of the premise that Mauritius has sovereignty over the Chagos Archipelago.[134] So, they were examined jointly by the Special Chamber. If the sovereignty dispute had been resolved before the seizin of the tribunal, the UK would have no legal interest at stake and the tribunal could not overstep its jurisdiction by rendering its judgment. If, on the other hand, the dispute was still extant, the UK was an indispensable third party in the sense of the *Monetary Gold* principle and the Special Chamber would have to exercise powers it did not possess, in order to determine incidentally which of the two States had a valid sovereign title over the Chagos Archipelago.

The Special Chamber held, rather surprisingly, that the sovereignty dispute ceased with the delivery of the *Chagos* advisory opinion. On the one hand, the Special Chamber affirms that the advisory opinion cannot have resolved the bilateral dispute due to the lack of consent of the disputing parties and at the same time that the necessary implication arising from the opinion is that Mauritius has sovereignty over the Chagos Archipelago.[135] In this way, the Special Chamber accepts that decolonization and sovereignty go hand-in-hand, and hence determination of the former necessarily entails determination of the latter.[136] Its reasoning comes down to a two-step logical argumentation, each step being interesting in its own right. The first has to do with the

---

132 *Monetary Gold*, is a procedural principle developed in ICJ jurisprudence. It requires the Court to abstain from deciding a case only where the legal interests of a non-consenting third state form "the very subject matter" of the case, and where the Court cannot decide the case before it without adjudicating on the international rights and obligation of a third state, ICJ, *Monetary Gold Removed from Rome in 1943* (*Italy v. France, UK and USA*), Judgment of 15 June 1954, ICJ Reports 1954, 32. It is likely that Mauritius submitted its claim to ITLOS and not to the ICJ, due to the latter's strict application of the *Monetary Gold* principle.

133 'Written Preliminary Objections of the Republic of Maldives under Article 294 of the United Nations Convention on the Law of the Sea and Article 97 of the Rules of the International Tribunal for the Law of the Sea', *Delimitation in the Indian Ocean*, annex 1, 19–20[59]–[62], 27[82] and 33[103].

134 *Delimitation in the Indian Ocean* 36 [114]–[115].

135 *Delimitation in the Indian Ocean* 51[168] and 53–4[174].

136 *Contra* Chris Monaghan who considers that the Advisory Opinion strengthened Mauritius' position but did not make a determination on sovereignty: Chris Monaghan, 'Reflections on the UK's Assertion of Sovereignty over the Chagos Archipelago in the Wake of the *Chagos* Advisory Opinion' in *The ICJ and Decolonization, supra* note 98, 144, 158.

capacity of an advisory opinion to produce an authoritative decision that produces legal effect and resolves a legal dispute. Relatedly, the second suggests that the positions of the disputing States are irrelevant in the determination of whether such a dispute is still in play or not.

Infamously, the tribunal based its finding that the sovereignty dispute had been effectively resolved by the *Chagos* opinion on a novel distinction between the binding character and the authoritative nature of an advisory opinion of the ICJ.[137] This was introduced in order to relieve a tension in the Special Chamber's reasoning that is hard to round off; on the one hand, the generally recognized non-binding nature of advisory opinions and on the other their capacity to produce "legal determinations [that] do have legal effect".[138] So, while an advice is just an advice that cannot and does not produce an obligation of compliance with the Court's findings,[139] due to the ICJ's position as the principal judicial organ of the United Nations, the Special Chamber concluded that "judicial determinations made in advisory opinions carry no less weight and authority than those in judgments".[140] The ICJ's position, according to the Special Chamber, is capable of producing legal effects analogous to that of substantive *res judicata*. This bold statement was not backed with a clear explanation of the normative basis on which it rests and hence the Special Chamber left it open to speculation what it means by 'authority' or 'legal effect'.[141]

From the outset one must distinguish between the legal and the moral effects of an advisory opinion. The authoritative nature of an advisory opinion mainly pertains to the latter and in and of itself is not a valid normative justification of the Special Chamber's conclusion. Having distinguished

137 *Delimitation in the Indian Ocean* 61–2[203].

138 Ibid 62[205]; Separate and Dissenting Opinion of Judge *ad hoc* Oxman, 14[36]; S Thin, 'The Curious Case of the 'Legal Effect' of ICJ Advisory Opinions in the Mauritius/Maldives Maritime Boundary Dispute', *EJIL:Talk!*, 5 February 2021; FS Eichberger, 'The Legal Effect of ICJ Advisory Opinions Redefined? The Mauritius/Maldives Delimitation Case – Judgment on Preliminary Objections' 22 (2021) *Melbourne Journal of International Law* 1.

139 R Jennings, 'Advisory Opinions of the International Court of Justice' in UNESCO (ed), *Boutros Boutros-Ghali Amicorum Discipulorumque Liber:* Paix, *Dévelopment, Démocratie* (Bruylant, 1998) 531, 532.

140 *Delimitation in the Indian Ocean*, [203].

141 Relevant criticisms by Eichberger, *supra* note 138, 16; Thin, *supra* note 138; N Lanzoni, 'The Authority of ICJ Advisory Opinions as Precedents: The Mauritius/Maldives Case' 2 (2022) *The Italian Review of International and Comparative Law* 1; Cr. Gaver, 'Dispute Concerning Delimitation of the Maritime Boundary between Mauritius and Maldives in the Indian Ocean (Mauritius/Maldives). Case No. 28. Judgment', 115 (2021) *AJIL* 521.

authority from bindingness, the Special Chamber can only have in mind authority as legitimacy, not as legal power. This is so, because ICJ advisory opinions do not possess binding force and they are only subsidiary means for the determination of the law according to Article 38(1)(d) of the ICJ Statute.[142] Hence, their formal *de jure* authority, or the authority they attract from the UN Charter, is limited.[143] To the contrary, their legitimising *de facto* authority to exert a powerful pull toward compliance on those to whom it is addressed, could be significant.[144] Advisory opinions are the result of a proper judicial process, they are covered by procedural guarantees and delivered in a reasoned form. They may not produce *res judicata* but that fact is not sufficient to deprive an advisory opinion "of all the moral consequences which are inherent in the dignity of the organ delivering the opinion or even of its legal consequences".[145] This is mainly why they procure policy changes. For example, the *Chagos* opinion has been the catalyst in altering the official position of more than 20 States in the UNGA to align with the Court's findings.[146] Further, an advisory opinion produces a justifying and legitimising effect, so that a State acting contrary to an advisory opinion would have to justify its actions.[147] And *a contrario*, no State can be considered to act in contradiction to international law if it complies with

142 H Thirlway, *The Sources of International Law* (OUP, 2014) 131.

143 Kolb argues that the formal authority of the advisory opinion extends to the requesting organ. To the extent that it is applying international law, it is obliged to apply the law as pronounced in the opinion, *supra* note 48, 1097–8.

144 T Franck, *The Power of Legitimacy among Nations* (OUP, 1990) 25. Lanzoni labels this legitimizing function as the 'normative authority' of advisory opinions, *supra* note 141, 12, and Alter Helfer and Rask Madsen as '*de facto* authority', K Alter, L Helfer and M Rask Madsen, 79 (2016) 'How context shapes the authority of international courts' *Law and Contemporary Problems* 1.

145 *Peace Treaties*, Separate Opinion of Judge Azevedo, 65. The Special Chamber held in the same vein that an ICJ advisory opinion "cannot be disregarded simply because [it] is not binding", *Delimitation in the Indian Ocean* 63 [205]. Thouvenin labels this as the *res deliberata*, JM Thouvenin, 'On Different *Res*: *Res Judicata, Res Interpretata, Res Praescripta* (or *Indicata*), *Res Deliberata*' 65 (2022) *Japanese Yearbook of International Law* 270.

146 On 22 June 2017, UNGA resolution 71/292 referring the matter to the ICJ was upheld with a 95–15 majority (65 abstentions). Following the court's ruling in 2019, UNGA resolution 73/295 that demanded the unconditional withdrawal of the UK from the archipelago within six months, was upheld with a 116–6 majority (56 abstentions).

147 K Oellers-Frahm, 'Lawmaking Through Advisory Opinions?' 12 (2011) *German Law Journal* 1033, 1051; G Bernabei, 'The Law-Making Effect of ICJ Advisory Opinons; A Survey of the *Chagos* Opinion' in PG Telés and MA Ribeiro (eds) *Case-Law and the Development of International Law* (Brill, 2021), 127, 132.

the findings of the Court in an advisory opinion.[148] Thus, by appealing to the authoritative character of the principal judicial organ of the UN, the Special Chamber can suggest, at best, that States have a strong moral responsibility to comply with the ICJ's findings.

The Special Chamber clearly decided to go beyond that and attributed formal authority to the ICJ advisory opinion. According to the most convincing interpretation, the Special Chamber implicitly accepted the judicial pronouncements of the advisory opinion as 'givens'.[149] The reference to 'givens' is to the exception to the *Monetary Gold* principle established by the arbitral tribunal in *Larsen v. Hawaiian Kingdom*, where it was stated that "if the legal finding against an absent third party could be taken as a given (for example, by reason of an authoritative decision of the Security Council on the point), the [*Monetary Gold*] principle may well not apply".[150] The basis of this assumption is that the Special Chamber is simply applying a legal finding (in this case: sovereignty over Chagos) which is already binding with respect to the UK. So, there can be no complaint of an overreach of competence as the Special Chamber is not really exercising its own competence but it is accepting a legal reality already determined by a competent body (in this case: the ICJ).[151] Having this in mind, the Special Chamber held that the ICJ opinion determined the issue of sovereignty and further that this determination resolved with legal force the dispute between the two States. Leaving aside the interpretative issue of whether the ICJ indeed clarified the sovereignty issue in its opinion, the normative weight attached to pronouncements made in advisory opinions is questionable.

In order to fully appreciate the Special Chamber's conclusion, it is important to take stock and reflect on the nature of advisory opinions and the ICJ's role when delivering them. What kind of determinations with legal effect – if any – does the ICJ make in the course of advisory proceedings? A starting point for an answer to the aforementioned question was given by the ICJ in

148 JA Frowein and K Oellers-Frahm, 'Article 65' in A Zimmermann, C Tomuschat, K Oellers-Frahm and Chr. Tams (eds), *The Statute of the International Court of Justice: A Commentary* (OUP, 2012) 1605, 1624.

149 This reading has been proposed by commentators, *see* D Akande, "Introduction to the Symposium on Zachary Mollengarden and Noam Zamir 'The Monetary Gold Principle: Back to Basics'" 115 (2021) *AJIL UNBOUND*, 140, 143; Eichberger, *supra* note 138, 17.

150 *Larsen v. Hawaiian Kingdom*, 119 (2001) ILR 566, 592[11.24].

151 For an analysis see M Paparinskis, "Long Live Monetary Gold *Terms and Conditions Apply", 115 (2021) *AJIL UNBOUND* 154, 156. The existence of the exception is one example of how the *Monetary Gold* doctrine does not, in appropriate cases, preclude adjudication of cases involving the legal interests of absent third parties.

Nuclear Weapons. According to that opinion, in advisory proceedings the Court's task is to engage "in its *normal judicial function* of ascertaining the existence or otherwise of legal principles and rules applicable to the" opinion at hand (emphasis added).[152] No clear definition of ascertainment of the law was provided by the ICJ. The Special Chamber's judgment provides no clarification in this respect either. Its argument, however, seems to be that since the ICJ can ascertain the law *erga omnes*, it can also determine whether that law is applicable with respect to the question posed. Then, the argument runs, this determination made in the context of an advisory opinion must be treated as binding law. In this way, the Special Chamber conflates the ICJ's capacity to state the law with the legal bindingness of such statements,[153] and its conclusion is in flat contradiction with the original assumption that advisory opinions cannot as such have binding force.[154] It is a *non-sequitur* to suggest that because the Court finds which legal rule is applicable in the question put to it, this renders the Court's determinations binding. Otherwise said: "the advisory opinion does not resolve the dispute, but establishes how the dispute should be resolved under international law".[155]

It is important nevertheless to understand how far can the ICJ engage with the law in advisory opinions, so as to determine whether the legal pronouncements rendered in advisory opinions can produce any legal effects. The only clarification made by the Court in *Nuclear Weapons* in this respect, suggests that law-ascertainment is different from legislation.[156] If by legislation, the Court understands a formal procedure resulting in the definition of rights and obligations binding upon all legal subjects then this is generally outside the purview of the Court's activity. Due to its nature as a judicial organ, the ICJ would highjack a function reserved for States in international law if it were to legislate. Despite it being distinguishable from legislation, the *contours* of law-ascertainment are not clear. To the extent that it requires the determination of the content of legal rules, law-ascertainment entails per force the develop-

152 *Nuclear Weapons* 237[18].

153 Thin, *supra* note 138; Rosenne, *supra* note 47 (vol. III), 1699.

154 According to an additional argument supporting this conclusion, since States cannot prevent the delivery of an ICJ advisory opinion, the latter cannot produce binding rights and obligations for States despite their consent, J Frowein and K Oellers-Frahm, 'Article 65' in A Zimmermann, Chr. Tomuschat and K Oellers-Frahm (eds) *The Statute of the International Court of Justice, A Commentary* (OUP, 2006), 1401, 1415.

155 Lanzoni, *supra* note 141, 22.

156 Ibid 'it states the existing law and does not legislate'. Jennings, *supra* note 139, 534; Sh. Rosenne, *The Law and Practice of the International Court 1920–2005* (vol. 3), (OUP, 2006) 1753.

ment of the law. And this, indisputably forms part of the ICJ's judicial function in advisory proceedings.[157] In order to guard its legitimate authority as an independent and objective court of law in advisory proceedings, the ICJ has shown caution and judicial restraint when (not) making pronouncements that go beyond the mere application of existing law. As Jennings put it, the Court tries to keep apart *jus dicere* from *jus dare*.[158] The infamous *non-liquet* in the *Nuclear Weapons* opinion has been the most dramatic instance in this respect.[159]

Relatedly, the ICJ cannot engage in any form of law-creation in advisory opinions. By law-creation here is meant the generation of a legal duty of compliance with the pronouncements of the Court, akin to that provided for in Article 94 of the UN Charter. As opposed to contentious proceedings where the Court resolves with binding force a dispute, advisory opinions are not binding on States, do not determine directly their rights and obligations, and, for that matter, do not contain operative clauses.[160] Because the Court cannot itself give binding force to judicial pronouncements made in advisory proceedings, they have to acquire such force externally; through the reception of the opinion from the international community by a voluntary act, usually via a collateral agreement.[161] So, the Special Chamber's unprece-

---

157 E Hambro, The Authority of the Advisory Opinions of the International Court of Justice, 3 (1954) *ICLQ* 87; L Boisson de Chazournes, Advisory Opinions and the Furtherance of the Common Interest of Mankind, in L Boisson de Chazournes, C Romano and R Mackenzie (eds) *International Organization and International Dispute Settlement: Trends and Prospects* (Brill, 2002) 105. Some commentators have labelled the process of determining the content of the law as 'law-making', when this requires a substantial departing from pre-existing law or even the creation of new rules, *see* Chr. Tams, 'The Development of International Law by the International Court of Justice', in Decisions of the ICJ as Sources of International Law? 2 (2018) *Gaetano Morelli Lectures Series* 63 at 67–9; T Mayr and J Mayr-Singer, 'Keep the Wheels Spinning: The Contributions of Advisory Opinions of the International Court of Justice to the Development of International Law' 76 (2016) *ZaöRV* 425, 434 ("a *prima facie* rejection of a law-making role of the Court coupled with the acceptance of a law-developing function is artificial and shows a blind adherence to semantics over reality")

158 RY Jennings, The Role of the International Court of Justice, 68 (1998) *BYBIL* 1, 41.

159 Oellers-Frahm, *supra* note 147, 1048.

160 This can be inferred *a contrario* from the absence of a provision equivalent to Article 94 of the UN Charter for advisory opinions, Rosenne, *supra* note 156, 1697.

161 *Eg.* Former Article XII(2) of the Statute of the ILO Administrative Tribunal provided for the delivery of binding ICJ advisory opinions. The contractually agreed binding effect 'goes beyond the scope attributed by the Charter and the Statute of the Court to an advisory opinion', *Judgments of the Administrative Tribunal of the ILO upon Complaints Made against UNESCO*, Advisory Opinion, ICJ Reports 1956, 84; *Difference Relating to Immunity from Legal Process of a Special Rapporteur of the Commission on Human Rights,*

dented move to attribute binding force to law-ascertaining pronouncements without an ensuing voluntary act can be problematic. Especially, when these pronouncements are strongly connected to bilateral issues as was the case in *Chagos*.

Nevertheless, there are different levels of judicial engagement with the development of the law. It is one thing for the Court to develop rules that pertain to the UN's institutional law and quite another to make direct pronouncements on legal questions that pertain to bilateral disputes. A characteristic example of the first category, has been the *Reparations* opinion.[162] In this opinion, through a teleological interpretation of the UN Charter, the Court asserted that the UN has the capacity to bring a claim against a State for injuries suffered by one of the organization's employees. The finding that the UN possesses a degree of legal personality was a watershed in the development of the law of international organisations as the common understanding at the time was that only States held any form of international legal personality.[163] As to the second category of opinions, the Court has occasionally gone beyond what could be understood as merely 'opining' on a particular matter and answered legal questions regarding responsibility issues that pertain to bilateral disputes.[164] The most striking example of this instance has been the *Wall* opinion, where the Court proceeded to consider forms of reparation resulting from Israel's unlawful actions.[165] In both occasions, the Court makes direct pronouncements on international legal questions by going beyond a mere assertion of pre-existing rules; its pronouncements contribute to the development of the substantive content of legal rules.[166]

But, giving binding force – or 'legal effect' as per the Special Chamber's terminology – to judicial *dicta* belonging to the second category turns advi-

ICJ Reports 1999, 77[25]: "A distinction should thus be drawn between the advisory nature of the Court's task and the particular effects that parties to an existing dispute may wish to attribute, in their mutual relations, to an advisory opinion of the Court".

162 ICJ, *Reparations for Injuries Suffered in the Service of the United Nations*, Advisory Opinion, ICJ Reports 1949, 174. Of the same nature were the following opinions: *Genocide* (*1951*), *Effects of Awards of Compensation* (*1954*), *Certain Expenses* (*1962*) and *Namibia* (*1971*).

163 J Klabbers, An Introduction to International Organizations Law (CUP, 2022), 46.

164 Lauterpacht, *supra* note 63, 354; Bordin, *supra* note 112, 96–104. Contesse names this function 'ruling through advice', J Contesse 'The Rule of Advice in International Human Rights Law' 115 (2021) *AJIL* 367–408.

165 *Wall*, [153].

166 Frowein and Oellers-Frahm, *supra* note 148, 1606 1622 and 1628.

sory opinions into dispute settlement mechanisms. In this way, the distinction between advisory and contentious proceedings is blurred to the point of collapse.[167] This has been the case in *Chagos* where the Court held that the UK has committed an internationally wrongful act that entails its international responsibility and also that all Member States must co-operate with the United Nations to complete the decolonization of Mauritius.[168] The competence of the Court to make such findings caused great controversy within the bench in *Chagos*,[169] but probably it was endorsed since the ICJ has made such determinations in past opinions.[170] Be that as it may, giving 'legal effect' to such statements and hence determining that they have resolved the underlying sovereignty dispute, can only mean that they acquire the force of material *res judicata*.[171] That is, they are recognised as binding on the disputing parties. *A contrario,* when the subject-matter of the requested opinion concerns the interpretation of UN texts, the binding force attached

167 The unprecedented conflation between contentious and advisory proceedings at the normative level, is different from their conflation at the procedural level when a bilateral dispute underpins the ICJ advisory proceedings. Three factors pertaining to procedural issues are testament to the latent contentious nature of the advisory proceedings in *Chagos*. First, both the UK and Mauritius were granted a longer time for their oral arguments than all other participants (three hours instead of forty minutes, *Chagos*, Verbatim Record of the 20th Public Sitting (3 September 2018) ICJ CR 2018/20, 26). Second, two members of the Court, Judges Crawford and Greenwood, abstained from participating on the bench by reason of their earlier activity, respectively as counsel and arbitrator, in the *Chagos Marine Protected Area* arbitration. Third, the acknowledgment by the UK to appoint an *ad hoc* judge should Mauritius make use of this prerogative. For different reasons, neither State made use of this possibility however, see *Chagos Opinion*, Written Statement of the United Kingdom, 3[1.7] note 9.

168 *Chagos* [182]. According to Hilpold, the Court could have applied the full range of obligations deriving from Article 41 of the ILC Articles on State Responsibility and pronounce the obligation of all States not to recognise the situation resulting from the continued violation of the right to self-determination. It refrained from doing so, Hilpold continues, in order to dodge the criticism that it is tackling a contentious case in the clothes of an advisory proceeding, P Hilpold, "Humanizing' the Law of Self-Determination – the Chagos Island Case' 91 (2022) *Nordic Journal of International Law* 189–215), 205–6. Taking the argument further, Higgins held in *Wall* not only that the ICJ can make such pronouncements, but also that the legal consequences from a finding on illegality in the context of an advisory opinion, were identical to those ensuing if the same finding was made in contentious proceedings, *Wall*, Separate Opinion of Judge Higgins, 216–7[38].

169 In favour: Au. Trindade *Separate Opinion* 257[333]; N Salam *Declaration* 339[6]; against: K Gevorgian *Declaration* 336[5], P Tomka *Declaration* 151[8].

170 E.g. *Namibia* [118].

171 Kolb, *supra* note 48, 1095 note 315: "the force of res judicata in the material sense means that the issue in dispute between the parties has been resolved."

to such opinions merely renders the ICJ the final arbiter on intra-organisational issues. Overall, the *Delimitation in the Indian Ocean* judgment brought the *limbo* of equally valid judicial interpretations about the sovereignty over Chagos to an end. It transformed a non-binding opinion into a legally binding decision,[172] hereby attaching unwarranted effects to ICJ advisory opinions and practically endorsed the PCIJ's *mentalité* on the delivery of such advice. It remains to be seen whether this approach will develop into a trend, followed by other courts and tribunals.

What is undisputable though, is that the Special Chamber's approach has affected the use of ICJ advisory opinions in the resolution of bilateral disputes. The next Section will showcase how States have strived to capitalize on advisory opinions, especially after the delivery of the Special Chamber's judgment and concomitantly how the ICJ's work may be influenced.

3.2 *Advisory Opinions as* de facto *Dispute Settlement Rulings*

As noted earlier in this Chapter, advisory opinions in the ICJ era have been resorted to less frequently than in the League of Nations era, since they have not been created to serve as a dispute settlement mechanism. And this conception has dictated their use up to date. When an inter-State dispute is underlying the request for an advisory opinion the latter is made in order to apply political pressure on the recalcitrant State and hence create an impetus to reach a negotiated settlement. There is seldom enough evidence to estimate the extent to which the pressure created by the Court's opinion influences the outcome of the dispute.[173] What can be inferred from their non-binding nature though, is that they were meant to be used as a means of external political pressure to abide with the specific interpretations of international law articulated by the Court.[174] And as noted in the previous Chapter advisory opinions are utilized as means, that is in order to strengthen the requesting party's position in other dispute settlement methods (judicial or not). Testament to the essentially political purpose of such pro-

172 N Klein, 'Chagos: A boundary dispute tips over a sovereignty ruling' *The Interpreter* (8 February 2021).

173 *Chr. Dominicé, 'Request of Advisory Opinions in Contentious Cases?' in International Organizations and International Dispute Settlement, supra* note, 91, 100; Giladi and Shany claim that this can be supported only by 'anecdotal evidence'; R Giladi and Y Shany, 'Assessing the Effectiveness of the International Court of Justice' in C Espósito and K Parlett (eds) *Cambridge Companion to the International Court of Justice* (CUP, 2023), 101, 116.

174 See e.g. D Sloss, 'Using International Court of Justice Advisory Opinions to Adjudicate Secessionist Claims', 42 (2001) *Santa Clara Law Review* 357.

ceedings is that the Court itself, that cherishes the opportunity to influence global affairs, will rely on the political will of the requesting UN organ. If, on the contrary, the Court is not willing 'to take into consideration the political process through which the request for the opinion was adopted' the advisory opinion will not contribute to the resolution of the political tension.[175] Overall, if the request forms part of an exercise in confrontation, and it is not a genuine effort to find an acceptable political solution of the problem, an advisory opinion may have limited consequences for the political development of the issue in connection with which it was requested.

However, judicial practice has altered the initial understanding on the nature of ICJ advisory opinions. This new understanding is evident not only from the legal effects of advisory opinions – analysed above – but also from their political ramifications, explained below. The preceding analysis brought to the fore two features of such opinions that bring them closer to a *de facto* dispute settlement mechanism when they pertain to a bilateral dispute. First, the lack of true discretion on their delivery and second, the readiness of other *fora* to attribute to them binding force. In turn, these features develop the potential of ICJ advisory opinions to accelerate the resolution of international disputes and hence their capacity to be used in the context of a multi-*forum* litigation strategy. It is argued here that, what has been redefined after *Chagos* is not only their nature, but consequently State expectations when instrumentalizing ICJ advisory opinions. States expect the Court to act as a rule-maker when delivering an advisory opinion and this perception will likely give new life to ICJ advisory opinions.

3.2.1 *Chagos* as a Watershed

The dispute around Chagos took a surprising turn after the delivery of the Special Chamber's judgment. At first, the UK government was adamant in its position that the judgment can have no effect for the UK since it was not a party in the proceedings and British sovereignty over the territory of the BIOT was not in doubt.[176] In effect, the UK reiterated the position it held after the delivery of the ICJ opinion. During the UNGA debates for the adoption of Resolution 73/295[177] and the parliamentary debates after the adoption

175 M Shaw, *Rosenne's Law and Practice of the International Court 1920–2015, vol. III* (5th ed. OUP, 2016), 1767.

176 Personal Question 148829 [BIOT: Navy], 8 February 2021.

177 UNGA, 83rd Plenary Meeting 22 May 2019, 73rd Session (2019), UN Doc. A/73/PV.83, 11 (Ms. Pierce).

of that resolution,[178] the UK emphasized the advisory nature of the opinion and the bilateral nature of the dispute which should not have been the object of an ICJ opinion. But after the Maldives changed its stance,[179] and the UK found itself isolated at the UN, the colonial power followed suit. On 3 November 2022, the UK Foreign Secretary said in a written ministerial statement that the countries "have decided to begin negotiations on the exercise of sovereignty over the British Indian Ocean Territory Chagos Archipelago."[180]

What prompted this change of heart is not entirely clear and neither the UK nor the Mauritian statement on the negotiations cite a reason for them. Several factors must have contributed to this development. For the purposes of the present analysis, it is important to understand to what extent this occurred because of the ICJ's pronouncements. To state that this was the case solely because of the legal effect attributed to the ICJ advisory opinion, would be to grossly overestimate the power of opinions to dictate policy changes. Analysts have argued that territorial disputes in the Indian Ocean, which also involve France and some of its former colonies, "open the door for islands to deepen their relationship with China."[181] So, resolving a longstanding territorial dispute and a point of disagreement in international law and UN opinion may form part of the UK's strategic shift towards the Indo-Pacific in response to China's growing economic, maritime, and military power.[182] Others suggest that Brexit and the ensuing need for trade alliances has been the precipitating factor for a negotiated settlement of the dispute.[183] What can be said with certainty is that *Chagos* was rendered at a time when the political environment was favorable for a shift in UK foreign policy.

178 House of Commons Debates, 3 July 2019, Column 584WH.

179 On 22 August 2022, the President of the Maldives sent an undisclosed letter to the Prime Minister of Mauritius stating that the Maldives would vote in favor of the UNGA Resolution entitled "Advisory opinion of the International Court of Justice on the legal consequences of the separation of the Chagos Archipelago from Mauritius in 1965", 'Government declines to disclose president's letter to Mauritius premier' *Atoll Times*, 25 October 2022.

180 House of Commons, Written Statement 354 (3 November 2022). Confirmed the same day by the Mauritian Prime Minister before his country's National Assembly, National Assembly, Hansard 3 November 2022, 19–20, available at: https://mauritiusassembly.govmu.org/Documents/Hansard/2022/hansard2722.pdf.

181 Carnegie Endowment for International Peace, 'We're thinking about the Indian Ocean all wrong' (2 May 2022).

182 P Loft, 'British Indian Ocean Territory: UK to negotiate sovereignty 2022/23', *House of Commons Library, Research Briefing 9673* (22 November 2022) 22–3.

183 O Alake, 'Britain will have to give up its last African colony thanks to the UN – and Brexit', *Quartz* (27 February 2019).

On the other hand, neither should one underestimate the capacity of ICJ advisory opinions to influence State policy, especially after *Chagos*. Because a new debate will likely open on the compliance pull of ICJ opinions. In general, most – if not virtually all – ICJ advisory opinions have been endorsed by resolutions of the bodies or agencies concerned. Therefore, problems of implementation that have been encountered in this area have involved not the ICJ's opinions themselves, but the alignment with the ensuing institutional action – usually UNGA resolutions – adopted in pursuance of those opinions. Two opinions stand out as examples of the limits of this pull. With respect to the 1988 opinion on the *Applicability of the Headquarters Agreement*, the US judiciary did not explicitly endorse the authority of the ICJ advisory opinion, nevertheless it found an elegant way to align with the ICJ's pronouncements.[184] To the contrary, the Israel Supreme Court declared the ICJ's *Wall* opinion to be authoritative, but did not endorse its findings as they rested – according to the Israel Supreme Court – on a different factual basis.[185] This perception is subject to change after the Special Chamber's judgment. Even if the legal effect of the opinion is not endorsed by the uncooperative party to the dispute, it will constitute an additional political factor pushing for a settlement in the direction dictated by the opinion. Otherwise said, binding determinations from a court are likely to increase the legitimacy of a settlement in accordance with them.[186] From a political perspective then, the legitimizing effect of advisory opinions coupled with the legal effect attributed to them, provide two strong cards to be played during the implementation phase. What the parties understand to be the likely result of any litigation that may come after the ICJ opinion, or the 'shadow of the law',[187] provides an additional bargaining chip and

---

184 *Dominicé, supra* note 173, 98. The domestic decision was *United States v. Palestine Liberation Organization*. U.S. District Court for the Southern District of New York, 27 (1988) *International Legal Materials* 1055. For an explanation of the implementation difficulties of the *Headquarters* opinion see Weckel, 'Les suites des décisions de la Cour internationale de Justice' 42 (1996) *Annuaire Français de Droit International* 428, 432

185 A Orakhelashvili, 'Legal Consequences of the Construction of a Wall in the Occupied Palestinian Territory: Opinion and Reaction' 11 (2006) *Journal of Conflict and Security Law*, 119. For the domestic decision see *infra* note 192.

186 B Simmons, 'Capacity, commitment and compliance: International law and the settlement of territorial disputes' 46 (2002) *Journal of Conflict Resolution* 829, 835.

187 R Mnookin and L Kornhauser, 'Bargaining in the Shadow of the Law: The Case of Divorce' 99 (1979) *Yale Law Journal* 950, 978. Pavone and Stiansen argue that policy makers alter policies in anticipation of possible judicial review, T Pavone and Ø. Stiansen, *The Shadow Effect of Courts: Judicial Review and the Politics of Preemptive Reform*, 116 (2022) *American Political Science Review* 322, 334 The shadow of international law may

will likely influence the future disposition of the parties towards settlement of the dispute.

Also, in cases that pertain to sensitive issues of national self-conception such as State sovereignty, pronouncements by international courts produce historical knowledge. Notwithstanding criticisms that elaboration of a comprehensive history should not be assumed by a judicial body,[188] it is indisputable that judicial pronouncements construct a historical narrative. Mainly ICJ judgments, but also advisory opinions, are based on a detailed examination of the factual background and consequently must produce an official account of relevant facts. In this way, judicial decisions perform a social function; they constitute a form of history-making and a means of either challenging or confirming a script of historical events.[189] Such an authoritative history elaborated via means of evidence will not be easily challenged and is eventually popularly understood and accepted. Arguably then, by making use of international legal processes (ITLOS and the ICJ) Mauritius attempted to produce and record its own authoritative historical account.[190] And, to a great extent it did so successfully. As demonstrated in Chapter 2, for the same reason – to debunk Russia's myth of genocidal acts on behalf of Ukraine in Donbas – it is so important for Ukraine to pursue its reverse compliance claim before the ICJ and to get the declaratory judgment it seeks.

Most probably, these factors have affected the UK stance towards Mauritius. The UK, like most States, takes great pride in underscoring its longstanding political commitment as a champion of the international rule of law. During the House of Commons debates that followed the adoption of the UNGA resolution calling the UK to unconditionally withdraw from the archipelago, the UK Foreign Secretary strongly emphasized that "no international court or tribunal has ever found our sovereignty to be in doubt" and at the same time that "the UK continues to be seen as one of the most promi-

---

not reach far, as Leonardsen argues, nevertheless it is present, E Leonhardsen, 'Trials of Ordeal in the International Court of Justice: Why States Seek Provisional Measures when non-Compliance Is to Be Expected, 5 (2014) *Journal of International Dispute Settlement* 306, 330–3.

188 H Arendt, *Eichmann in Jerusalem: A Report on the Banality of Evil* (Rev. and Enlarged, 1964) 253.

189 V Kumar, 'On Scripts and Sensibility: Cold War International Law and Revolutionary Caribbean Subjects' 21 (2020) *German Law Journal* 1541, 1542.

190 D Guilfoyle, 'The Chagos Archipelago before International Tribunals: Strategic Litigation and the Production of Historical Knowledge' 21 (2021) *Melbourne Journal of International Law* 749.

nent international champions of the rule of law across the globe".[191] In this way, the government implicitly accepted that should a judicial *forum* make such a finding, the UK will abide by it. So, sustaining the same line of defence after the Special Chamber's judgment – and the view expressed therein on the legal effect of the ICJ advisory opinion – would have exposed the UK as inconsistent in its political stance. And, it would have equated it with States like Israel and Serbia that have undermined ICJ advisory opinions rendered in the context of underlying bilateral disputes.[192] Further, the Special Chamber's judgment made it even harder for the UK to disregard the *Chagos* opinion, because it effectively removed from the UK the luxury to rely on the non-binding effect of the advisory opinion. All in all, the UN's stance, was a factor that weighed in heavily on the decision for a negotiated solution to the long-standing dispute.

Even if the Special Chamber's judgment remains an isolated incident, it is expected that States will capitalize on advisory opinions and employ them in a dispute settlement strategy. As long as this perception on the formal authority of ICJ advisory opinions is not overturned, States expect the ICJ to act as a *de facto* legal dispute settler. Given the pivotal position of the main judicial body of the UN in the constellation of international dispute settlement institutions, States will endeavour not only to lobby for ICJ advisory opinions on disputed issues, but mainly to instrumentalise these advisory opinions in subsequent judicial proceedings.[193] Nevertheless, international courts are treading on thin ice should they embrace the Special Chamber's approach in the future. As noted above, the political pressure exercised by an advisory opinion, is exacerbated when it is perceived as producing *res judicata* effects. And this pressure could either provoke greater compliance with the pronouncements rendered in such opinions – as has been the case in Chagos – or accelerate State backlash. An *exemplaire* of the latter reaction is provided by the recent

191 House of Commons Debates, 3 July 2019, Column 586WH.

192 Serbia criticised the *Kosovo* advisory opinion as leaving room 'for a dangerous misinterpretation of the Court's view as having legalized the ethnic Albanians'attempt at unilateral secession', UNSC Official Record, 6367th meeting, UN Doc S/PV.6367 (3 August 2010) 7. And the Israeli Supreme Court resisted the influence of the *Wall* advisory opinion on domestic proceedings by arguing that the ICJ's conclusion, while authoritative, rested on a different factual basis, Israeli Supreme Court, hcj 7957/04, *Zaharan Yunis Muhammad Mara'abe et al. v. The Prime Minister of Israel et al.*, 15 September 2005, [37]–[74].

193 Eichberger, *supra* note 138, 12; Lanzoni, *supra* note 141, 26–7; V Rezadoost, 'Unveiling the 'author' of international law-The 'legal effect' of ICJ's advisory opinions' (2024) *Journal of International Dispute Settlement* 1, 23–4 (published as 'advance article').

attempt by Palestine to bring its long-standing dispute with Israel before the ICJ for an advisory opinion.

3.2.2 The Political Ramifications of ICJ Advisory Opinions after *Chagos*

Palestine has been the first State to use an ICJ advisory opinion in a litigation strategy after *Chagos*.[194] In its dispute with Israel, Palestine's main claim has been to gain international recognition as a full sovereign member State of the international community. This necessarily entails the termination of Israeli occupation of Palestinian territory and the realization of the Palestinian people's right to self-determination. To this end, during the last twenty years, Palestine has been consistent in its effort to internationalize the conflict "as a legal matter, not only a political one."[195] In this context, on 30 December 2022, the UNGA voted in favor of resolution 77/247 entitled 'Israeli practices affecting the human rights of the Palestinian people in the Occupied Palestinian Territory, including East Jerusalem'.[196] Paragraph 18 of the resolution reads:

> [The UNGA] [*d*]*ecides*, in accordance with Article 96 of the Charter of the United Nations, to request the International Court of Justice, pursuant to Article 65 of the Statute of the Court, to render an advisory opinion on the following questions, considering the rules and principles of international law, including the Charter of the United Nations, international humanitarian law, international human rights law, relevant resolutions of the Security Council, the General Assembly and the Human Rights Council, and the advisory opinion of the Court of 9 July 2004:
> (a) What are the legal consequences arising from the ongoing violation by Israel of the right of the Palestinian people to self-determination, from its prolonged occupation, settlement and annexation of the Palestinian territory occupied since 1967, including measures aimed at altering the demographic composition, character and status of the Holy City of Jerusalem, and from its adoption of related discriminatory legislation and measures?

---

194 By 'Palestine' here is meant the PLO-controlled Palestinian Authority that has been accorded non-member observer State status in the UN by UNGA resolution 67/19.

195 M Abbas, '*The Long Overdue Palestinian State' New York Times* (16 May 2011).

196 UN Doc. A/Res/77/247, The resolution was approved with 87 votes in favor and 26 votes against, with 53 abstentions.

> (b) How do the policies and practices of Israel referred to in paragraph 18 (a) above affect the legal status of the occupation, and what are the legal consequences that arise for all States and the United Nations from this status?"

Once more, the ICJ has been asked to render an opinion on a bilateral dispute and to pronounce on the responsibility issues that arise therefrom.

What is of acute interest in this particular request, is its interrelationship with the previous 2004 *Wall* opinion and how this may impact on the Court's discretion to deliver the opinion. It is worth noting at this point, that the *Wall* opinion and the ensuing UNGA resolutions endorsing it, have not been implemented to date. As noted in [6] of resolution 77/247, the construction of the wall is one of the many settlement activities of Israel in the Occupied Palestinian Territory. Also, the findings of the 2004 opinion have been noted and recalled in the resolution's preamble and, the *Wall* opinion was a factor taken into account by the UNGA before making the new request. Two considerations are likely to determine the role that these findings will play in the delivery of the new opinion; first, the extent to which the opinions are *res judicata* for the Court itself and second whether any legal or factual developments justify a new position by the Court.[197] Given the firm stance of the UN on this particular dispute[198] and the ICJ's tendency to attach the value of precedent to its previous advisory opinions,[199] it is expected that the ICJ will use the 2004 findings as 'givens'. What remains to be determined, is the extent of the overlap between the two requests and the willingness of the Court to answer the same question twice.[200] The Court has anticipated such a situation in its previous opinion where it clarified that it "is indeed aware that the question of the wall is part of a greater whole, and it would take this circumstance carefully into account in any opinion it might give".[201] It is likely then, that the ICJ will not decline to deliver the new opinion since the general issues that underlie the new request have been examined in *Wall* only to the extent that they might be necessary to its consideration of the question put to it.[202]

197 Kolb, *supra* note 48, 1096.

198 UNGA Res 77/247 [6].

199 Kolb, *supra* note 48, 1096. I Scobbie, 'Res Judicata, Precedent and the International Court: A Preliminary Sketch' (1999) 20 *Australian Yearbook of International Law* 299, 312–4.

200 This has never been the case in the Court's history as noted by d'Argent, *supra* note 93, 1809.

201 *Wall* 160[54].

202 *Ibid.*

The tactical decision by Palestine to employ an ICJ advisory opinion in this long-standing dispute despite Israel's willingness to settle the dispute via bilateral negotiations, has provoked a severe reaction by Israel. It endorsed an extreme rhetoric discrediting the legitimacy of the UN as an institution by and large,[203] hinted that it will not cooperate with the ICJ[204] and implemented a series of sanctions against Palestine.[205] What stands out from this reaction is the Israeli Prime Minister's characterization of Palestine's recourse to the ICJ as 'legal war' and his resolve that Israel will not be bound by the findings of the ICJ. Israel's backlash affirms non-implementation of any ICJ ruling, implies non-participation in ICJ proceedings, while it has not yet reached at the level of withdrawal from the UN altogether.[206] This reaction underscores that the ICJ's pronouncements do have authority and do matter for the effective resolution of the dispute. But Israel does not view Palestine's recourse to the ICJ as a genuine attempt to promote the political resolution of the dispute, rather as an attempt to exploit the Court, "as a weapon of mass destruction in their jihad war of Israel demonization".[207] And it is aware that the advisory opinion could be a precipitating factor in its future negotiations with Palestine if it finds itself politically isolated at the UN, like the UK has been after Chagos. It remains to be seen whether, and to what extent, this politically-charged advisory opinion will affect a bilateral solution to the dispute, when the last negotiatory attempt collapsed in 2014.

The Court had to deal with a related argument, in the context of the 2004 opinion. Some participants argued that the ICJ should decline to exercise its

203 Ambassador Erdan, Isreali representative to the UNGA before the voting procedure: '[...] the despicable decision expected to be passed today is a moral stain to the UN and to any country that supports it [...]. Any decision from a judicial body which receives its mandate from the morally bankrupt and politicized UN is completely illegitimate', full speech available at Ambassador Erdan's 'X' media account.

204 Ibid: 'We will not take part in this disgrace and show of lies.'

205 The measures were announced by the Prime Minister via social media and include, *inter alia*, the use of Palestinian money to compensate the families of Israeli settlers and soldiers who were attacked by Palestinians, and the imposition of a moratorium on Palestinian construction in some areas of the Israeli-occupied West Bank, Deutsce Welle 'Israel to Sanction Palestinian Authority After UN Vote', 6/1/2023 available at: https://www.dw.com/en/israel-to-sanction-palestinian-authority-after-un-vote/a-64311273.

206 It is worth noting that Israel withdrew from the compulsory jurisdiction of the ICJ on 21 November 1985, https://treaties.un.org/pages/ViewDetails.aspx?src=IND&mtdsg_no=I-4&chapter=1&clang=_en#3, endnote 3.

207 'Fourth Committee Hears Support for Referring Question of Palestine to International Court of Justice for Advisory Opinion – Press Release', *UN Doc.* GA/SPD/770.

jurisdiction since its opinion could impede a political, negotiated solution to the Israeli-Palestinian conflict.[208] At that time, the 'Roadmap to a Permanent Two-State Solution' negotiations were underway and some States have anticipated a recalcitrant stance in these negotiations from the losing side after the delivery of the opinion.[209] The Court dismissed this contention and refused to assess the political ramifications of its advisory opinion as a relevant factor in the exercise of its discretion.[210] Arguably, the ICJ would undermine its position as a judicial body if it were to speculate on political issues. It is rather the requesting organ that should have given more credence to this argument. The UNGA must be very careful in evaluating the political circumstances before making a request for an advisory opinion; the inclination of the ICJ to give an opinion to the almost total disregard of its discretion to refuse, underscores the point that State interests and the existence of genuine consent to jurisdiction are likely to influence the motivation to implement the opinion's findings, and constrain ICJ and UNGA effectiveness. Especially, since advisory opinions are in fact used for political purposes, their dramatic political ramifications could be at the root of non-compliance.[211]

Palestine's recourse to the ICJ forms part of a series of actions before international courts and tribunals all of which attempt to apply political pressure on Israel. In the course of this strategy, Palestine has resorted to several UN organs and its campaign has been quite impactful.[212] Three of these judicial procedures, run in parallel with the advisory proceedings, and it is likely that they will continue to be pending after the delivery of the ICJ opinion. If this is the case, Palestine will most certainly intend to may make use of the ICJ's findings in these judicial *fora*. The first court of interest is the International Criminal Court (ICC), where a prosecutorial investigation on

---

208 *Wall* 159[51].

209 *Ibid* 147[22] and 160[52]–[53].

210 *Ibid* 160[53]; *Nuclear Weapons* 23 [17]: "The Court is aware that, no matter what might be its conclusions in any opinion it might give, they would have relevance for the continuing debate on the matter in the General Assembly and would present an additional element in the negotiations on the matter. Beyond that, the effect of the opinion is a matter of appreciation. The Court has heard contrary positions advanced and there are no evident criteria by which it can prefer one assessment to another." Aust has argued that in its decision to undertake the request, the ICJ should look into the motive behind the request and assess whether the opinion would really help in solving the underlying problem, A Aust 'Advisory Opinions' 1 (2010) *Journal of International Dispute Settlement* 123.

211 Giladi and Shany, *supra* note 173, 14.

212 O Kittrie, *Lawfare* (OUP, 2016) Chapter 5.

the situation in Palestine is ongoing.[213] The sustained attempts by Palestinians to engage the ICC culminated on 5 February 2021, when the ICC's Pre-Trial Chamber held that this court's territorial jurisdiction covers the Occupied Palestinian Territory as defined by the UNGA resolution 67/19.[214] Despite the clear disclaimer on the Pre-Trial Chamber's part that its determinations have no bearing on neither the scope of Palestine's territory nor on its status under international law,[215] this decision undoubtedly strengthens Palestine's recognition claim. And the awaited judgment(s) of the ICC on the merits will likely draw inferences from the ICJ's pronouncements on occupation, settlement and annexation of Palestinian territory – should the ICJ decide to exercise its discretion and deliver its opinion before the ICC decides any case on the merits.

Further, a contentious case between Palestine and the United States is pending before the ICJ.[216] Palestine alleges that the 2018 relocation of the United States embassy in Israel (from Tel Aviv) to Jerusalem is in breach of the Vienna Convention on Diplomatic Relations. Palestine asserts Jerusalem as a city under international governance by virtue of UNGA resolution 181 (1947) and bases its application on this understanding.[217] Israel to the contrary, that claims Jerusalem as part of its territory, is not a party to these proceedings. And this may render the *Monetary Gold* principle particularly pertinent for the Court's competence (not) to entertain the case.[218] It will be interesting to see whether the ICJ will get around this principle and apply the related findings from the 2004 opinion – and the new opinion if it is decided by that time – as 'givens'. Only once in its history the ICJ had to consider the effect of its advisory opinion on a contentious case, in the preliminary objections phase of the *South West Africa Cases*.[219] In this case, the Court upheld the applicability of the *International Status of South West Africa Advisory Opinion*, so it is possi-

---

213 This covers crimes falling within the jurisdiction of the ICJ committed since 13 June 2014, with no end date and in all parts of the territory of the State of Palestine, 'Referral by the State of Palestine Pursuant to Articles l3(a) and 14 of the Rome Statute' 15 May 2018, Ref: PAL-180515-Ref.

214 ICJ, Pre-Trial Chamber, *Situation in the State of Palestine*, ICC-01/18–143, [116]–[118].

215 Ibid 29[62] and 45[102].

216 ICJ, *Relocation of the United States Embassy to Jerusalem (Palestine v. United States of America), Application Instituting Proceedings, 28 September 2018*

217 *Ibid* 3[5]–[6].

218 See the relevant debate in *Ejil:talk*, M Milanovic, 'Palestine Sues the United States in the ICJ re Jerusalem Embassy' (30 September 2018) and A Miron, Palestine's Application the ICJ, neither Groundless nor Hopeless. A Reply to Marko Milanovic (8 October 2018).

219 ICJ, *South West Africa Cases* (*Ethiopia v. South Africa; Liberia v. South Africa*) [1962] ICJ Reports 319, 333–4.

ble that it will follow this precedent in the Palestine-United States case. The development of the latter case is however uncertain as the US has denied to participate in the proceedings and the Court has not yet adopted a decision for the organization of public hearings.

Finally, Palestine has been the first State to file an inter-State complaint under the compulsory mechanism of the International Convention on the Elimination of All Forms of Racial Discrimination (CERD).[220] Palestine alleged violations of Articles 2, 3 and 5 CERD on the part of Israel within the Occupied Palestinian Territory, the gravest allegation being that of a violation of Article 3 regarding the prohibition of racial segregation and apartheid. Like the case before the ICC, the CERD communication is pending at the merits stage.[221] A close 'judicial dialogue' between the ICJ and the CERD organs is expected for two reasons: institutionally, both form part of the UN machinery and also the subject matter in both pending proceedings overlaps greatly as the ICJ in the advisory opinion will pronounce on 'discriminatory legislation and measures' adopted by Israel. Nevertheless, the latest public statement of Israel's representative to the UNGA discrediting the UN as an organization altogether casts a shadow on Israel's further participation in the CERD proceedings.[222]

All the cases cited above constitute an exercise in constructing and furthering a particular narrative. That of a law-abiding State willing to rely on international law against powerful adversaries, who are unwilling to submit themselves to binding dispute resolution.[223] Engaging the ICJ in this strategy is a move that bolsters this narrative and applies pressure on Israel in a twofold way. First, by the possibility of a favorable ICJ ruling for Palestine that will further isolate Israel at the UN and second, by the potential use of this ruling as a binding precedent in other *fora*. The circumvention of Israel's

---

220 *Interstate Complaint under Articles 11–13 of the International Convention for the Elimination of All Forms of Racial Discrimination State of Palestine versus Israel* (23 April 2018), available at: https://tbinternet.ohchr.org/_layouts/15/treatybodyexternal/Download.aspx?symbolno=INT%2fCERD%2fISC%2f9325&Lang=en

221 Articles 11–13 ICERD provide for a two-stage inter-State communication procedure before the CERD Committee (examination of the preliminary questions of jurisdiction and admissibility) and subsequently before an *ad hoc* Conciliation Commission (examination of the merits). Set up in February 2022, the Conciliation Commission has held three in-person meetings with representatives from both sides, but the content of these meetings is not public, *UN Committee on the Elimination of Racial Discrimination (CERD) Sets Up Ad Hoc Conciliation Commission – Press Release,* 17 February 2022, available at: https://www.un.org/unispal/document/un-committee-on-the-elimination-of-racial-discrimination-cerd-sets-up-ad-hoc-conciliation-commission-press-release/.

222 Ambassador Erdan, *supra* note 203.

223 M Milanovic, *supra* note 27.

consent though, along with the pressure exercised by a multitude of judicial pronouncements could trigger a recalcitrant stance from Israel's part. So, instead of precipitating compliance with the ICJ's pronouncements, the political ramifications of the advisory opinion may yield the opposite result.

State resistance or backlash towards the ICJ and its rulings, impacts the attribute on which the Court relies the most when expecting implementation of its advisory opinions; its legitimizing *de jure* authority. Arguably, the authority of any court depends upon its interaction with engaged audiences.[224] Otherwise said, the subjective beliefs of interested actors regarding the court's authority, or a court's sociological legitimacy, may impact its *de jure* authority.[225] So, extraordinary critique by States, that is, a critique of not only law but also of the very institution, the Court,[226] will inevitably undermine the authority of the ICJ. This undermining of its authority may spring from the Court's involvement with bilateral disputes, but it will affect the compliance pull of opinions that pertain to issues of general interest, such as the prospective advisory opinion on climate change.[227]

In its turn, the ICJ is not expected to accept this passively, but to react preemptively in order to prevent backlash. Judge *ad hoc* Oxman, in his separate and dissenting opinion in *Delimitation in the Indian Ocean* has prophetically warned on the unintended consequences of attributing formal authority to ICJ advisory opinions and held that 'it risks complicating ... the exercise by the ICJ of its discretion with respect to requests for Advisory Opinions.'[228] The preemptive move by the Court will probably be to think twice before undertaking in the future Advisory Opinions that pertain to bilateral disputes. Especially, since other tribunals have the tendency to view such opinions as binding.

224 Alter Helfer and Rask Madsen, *supra* note 144, 22ff.

225 Justifications of authority of international courts on the basis of sociology have been endorsed by many authors, see A Buchanan and R O Keohane, 'The Legitimacy of Global Governance Institutions' 20 (2006) *Ethics and International Affairs* 405. All relevant accounts are adaptations of Weber's theory on legitimacy, M Weber, *Economy and Society: An Outline of Interpretative Sociology* vol 1 (University of California Press, 1978), 215.

226 M Rask Madsen, P Cebulak and M Wiebusch, 'Backlash against international courts: explaining the forms and patterns of resistance to international courts' 14 (2018) *International Journal of Law in Context* 197, 199.

227 Initiated by Vanuatu, a coalition of States is seeking an ICJ Advisory Opinion on climate change. On 29 November 2022, sixteen States circulated a draft UNGA resolution to kickstart the consultation process that will lead to a UNGA vote at the 77th session, see https://www.vanuatuicj.com/home.

228 Separate and Dissenting Opinion of Judge ad hoc Oxman, *Delimitation in the Indian Ocean*, 129[32].

Should this promote a trend of reactions equivalent to that of Israel, the ICJ will eventually have to pay deference to State consent and abandon its approach to advise on any dispute irrespective of the particular circumstances surrounding the request for the opinion. For, however trite this may be, a gap between judicial outcomes and constituency preferences could result in the erosion of a court's authority; because such outcomes are often not complied with, and even isolated instances of non-compliance may trigger a domino of unexecuted decisions.[229] Comparable considerations have pressured the Inter-American Court of Human Rights to reject requests for advisory opinions addressing sensitive political issues.[230] Since the ICJ cannot dictate how other tribunals will perceive its advisory opinions, it will have to be more attentive to State interests when deciding whether it will opine on issues that States do not want to subsume under judicial scrutiny.[231] This consideration of course, applies also to the UNGA and the exercise of its political discretion to request Advisory Opinions on sensitive matters. However, for the Court, rethinking its discretion to deliver an Advisory Opinion in order to save its authority may effectively be a policy decision, albeit one that must be dressed in a legal garment. It is interesting to see whether this jurisprudential change will take place and under what legal justification.

4 Beyond the ICJ: IACtHR Advisory Opinions as Part of a Multi-*forum* Litigation Strategy

The ICJ is not the only judicial *forum* used by States for the delivery of authoritative advisory opinions in the framework of settling their international disputes. Requests for advisory opinions made to the Inter-American Court of Human Rights (IACtHR) have also been made in order to further political objectives in inter-State disputes. Nevertheless, advisory proceedings before other international courts of limited jurisdiction have not been instrumentalised in this way, mainly for reasons of competence. For example, under Article 47 and Protocol 16 of the European Convention for Human Rights, a State's

229 Y Shany, 'International Courts in a Politicized World' in Charles N Brower et al. (eds) *By Peaceful Means: International Adjudication and Arbitration* (OUP, 2024) 83, 88; Sh. Dothan, *Reputation and Judicial Tactics: A Theory of National and International Courts* (Cambridge University Press 2016) 89.

230 C Bailliet, 'The Strategic Prudence of the Inter-American Court of Human Rights: Rejection of Requests for an Advisory Opinion', 15 (2018) *Brazilian Journal of International Law* 254.

231 Lanzoni, *supra* note 141, 27.

executive power may not request an opinion from the European Court of Human Rights. And the judiciary, that is entitled by virtue of Protocol 16 to make such requests, does not initiate strategic litigation for the resolution of international disputes. Similarly, the advisory competence of ITLOS as a full tribunal is not expressly provided for in UNCLOS,[232] it rather relies, according to ITLOS, on a permissive interpretation of Article 21 of this convention.[233] The unfavourable State reaction to this approach suggests that a new request will probably prompt similar criticism and explains why the use of this procedure may be counter-intuitive for States.[234] It could lead the Tribunal to adopt a cautious and narrow approach to the scope of its advisory jurisdiction and in this way undermine the authority of an advisory opinion.[235]

The IACtHR is the most active international court exercising advisory jurisdiction today.[236] And three pertinent factors are at the roots of this. First, the IACtHR views its advisory opinions as producing legal effects. Having declared initially in 1997 that its advisory opinions have 'undeniable legal effects',[237] the IACtHR holds consistently since 2014, that its advisory opinions have legal relevance for all States that have adopted the 1948 American Declaration on the Rights and Duties of Man, whether or not they are parties to the American Convention on Human Rights – the regional treaty that gives jurisdiction to the Court.[238] Second, advisory opinions under the inter-American human rights regime have served as a substitute for IACtHR inter-State contentious

232 Expressly, only the Seabed Disputes Chamber of ITLOS may issue an advisory opinion with respect to matters related to "the Area", *see* Articles 187 and 191 UNCLOS.

233 *Sub-Regional Fisheries Commission*, Case No. 21, Advisory Opinion, 2 April 2015 ITLOS Rep. 4, [53]–[59].

234 See Rep. 23rd Meeting of States Parties to UNCLOS [21] *U.N. Doc. SPLOS/263* (July 8, 2013); 24th Meeting [37] *UN Doc. SPLOS/277* (July 14, 2014); 25th Meeting [23] *UN Doc. SPLOS/287* (July 13, 2015); 26th Meeting [25] *UN Doc. SPLOS/303* (Aug. 2, 2016).

235 B Mayer, 'International Advisory Proceedings on Climate Change' 44 (2023) *Michigan Journal of International Law* (forthcoming), *The Chinese University of Hong Kong Faculty of Law Research Paper No. 2022–43*, available at: https://ssrn com/abstract=4086761, 1, 35.

236 Since 1978, the Inter-American Court of Human Rights has issued twenty-six advisory opinions, while the ICJ twenty-seven since 1948. The African Court on Human and People's Rights has dealt with 15 requests since 2006, but it has issued only five as the rest were either struck out of the docket or declared inadmissible.

237 *Advisory Opinion OC-15/97*, Inter-American Court of Human Rights (ser. A) No. 15, [26] (Nov. 14, 1997).

238 Rights and Guarantees of Children in the Context of Migration and/or in Need of International Protection, Advisory Opinion OC-21/14, Inter-Am. Ct. H.R. (ser. A) No. 21, [32] (Aug. 19, 2014); Advisory Opinion OC-22/16, Inter-Am. Ct. H.R. (ser. A) No. 22, [25] (Feb. 26, 2016). This is supported by Article 64 of the American Convention that gives the right to all OAS members to request an opinion from the IACtHR.

cases which have not been popular.[239] Some States seek advisory opinions as a way of confronting other States without necessarily mentioning them. Thus, these opinions could be considered as 'covert' or disguised' inter-State contentious proceedings.[240] Third, the IACtHR understands in the broadest possible terms its advisory jurisdiction. In particular, this extends "to any provision dealing with the protection of human rights set forth in any international treaty applicable in the American States".[241] Hence, this procedure has been appealing to member States of the Organization of American States and they have used it twice in order to influence disputes that made their way to the ICJ.

The first related to the ICJ consular assistance cases that ultimately caused the United States' withdrawal from the Optional Protocol to the Vienna Convention on Consular Relations Concerning the Compulsory Settlement of Disputes.[242] In 1997, Mexico sought the IACtHR's opinion "on behalf of some of its nationals, whom the host State had allegedly not informed of their right to communicate with Mexican consular authorities and who had been sentenced to death in ten States in the United States".[243] The opinion sought obviously had a respondent State, even though the United States had not – and has not – ratified the American Convention. While the advisory proceedings were underway, Paraguay brought a case on identical grounds before the ICJ,[244] and right after that case was discontinued, Germany took the United

239 Only two inter-State communications have been brought before the Inter-American Commission on Human Rights (IACmHR). One was declared inadmissible (IACmHR, Report No. 11/07, Interstate case 01/06, *Nicaragua vs. Costa Rica*, 8 March 2007) and the other ended in an amicable solution (IACmHR, Report No. 96/13, Decision to archive, Interstate case 12.779, *Ecuador vs. Colombia*, 4 November 2013).

240 J Contesse, 'Inter-State Cases in Disguise under Inter-American Human Rights Law, Advisory Opinions as Inter-State Disputes', *Völkerrechtsblog* (27 April 2021).

241 "Other Treaties" Subject to the Consultative Jurisdiction of the Court (Art. 64 American Convention on Human Rights), Advisory Opinion OC-1/82, IACtHR (ser. A) No. 1, Op. [1] (Sept. 24, 1982).

242 For an overview of the judicial and political drama that unfolded see J Quigley, The United States' Withdrawal from International Court of Justice Jurisdiction in Consular Cases: Reasons and Consequences, 19 (2009) *Duke Journal of Comparative and International Law* 263–306.

243 IACtHR, Advisory Opinion OC-16/99 requested by Mexico (1 October 1999) *The Right to Information on Consular Assistance in the Framework of the Guarantees of the Due Process of Law* Ser. A, No. 16, [2].

244 ICJ, *Vienna Convention on Consular Relations* (*Paraguay v. United States of America*), Application Instituting Proceedings, 3 April 1998. The case was discontinued because Mr. Breard, the Paraguayan whose rights were allegedly violated, was executed by the

States to the Court with respect to the same legal issue.[245] While the United States in its written comments to the IACtHR argued that it should defer consideration on this request for reasons of prudence or comity,[246] the regional court was undeterred. It highlighted its autonomous standing, took knowingly the risk of fragmenting international law and stated with audacity that it cannot be restrained from exercising its advisory jurisdiction because of contentious cases filed with the ICJ.[247] Unsurprisingly, the IACtHR found that the Vienna Convention on Consular Relations confers rights upon detained foreign nationals, among them the right to information on consular assistance, and that said rights carry with them correlative obligations for the host State.

It is doubtful whether Mexico had in mind a litigation strategy that involved the use of the advisory opinion as a precursor to its ensuing ICJ application in *Avena*.[248] It is very likely though that it anticipated the IACtHR's ruling. Nevertheless, it appealed to the IACtHR's favorable interpretation of the Vienna Convention on Consular Relations in its ICJ application.[249] The ICJ arrived at similar conclusions, but its judgment made no reference to the advisory opinion so one can only speculate on the level of influence exercised by the IACtHR on the outcome of the case. All in all, the IACtHR's stance to pronounce on all situations that concern the protection of human rights in the region paved the way for its use in subsequent disputes.

Colombia is another State that resorted to advisory proceedings in order to influence a bilateral international dispute. In its dispute with Nicaragua, brought by Nicaragua before the ICJ, Colombia claims that the interoceanic channel that Nicaraguan authorities desire to build, and other actions, could have harmful environmental impacts on Colombian waters and impact its population. To strengthen its case before the UN court, Colombia requested and obtained an advisory opinion by the IACtHR on the right to a healthy environment.[250] In addition to presenting questions related to environmen-

---

state of Virginia, ICJ, *Vienna Convention on Consular Relations* (*Paraguay v. United States of America*), Order of 1 November 1998.

245 ICJ, *LaGrand* (*Germany v. United States of America*), Application Instituting Proceedings, 2 March 1999.

246 *Information on Consular Assistance*, [46].

247 *Ibid* [57]–[61]. For a critique of this stance see Sh. Rosenne, *The World Court: What it Is and How It Works*, T Gill (ed) (Martinus Nijhoff, 2003), 240.

248 ICJ, *Case Concerning Avena and Other Mexican Nationals* (*Mexico v. United States of America*), Judgment 31 March 2004, ICJ Reports 2012, 12.

249 *Avena*, Application Instituting Proceedings, 13[65] and 41[271].

250 IACtHR, Advisory Opinion OC-23/17 requested by Colombia, (15 November 2017) *The Environment and Human Rights*, Ser. A, No. 23.

tal impact and human rights before the IACtHR, the Colombian agents submitted four counter-claims against Nicaragua before the ICJ, the first two of which had clear environmental implications. However, in November 2017 the ICJ declared those two claims inadmissible.[251] Yet, it is clear that the state of Colombia considered that, had they been declared admissible, the opinion of the IACtHR – which foreseeably would be favourable to environmental human rights concerns, as it indeed was – could increase the chances of having a successful case before the ICJ. So, with respect to this advisory opinion, there is little room to speculate on the rationale behind the request; it clearly reflects the desire to achieve policy objectives in relation to the pending ICJ procedure.[252] This instrumentalization of the IACtHR by Colombia was pointed out during the public hearing as a reason for the Court to decline to exercise its jurisdiction.[253] Nonetheless, the IACtHR did not consider such underlying political considerations as pertinent factors, reaffirming thus its previous position in *Information on Consular Assistance*.[254]

Up to this date, the impact of IACtHR advisory opinions in determining the resolution of inter-State disputes has been limited. Especially, when compared to that produced by ICJ opinions. The IACtHR's broad understanding of its advisory jurisdiction will probably not change this, as the willingness to undertake any request pertaining to human rights in the American region does not help bolster the court's legitimate authority. In all fairness though, the IACtHR has, unlike the ICJ, exercised its discretion and rejected five requests to render an advisory opinion, so it is attentive to the political context surrounding the request.[255] Albeit, the *national* political context; all rejections pertain to political issues which are contentious at the national level, so political ramifications at the international level do not seem to affect the IACtHR's advisory competence as evidenced by both opinions analysed above. The significant advantage of advisory opinions, when compared to contentious proceedings, is that they present a disaggregated analysis of State action. And the willingness of the IACtHR to undertake such analysis may render its advisory opinions a fitting choice for States wishing to accom-

251 ICJ, *Alleged Violations of Sovereign Rights and Maritime Spaces in the Caribbean Sea (Nicaragua v. Colombia)*, Order of 15 November 2017.

252 N Carrillo-Santarelli, 'The Politics behind the Latest Advisory Opinions of the Inter-American Court of Human Rights' *I·CONnect* (24 February 2018).

253 *The Environment and Human Rights*, 14[25].

254 *Ibid* [26].

255 A list with all rejections is available at: https://www.corteidh.or.cr/rechazo_solicitud_opiniones_consultivas.cfm?lang=en.

plish policy objectives in their international disputes.[256] But, the compliance pull of these opinions will ultimately depend on the *de jure* and *de facto* authority of the issuing institution. In this respect, the ICJ has clearly the upper hand when compared to the IACtHR. Even if OAS member States generally support the Court's authority in the region,[257] the activist label it carries makes the instrumentalization of its advisory opinions in other proceedings rather unlikely.

5 The Court as a Rule-Maker: a New Golden Era for ICJ Advisory Opinions?

In the aftermath of the *Wall* opinion, the ICJ President at the time addressed the UNGA. His speech was devoted to "the Court's generally less known but nonetheless extremely important advisory function, which was underutilized but could be an extremely valuable tool for United Nations bodies".[258] He went on to suggest that recourse to the advisory function should be encouraged, *inter alia* because "the advisory procedure could also play an indirect role in preventing disputes or conflicts from developing".[259] Twenty years later, his remarks are particularly apposite as ICJ advisory opinions not only prevent disputes but play an active role in their resolution. The necessary impetus for an extended use of the advisory procedure as a means of addressing international problems, lacking in 2004, might have been given in the context of the Chagos saga. The reasoning of the ITLOS Special Chamber in *Delimitation in the Indian Ocean* recognizing legal effects to the *Chagos* ICJ opinion has put forward a new understanding of the function and nature of ICJ advisory opinions. An understanding that implants in the Court a new role: that of a rule-maker. And when advisory opinions are instrumentalized in the course of a strategy for the resolution of a bilateral dispute, the expectation is that the Court will act as a *de facto* legal dispute settler. This will

256 In its latest rejection up to date, the IACtHR declined to answer a question on possible distortions of the impeachment mechanism that could result in a parliamentary coup d'état, because in order to do so it would be called to decide factual questions which lies outside the purposes of its advisory function, IACtHR, Order of 29 May 2018, *Request for an Advisory Opinion by the Inter-American Commission on Human Rights*, 9[13].

257 PBM da Cruz, 'Trackers and Trailblazers: Dynamic Interactions and Institutional Design in the Inter-American Court of Human Rights' 11 (2020) *Journal of International Dispute Settlement*, 69, 85.

258 UN Doc. A/C.6/59/SR.21 (5 November 2004) [65].

259 Ibid [72]–[73].

prompt States to actively lobby for new opinions and may herald a new era in international dispute settlement.

As evinced by the development of the sovereignty dispute between the UK and Mauritius after *Chagos*, an ICJ advisory opinion may constitute a watershed in promoting a solution to a stalemated issue. Both as an authoritative ascertainment of the law by the principal judicial organ of the UN and further as a decision with *res judicata* effects for other judicial *fora*. Thus, when incorporated in a multi-*forum* litigation strategy, an ICJ advisory opinion has the potential to exert pressure on other courts to base their rulings on the ICJ's pronouncements and on disputing States to align their policies with the Court's opinion. Especially when, by confirming the illegality of certain conduct, it confers a certain stigma on the violator – in *Chagos* the UK is portrayed as an illegal colonial occupier[260] – then the potential to replicate this stigma in other *fora* fosters the possibility of political change. The conclusion of bilateral negotiations between the UK and Mauritius on 3 October 2024 is testament to the effectiveness of advisory opinions as a mechanism of political pressure. Mauritius has emerged victorious as the UK has conceded that Mauritius is sovereign over the archipelago, and 'Mauritius will now be free to implement a programme of resettlement on the islands of the Chagos Archipelago, other than Diego Garcia'.[261] It is no wonder then, that on 23 August 2019, the Prime Minister of Mauritius, unveiled the country's latest postal stamps and souvenirs, depicting the Peace Palace in the Netherlands, the seat of the ICJ.[262] The ICJ influenced also the attitude of UN agencies towards the disputing States; the United Nations World Map depicted the Chagos Archipelago as Mauritian territory since 2020,[263] and the Universal Postal Union declared the use of British stamps in the Chagos Islands invalid.[264] Also, it influenced noticeably the attitude of third States towards

260 D Guilfoyle, 'Litigation as Statecraft: Small States and the Law of the Sea' (2023) *British Yearbook of International Law* 1, 31.

261 Press Release, *supra* note 2.

262 *Prime Minister launches first day cover, stamps and souvenir sheet on ICJ Advisory Opinion on Decolonisation,* 23 August 2019, available at: http://www.govmu.org/English/News/Pages/Prime-Minister-launches-first-day-cover,-stamps-and-souvenir-sheet-on-ICJ-Advisory-Opinion-on-Decolonisation.aspx.

263 Government Information Service (Mauritius), 'Chagos Archipelago depicted as Mauritian territory by new UN world map' (22 May 2020), available at: https://dha.govmu.org/Slider/SitePages/Chagos-Archipelago-depicted-as-Mauritian-territory-by-new-UN-world-map.aspx

264 Universal Postal Union, 'UPU adopts UN resolution on Chagos Archipelago', 27 August 2021, available at: https://www.upu.int/en/Press-Release/2021/Press-release-UPUadopts-UN-resolution-on-Chagos-Archipelago .

the Mauritian position and the UNGA resolution implementing the opinion is testament to that. The legitimising *de facto* authority of *Chagos* slowly but steadily chipped away the legitimacy of the UK position and firmly established the ICJ's position as the overwhelming 'legal truth' in international discourse.

This pull towards compliance with the Court's advisory opinion was effectuated despite the UK's lack of consent to have the dispute brought before an international tribunal. The circumvention of consent is perhaps what renders ICJ advisory opinions such an appealing judicial mechanism for States. This and the Court's tendency to deliver an opinion irrespective of the circumstances surrounding the request. The jurisprudential attitude of the Court to exercise its advisory jurisdiction without further ado, is however a two-edged knife. Instead of precipitating compliance, the political ramifications of an advisory opinion rendered despite the consent of a recalcitrant State may yield the opposite outcome. The Israel-Palestine dispute showcases how the disregard of a State's interests may backfire and provoke backlash. Because the same circumstances could trigger a different reaction depending on the participating actors, the dividing line separating implementation from backlash is thin. And what may have been a success story for the Court, could end up as a story of unintended implications. It falls upon the ICJ to find how much – and for how long – it can rest on its authority and sustain an attitude of indifference towards State interests. The IACtHR, a court particularly active in delivering advisory opinions, but with considerably less influence and legitimate authority when exercising its advisory jurisdiction, has been more attentive to the political context; it exercised its discretion and refused to deliver opinions that may have caused extreme backlash from OAS members and hence undermined the IACtHR's authority. Time will tell whether ICJ advisory opinions will properly transform into a consequential mechanism of *de facto* international adjudication or the latest developments after *Chagos* have gone the limited formal *de jure* authority they attract from the UN Charter beyond breaking point. Time will eventually tell whether the international legal order is already witnessing a new era for the use of advisory opinions as a litigation mechanism.

CHAPTER 5

The Many Roles of the Court in the Changing Landscape of Inter-state Litigation

An account of the role of the Permanent Court of International Justice in the political history of the League of Nations suggested that 'the Permanent Court is but a footnote, partly because it did not deal with the main political issues of the day'.[1] The ICJ is nowadays called to confront such issues. The way it accommodates them shall determine its legacy. Most high-stakes crises of today make their way to the Court as part of a multi-*forum* litigation strategy. States resort to multi-*forum* litigation strategy for they do not expect that the ICJ will resolve their dispute single-handedly by rendering a decision (a judgment, an advisory opinion or a provisional measures order). So, they exploit the added pressure accumulated by the proceedings before and the pronouncements of other judicial *fora*. Such strategy capitalizes on the prolific use of judicial institutions with the ICJ usually on the driver's seat. The accumulating number of broader disputes where it has been pursued suggests that multi-*forum* litigation is turning into a strategic trend in inter-State litigation. Seemingly, multi-*forum* litigation as a strategic choice is here to stay.

Engaged constituencies probably have mixed feelings about this over-use of international judicial institutions. International lawyers have reasons to be content with this surge of interest in their profession. They appear on media, some of them appear before courts, and their writings get increasing attention. ICJ judges may have mixed feelings for this development. On the one hand, the renewed interest in international adjudication renders their work relevant in addressing contemporary issues that matter. On the other, the workload is such that may debase the quality of their work and trigger criticism. The court's overfilled docket, the protracted proceedings, the number of requests for provisional measures and the limited budget to tackle all the above do not do any favors to the way the Court is viewed by external observers. For all those engaged with the discipline finally, it may be seen as a blessing, international law becomes relevant in shaping world politics.

This book's aim is to address the legal and policy issues that arise from the utilization of the ICJ as part of a multi-*forum* litigation strategy. The concomi-

1 O Spiermann, *International Legal Argument in the Permanent Court of International Justice: The Rise of the International Judiciary* (CUP, 2005), 132.

 | DOI:10.1163/9789004704565_006

tant analysis has been two-tiered: first, the book explored the limits of ICJ instrumentalization in the context of a multi-*forum* litigation strategy. What are the policy objectives States pursue when instrumentalizing the ICJ in the course of such a strategy, and whether the latter constitutes an effective strategy for the promotion of these objectives. Then, the book analyzed the ramifications from the employment of such strategy. What roles are attributed to the Court when instrumentalized in this context and what impact does this have on the Court's authority. Table 5.1 outlines most of these findings.

In this concluding Chapter the intention is twofold. First, to summarise the main findings from the previous Chapters regarding the Court's authority. Especially, how it is affected when each type of ICJ jurisdiction is engaged in the course of a multi-*forum* litigation strategy. And in their synthesis, provide a comprehensive account of the Court's authority as a judicial institution. In a world where inter-State multi forum litigation multiplies, so does the risk of the ICJ becoming another diplomatic platform to air State grievances. Second, to examine whether this discussion may pivot to the authority of international law as a system of rules with a normative claim. Given the ICJ's critical role in preserving the perception of international law as a legitimate means of regulating international relations, such concerns may be generalized and affect the authority of international law as a normative regulator. Evidently, these issues are inter-connected and they will be examined in turn.

On the first issue, it is important to note from the outset that authority does not necessarily go hand-in-hand with reliance on the Court, and neither does trust. Seen also as an after-effect of the extensive use of multi-*forum* litigation, reliance on the Court is undisputably proven by the Court's recently inflated docket. For the incumbent ICJ president and his predecessor, this growing reliance on the Court for the delivery of international justice testifies to the international community's trust in the Court.[2] The book takes issue with this uncritical connection between reliance and trust. To examine whether State reliance on the ICJ goes hand-in-hand i) with trust in it and ii) with a bolstered legitimate authority of the ICJ, it is important to dig a little bit deeper and ask: 'reliance on the Court to do what?'. The analysis of ICJ instrumentalization in Chapters 2, 3 and 4 sheds light to this; that is, to the expectations States have

2 Speech of HE Judge Nawaf Salam, *On the Occasion of the Seventy-Eighth Session of the United Nations General Assembly*, 24 October 2024, available at: https://www.icj-cij.org/sites/default/files/press-releases/0/000-20241024-sta-01-00-en.pdf, 13; Speech of HE Judge Joan E Donoghue, *What Lies Ahead for the International Court of Justice?* UNGA Sixth Committee, 25 October 2023, available at: https://www.icj-cij.org/sites/default/files/press-releases/0/000-20231025-sta-01-00-en.pdf, 5.

TABLE 5.1 Instrumentalization of the ICJ in the context of a multi-*forum* litigation strategy

Aspect of ICJ jurisdiction	Policy objectives pursued	Feature(s) of ICJ jurisdiction instrumentalized	Instrumentalization of legitimate authority vs. instrumentalization as a forum for political advocacy	Role implanted in the Court
All	Legitimization via domino-effect of like-minded rulings		Legitimate authority	Pivotal Judicial Institution
All	Legitimization via construction of a narrative		Forum for political advocacy	Political Dispute-Settler
Main proceedings	Multilateralization of the Dispute	Low threshold for third-party interventions	Forum for political advocacy	Political Dispute-Settler
Provisional Measures	Dispute resolution via influencing non-legal proceedings (e.g. negotiations)	*Prima facie* examination of jurisdiction + indication of extensive measures + disruptive nature	Legitimate authority	Crisis-Manager
Advisory Opinion	Dispute resolution	Circumvention of consent + [externally] attributed legal effect	Legitimate authority	Rule-Maker (*de facto* Dispute-Settler)

from the engagement of the ICJ in a multi-*forum* litigation strategy. And because expectations form roles, the book outlines the different roles implanted in the Court when utilized strategically in this way.

In general, a judicial body is instrumentalized in either of two ways: i) as an institution capable of producing normative commands ('instrumentalization of legitimate authority'), or ii) as a *forum* for political advocacy. During its early days, the ICJ was utilized for its legitimate authority. Lately however, it is increasingly instrumentalized as a *forum* for political advocacy. The proliferation of multi-*forum* litigation strategies where the ICJ is engaged is an indication of such instrumentalization.

Until the mid-1990's States instrumentalized the ICJ chiefly as an institution capable of producing normative commands. States resorted to the Court with the expectation that it will effectively fulfil its dispute settlement role. And because it is a judicial institution, this role was – and still is – connected to its ability to produce normative commands. Hence, the influx of cases brought before the Court was an indicator of the international community's trust in its ability to effectively perform this role via the rendering of normative commands. A full docket was further an indicator that the ICJ was perceived as an authoritative institution, because only such an institution can produce effective normative commands. In other words, reliance meant trust, which in turn meant widespread sociological legitimacy. Also, this explains the revolving State reliance on the ICJ from 1948 to the mid-1990's. Whenever States perceived the Court to be failing in its dispute settlement role, resort to the Court would slow down. The willingness to condemn the UK in its first contentious case inspired confidence in the impartiality of the institution and its resistance to real or apprehended political pressures.[3] So, the ICJ was quite active during its first two decades. Its failure to condemn the apartheid regime in the mid-1960s was followed by a drought that lasted two decades.[4] Confidence only began to be restored in the Court when it ruled in favour of Nicaragua and against the United States in 1986. Judicial activity proliferated thereafter.

Lately however, States increasingly instrumentalize the Court as a *forum* for public advocacy, not only as a producer of normative commands. Due to this, the influx of cases does not necessarily go together with a concomitant trust in

---

3 W Schabas, 'Introduction' in W Schabas and Sh. Murphy (eds) *Research Handbook on International Courts and Tribunals* (Edward Elgar, 2017) 1, 35.

4 For the 'crisis of confidence' in the Court during this period, see RP Anand, 'Role of International Adjudication' in L Gross (ed.) *The Future of the International Court of Justice* (Oceana, 1976), 1, 2.

the Court's dispute settlement role. In essence, if a State is interested in utilizing the Court as a *medium* of communication, whether the Court will effectively fulfil its dispute settlement role is not a consideration that will weigh in its decision to sue. Yugoslavia's applications in *Use of Force* have been the most characteristic example to date, but, *inter alia*, Azerbaijan's resort to the Court against Armenia was undoubtedly animated by such considerations. The fact that cases continue to arrive at a growing pace irrespective of the Court's record in effectively performing its overarching dispute settlement role is a strong indication that the Court is instrumentalized for reasons unconnected to its capacity to settle a dispute. For example, small was the impact of the *Nuclear Weapons* and *Kosovo* advisory opinions, or of the *Lockerbie* and *Georgia v. Russia* cases in the Court's docket. At the same time, symptoms of lack of trust in the Court's work are proliferating. Out of 193 States entitled to appear before the ICJ, seventy-four have deposited an optional clause declaration under Article 36(2) ICJ Statute, and most of them are riddled with wide and far-reaching reservations. The practice of non-appearance has been resorted to by States called to appear as defendants on the basis of compulsory settlement provisions.[5] Compliance rates are progressively declining and the ICJ spends all the more time in dealing with preliminary objections to its jurisdiction. All the above are *indicia* testifying to an ensuing lack of State trust in the Court as a legal dispute settler. The growing reliance on the Court despite the limited trust States place in it to perform its dispute settlement role, is a sign that States resort to it while having other expectations in mind.

Likely, instrumentalization of legitimate authority and instrumentalization as a *forum* for political advocacy coexist as animating factors in most decisions to sue before the ICJ. The argument presented here is that the latter type is all the more prevalent lately and States increasingly rely on litigation as part of a broader advocacy campaign. The book demonstrated that ICJ instrumentalization in the context of a multi-*forum* litigation strategy targets both the Court's legitimate authority and its capacity to act as a *forum* for political advocacy. The former is in play when States engage a multitude of judicial *fora* because they wish to capitalize on the legitimating power of a domino-effect of like-minded rulings. The latter when a State expects to construct a narrative and to this end it utilizes different judicial bodies as communication *media*. Relatedly, two roles are implanted in the Court. That of a pivotal judicial institution in the constellation of international dispute settlement capa-

5 T Treves, 'Litigating global crises. Setting the scene: Legal and political hurdles for State-to-State disputes' 85 (2001) *Questions of International Law, Zoom-out* 5, 9.

ble of influencing other *fora*. And that of a political dispute settler capable of exercising public diplomacy by communicating claims to many audiences.

Authority-wise this points to two different directions. On the one hand, State trust in the Court's capacity to influence the decisions of other judicial organs is a clear sign that it is perceived as a *de facto* authoritative institution. A strong legitimate authority accompanies ICJ pronouncements so that other judicial organs can justifiably rely on them.[6] On the other hand, the wish to capitalize on the exercise of the Court's judicial or advisory function as a political *medium* and not as a method for legal dispute settlement is in tension with the preponderant role incumbent upon a judicial institution. This is why, instrumentalization as a *forum* for political advocacy may erode the Court's legitimate authority. The allegations by Russia regarding the inadmissibility of the applications for intervention,[7] the claims by the UAE on the purpose behind Qatar's interim protection requests[8] and Armenia's contention that Azerbaijan is abusively resorting to the Court,[9] all point to the same direction; the Court is instrumentalized as a *forum* for political advocacy. As explained in Chapter 2, such rhetorical ploys do not have legal value *per se*. The Court cannot, is not supposed to, take them into consideration when adjudicating. They constitute however a reason for concern.

This is so because they may herald a change in perception on the Court's role. A perception whereby the ICJ is reliable to exercise the role of a political *medium* or that of a political dispute settler. And these roles are in tension with its dispute settlement role and hence its legal function. Whether this will affect the sociological legitimacy of the Court and hence its authority remains to be seen. The only meaningful thing to be said at this point is that it promotes an understanding of the Court as a multi-role actor. Again, it is unclear whether this understanding will solidify, as at this point the ICJ enjoys a large measure of sociological legitimacy. However, if judicial bodies are perceived as exercising both legal and political functions, the normative force of their legal outputs is relativized. If States perceive the Court as an illegitimate institution because it plays a role unbecoming for a judicial body (e.g. the role of a negotiator or that of a platform of communication), this will impact the

6 Characteristic is the ECtHR's reliance in *Ukraine v. Russia* (*re Crimea*) on the factual background established by the ICJ in its relevant judgment on Crimea, see *supra* Chapter 2, Section 4(B).

7 See *supra* Chapter 2, Section 5.

8 See *supra* Chapter 3, Section 2(B)(ii)(a).

9 See *supra* Chapter 3, Section 3(A)(ii)(b).

ICJ's capacity to deliver authoritative pronouncements and demand compliance with them. And once this perception consolidates, it is hard to reverse it.

The book further suggested that peculiar features of ICJ jurisdiction can be instrumentalized in the course of multi-*forum* litigation. Because of the low admissibility threshold, interventions during main proceedings may be staged in order to multilateralize a dispute. Such an attempt to demonstrate political support in one's case, targets the Court's ability to promote dispute-settlement by building-up external political pressure. In this way, it implants in the Court the role of a political dispute-settler, a role unbecoming for a judicial body. As to provisional measures, the combined effect of their highly disruptive nature, of the cursory examination of jurisdiction, and of the indication of measures that go beyond the preservation of the parties' rights points to a fast-track dispute settlement mechanism. A mechanism that can be used to influence other ongoing proceedings. Albeit, the role of a crisis-manager implanted in the Court is a role becoming for a legal institution, so long as this management of the crisis ensues via normative commands. Finally, the Court's very strict conditions on refusing the delivery of an advisory opinion along with the attributed legal effect by other judicial bodies, render advisory opinions amenable to instrumentalization as definitive dispute resolution rulings. The role of a rule-maker is congruent with the Court's overall legal function, but it exceeds the ICJ's advisory competence per Article 65 ICJ Statute.

The different roles the Court is expected to fulfil may be impactful on the consolidation of the Court's authority in two ways. Firstly, as noted above, because the roles implanted in the Court may lie in tension with the ICJ's legal nature. This effect of instrumentalization may affect the Court's sociological legitimacy and curb the normative value of its outputs. Secondly, because the fulfilment of these roles may depend on stretching the Court's legal powers. For example, it is the Court's use of its advisory jurisdiction despite State consent and irrespective of the political circumstances surrounding the request that portrays the ICJ as a *de facto* dispute-settler when delivering an advisory opinion. Ditto, the Court is perceived as a manager of a developing situation when indicating provisional measures, *inter alia* because it is willing to go beyond the purposes incorporated in its Statute. In such cases, the international community will likely question the Court's legitimacy to effectively perform its judicial function because its decisions ignore State interests or because it exceeds its powers when delivering advisory opinions and provisional measures. In such instances, legitimacy concerns do not arise because of court instrumentalization, rather because of the Court's own behavior.

Whether ICJ legitimate authority is chipped away because of the Court's instrumentalization or because of the Court's own stance is critical. In the latter case it falls upon the Court to address legitimacy concerns. It depends on its willingness to pay attention to a changing international landscape. Chapters 3 and 4 held that the Court demonstrates a variable attentiveness to these changes. According to Chapter 3, the ICJ is modifying its engagement with provisional measures requests because it wants to put the brakes on States who exceedingly instrumentalize provisional measures.[10] While Chapter 4 suggested that the Court should be more attentive to State interests when delivering advisory opinions in order to anticipate unintended consequences. To the contrary, the ICJ possesses limited ability to address legitimacy concerns in the former case. That is, when multiple third-party interventions are sought or when the ICJ is used as platform for communication. On such occasions, these concerns spring out of the behavior of an indefinite number of actors the Court has no control over. To address them would require a long-term change in the attitude of States and in their perception over the Court's role.

As an interim conclusion, a word of caution is in order. The Court enjoys extensive legitimate authority as a judicial institution and this is not expected to change overnight. However, the over-use of multi-*forum* litigation strategies puts on the table a twofold erosion of the ICJ's authority. One is connected to the exercise of its functions. The other ensues from the Court's instrumentalization as a *medium* for political advocacy. And the latter is more worrisome because there are few things the Court can do to reverse it.

These concerns over the Court's authority must be understood in the institutional context within which the Court operates. The ICJ forms part of a dispute settlement machinery. For at least a century, this machinery has proved resilient.[11] Today, international courts bear the brunt of delivering the promise of international law for justice.[12] However, the environment in which they are to fulfil this task is changing to 'become considerably more hostile to [their] enterprise'.[13] Certain *indicia* of this change were outlined throughout the book (backlash against decisions, lack of trust in judicial institutions). In this changing landscape, the growing judicialization of

10 See Chapter 3, Section 4.

11 J Crawford, 'Continuity and discontinuity in international dispute settlement: An inaugural lecture' 1 (2010) *Journal of International Dispute Settlement*, 3.

12 J Dunoff, 'International Justice Cannot Stop the War. What Can?' 107 (2024) *Questions of International Law* 5, 6.

13 C Romano, 'Legitimacy, authority, and performance: Contemporary anxieties of international courts and tribunals' 114 (2020) *American Journal of International Law* 149, 162.

international law, of which multi-*forum* litigation is a feature, has perhaps another role to play; to contribute to the legalization of international governance.[14] To consolidate international law as a normative language that frames the political will of States and provides the necessary context to assess international consensus.

This observation is connected to the second question posed above regarding the significance of the utilization of multi-*forum* litigation strategy on the authority of international law as a system of normative claims. The Court is not just a part in the international dispute settlement machinery. Its role in this machinery is far more instrumental than that. The ICJ 'epitomises the social reality of the society of which it is an institution [and] epitomises the legal reality whose legal relations it enforces.'[15] Unlike arbitral tribunals, its permanence and incorporation in the environment of a global organization 'contribute to a sense of deciding [...] as part of an international legal system'.[16] And as such it is instrumentalized in the context of a multi-*forum* litigation strategy. Had the Special Chamber not pronounced upon the legal effects of ICJ advisory opinions, *Chagos* would not have exerted such a compliance pull over the UK. Had Ukraine not prompted Ukrainian investors to make arbitral claims and had Qatar not resorted to WTO proceedings, the pressure upon Russia and the Quartet respectively would not have been the same.

Due to its position, the ICJ plays a systemic role in international dispute settlement and the exercise of its functions promotes systemic objectives. It safeguards the coherence of the international legal system.[17] And by representing the idea of legality, its work is instrumental in preserving the perception of international law as a legitimate means of regulating international relations.[18] It preserves and legitimizes the role of international law as a normative regulator. The separation of law from politics effected via adjudication portrays 'resort to adjudication [...] as a faith in the rule of law writ large'.[19] So, the ICJ symbolizes the continuing promise of international adju-

14 Gl. Hernandez, 'The judicialization of international law: Reflections on the empirical turn' 25(2014) *European Journal of International Law* 919, 923.

15 P Allott, *Eunomia: A New Order for a New World* (OUP, 1990) 241.

16 P Webb, *International Judicial Integration and Fragmentation* (OUP, 2013) 152.

17 Gl. Hernandez, The International Court of Justice and the Judicial Function (OUP, 2014) 1.

18 R Giladi and Y Shany, 'Assessing the Effectiveness of the International Court of Justice' in C Esposito and K Parlett, *The Cambridge Companion to the International Court of Justice* (CUP, 2023), 101, 119.

19 Hernandez, *supra* note 17, 3.

dication to uphold the identity of international law as a normative system. Or, better said: '[the ICJ] captures [...] the aspirations of the international legal profession as to the transformative effects of international adjudication for law-enforcement, law-development, and legitimating laws and institutions'.[20]

Should multi-*forum* litigation strategies continue to be employed in the coming years, an issue of a somewhat existential nature for international law may come to the forefront. Should the concerns over the Court's authority as an institution be generalized, the continuous attempt to make the ICJ a front-runner in influencing international crises for the political role it fulfils may bring the law applied by it into disrepute. Or, such an instrumentalization of international law may have an inflationary effect on the normative force of the legal order itself. The over-use of a pivotal international judicial institution as a political *medium* can produce bad 'international law' coinage. In turn, this may impact international law's capacity to be understood as a mechanism creating normative commands. We are far away from this grim picture today, but in the era of whataboutism, the relativization of the normative value of rules may come about at a fast pace.

Nevertheless, there is also the bright side of the moon, the one that many international lawyers focus on today. The capacity of international law to regulate global affairs is indeed questioned, but this has always been the case and such criticism is to be expected when the Court engages with the main political issues of the day.[21] International law has taken center-stage in the mosh pit of world politics and it can produce just claims based on universally accepted values.[22] Seen in this light, the reliance placed on the Court to deliver justice (via legal and political means) is not a sign of trust, but rather one of hope.[23] Turning hope into reality is a challenge international law has to face.

I will finish this book by reflecting on the book's opening remarks. Elusive while it may be, justice provides a framework for thinking about the rights and duties of States. To set up this framework at the international level, some institutionalization is required. How this institutionalization will materialize depends on the cooperation and coordination of a multitude of actors. Chiefly

20 Giladi and Shany, *supra* note 18, 119.

21 Dunoff, *supra* note 12, 5: "much scholarship today is quicker to link international law to global injustice than to justice".

22 P d'Argent, 'International Law as a System of Claims. What Can International Law Do to Stop the War?' 107 (2024) *Questions of International Law* 9.

23 P Webb, 'From Crisis to Epoch: How to Understand this Era of International Law? 25 (2024) *Melbourne Journal of International Law* (forthcoming issue, advance copy), 1.

of States and judicial institutions. While these institutions do not exhaust the category of international justice, they perform an instrumental role in its delivery. All the more the ICJ. This book argued that how States understand the Court's role in this ('instrumentalization'), and further how the ICJ reacts to its instrumentalization can have implications as to the Court's legitimate authority and international law's normative authority. The latest trend to instrumentalize the Court as part of a multi-*forum* litigation strategy portrays the Court as a multi-role actor, and pushes it to rethink the exercise of its judicial function. I hope this is done in the best interests of justice.

Index

www.ingramcontent.com/pod-product-compliance
Lightning Source LLC
LaVergne TN
LVHW102105300926
849161LV00001B/28

* 9 7 8 9 0 0 4 7 0 4 5 5 8 *